# CAREER AND VOCATIONAL EDUCATION
# FOR THE MILDLY HANDICAPPED

# CAREER AND VOCATIONAL EDUCATION FOR THE MILDLY HANDICAPPED

By

## RHODA WOODS CUMMINGS, Ed.D.

*Assistant Professor*
*College of Education*
*University of Nevada, Reno*
*Reno, Nevada*

and

## CLEBORNE D. MADDUX, Ph.D.

*Associate Professor*
*Center for Excellence in Education*
*Northern Arizona University*
*Flagstaff, Arizona*

CHARLES C THOMAS • PUBLISHER
*Springfield • Illinois • U.S.A.*

*Published and Distributed Throughout the World by*

CHARLES C THOMAS • PUBLISHER

2600 South First Street

Springfield, Illinois 62794-9265

© *1987 by* CHARLES C THOMAS • PUBLISHER

ISBN 0-398-05344-8

Library of Congress Catalog Card Number: 87-6436

*Printed in the United States of America*

*Q-R-3*

*Library of Congress Cataloging in Publication Data*

Cummings, Rhoda Woods.
    Career and vocational education for the mildly handi-
capped.

    Bibliography: p.
    Includes index.
    1. Handicapped youth — Vocational education —
United States. 2. Career education — United States.
I. Maddux, Cleborn D., 1942-      . II. Title.
LC4019.7.C86   1987          371.9'044          87-6436
ISBN 0-398-05344-8

*To the writers and researchers whose work have made this book possible, and to scholars everywhere who expend the extra effort and make the sacrifices required in the pursuit of knowledge.*

# PREFACE

TODAY THE field of Special Education is facing a *major crisis*. This crisis is related to education for *mildly handicapped students* and results from the failure to adequately prepare them for adult living.

Traditionally, special education has done an acceptable job of preparing more severely handicapped students for work. For many of these individuals, planning for their future begins at an early age. In fact, immediately after parents are told their child is handicapped, they often receive professional advice that they should begin planning for the child's future. The usual next steps are to enroll the child first in an infant stimulation program, then in an early childhood program, and finally in a public or private school special education program. *From kindergarten on,* these programs emphasize the development of self-help, vocational, and other independent living skills. The ultimate goal of such programs is to equip students with skills for adult living.

What awaits the participants of these programs once they leave school? Many have access to group homes where, under the guidance of a trained supervisor, they are able to interact with peers, and they are assigned specific responsibilities necessary for the efficient operation of the home. In addition, they have companionship, and the opportunity to make friends with whom they can visit at the end of a day. Because of the skills many of them have acquired during their school years, they have part- or full-time jobs, depending on the extent of their disability. Many of them have access to community services, receive discounts on public transportation, and attend community-sponsored events such as dances, circuses, and such. They participate in summer and winter special olympics. In short, many moderately and some severely handicapped individuals lead active and fulfilling lives as adults.

Unfortunately, the same has not been true for many *mildly* handicapped youth. Many of these individuals have grown up, left the public schools, and are attempting to become integrated into adult society.

However, as the literature has recently begun to show, large numbers of these individuals continue to suffer from the effects of their disability. In fact, for many of them, their handicap has become even more of a problem as they have grown older. Researchers are now beginning to look at some of the problems encountered by this group after they leave school, and they are discovering some alarming facts!

Many mildly handicapped students are leaving schools unprepared either for college, vocational/technical school, or employment. They often have difficulty finding employment, and if they do find a job, they often cannot keep it because of their poor work habits and inadequate interpersonal skills. It has been said that many become victims of an invisible handicap which neither they nor their employers understand. They may live their lives in frustration, isolation, depression, and at levels far below their potential. If they do find and keep employment, it may be in dead-end jobs that are boring and do not make use of their full capabilities.

As a result, public school officials are beginning to recognize that academic remediation alone will not solve the problems of this handicapped population. Because of this realization, some initial attempts are being made to provide mildly handicapped students with career/vocational as well as academic instruction. However, many of these programs are often inappropriate.

We believe a major factor underlying all of these difficulties is the lack of a firm, theoretical foundation in career/vocational education. We fear this atheoretical orientation has characterized much of program development in vocational and career education, both for handicapped and nonhandicapped populations. The result has been a lack of clearly-defined models from which excellent career/vocational education programs could be developed.

Thus, the purpose for writing this book is to present a plan for career/vocational education program development grounded firmly in a theoretical framework that has withstood the scrutiny of research and the test of time. We have chosen John Holland's Theory of Vocational Personalities and Work Environments. This theory will be used as the framework for a career/vocational education program designed to prepare mildly handicapped students for a variety of potentially fulfilling occupations.

In summary, we believe that the majority of mildly handicapped students will not succeed without this kind of extensive, well-planned, appropriate, *theory-based* public school preparation. It is for this group that a need exists for drastic reforms in Special Education.

# ACKNOWLEDGMENTS

WE WISH TO acknowledge two colleagues who have had an indirect, yet positive impact on the content of this book. We are indebted to Dr. Jane Winer who was responsible for introducing us to the concept of career development theory, and to Dr. Corrine Kass, a pioneer in the field of learning disabilities, who has been an exemplary model of scholarship and a continuing source of inspiration.

# CONTENTS

# CAREER AND VOCATIONAL EDUCATION
# FOR THE MILDLY HANDICAPPED

Chapter One

# THE MILDLY HANDICAPPED

T HE SUBJECT of this book is vocational special education for the mildly handicapped. Brief consideration of this topic will probably lead the reader to at least two initial questions:

1. Who are the mildly handicapped?
2. Why do the mildly handicapped need a special vocational education program?

We will begin by answering both questions in a cursory fashion. The remainder of this chapter will then explore these answers in depth.

First, mildly handicapped individuals as defined in this book are those with learning disabilities, mild mental retardation, or mild emotional disturbance.

Second, they need a special vocational education program because the experiences of the authors as well as the results of a growing body of research studies indicate that these individuals are not being adequately prepared for life after public school. They usually do not receive adequate vocational training, and they have problems interacting with employers and coworkers. Consequently, they have difficulty finding and keeping a job, and they are often unemployed or underemployed. This state of affairs is extremely wasteful, costing our nation millions of dollars and subjecting our handicapped citizens to untold and largely unnecessary frustration and suffering.

## THE MILDLY HANDICAPPED

The term *mildly handicapped* is poorly chosen from one point of view. Someone once observed that a *mild handicap* is similar to a *minor operation,*

in that *minor* operations are restricted only to those performed on someone else! Similarly, *mild* handicaps can occur only to other people's children, never our own.

Nevertheless, it is important to recognize that all handicapping conditions can be viewed as falling along a continuum of severity ranging
from mild to severe (Kirk & Gallagher, 1983). The individuals about
whom this book is written fall somewhere toward the mild end of this
continuum. We will begin our discussion of the mildly handicapped by
defining learning disabilities, mental retardation, and emotional disturbance.

## The Learning Disabled

The newest and most controversial category of handicapping conditions is that of *learning disabilities*. The term is currently recognized in
federal law and is applied to a wide variety of learning problems that occur in otherwise normal individuals. Although there have always been
learning disabled people, the term was not coined until the early 1960s
when Sam Kirk used it at a professional meeting. Prior to that time,
various terms were used including brain injured, brain damaged, hy-
peractive, and neurologically impaired. Kirk preferred the new term because he and other authorities felt the older terms emphasized causation,
were not scientifically sound, and provided an excuse not to teach such
children.

### The Crisis in Learning Disabilities

The authors feel that the learning disabilities movement is currently
in the midst of a crisis that threatens its very existence. The field is under attack from without by lawmakers, regular educators and other professionals and it is torn from within by petty and unprofessional
rivalries, jealousies, and power brokering. Classrooms for learning disabled children are bursting at the seams with students who are not handicapped and who should not be in special education programs, and
many young LD teachers have never had a classically learning disabled
child placed in their programs. To understand how this sad state of affairs has come to pass, it is necessary to present a brief history of the field
of learning disabilities. Interested readers who desire more detailed information are referred to our earlier text on parenting the learning disabled (Cummings & Maddux, 1985b).

## Overidentification

Although there are many problems and controversies in learning disabilities, we believe that the most serious is the problem of overidentification of learning disabled children. Ironically, overidentification has been a problem in learning disabilities almost from the moment the field was created.

The term *learning disabilities* caught on immediately after Kirk coined it in the early sixties. After all, it was far less noxious than any of the previously-used terms that emphasized causation and seemed to imply more serious physical and mental impairment. This "softening" of terms was welcomed by parents, school administrators, physicians, and other child service professionals. At their urging, state and federal officials began passing laws that recognized the *new* condition. These laws, most of which were passed in the 1960s and early 1970s, made special funding available for school districts that instituted programs for learning disabled students. Typically, these laws added to district budgets a substantial amount of money for each child identified as learning disabled. Consequently, the 1960s and 1970s were periods of great growth in terms of the numbers of children who were identified as learning disabled (Cummings & Maddux, 1985b). School districts across the country began identifying larger and larger percentages of their students as learning disabled. In fact, many school administrators seemed more concerned with obtaining additional special education funding than with ensuring that accurate identification procedures were in place in their districts.

Students were labeled LD and then placed in special classrooms to be taught by teachers who were supposedly experts in the field of learning disabilities. However, the speed with which children were being identified and placed far surpassed the ability of colleges and universities to turn out properly prepared specialists. The result was an acute shortage of teachers certified in learning disabilities.

Overidentification thus spawned a different, though related problem; that of inadequate training of teachers. School district officials across the country were experiencing difficulty in locating and recruiting certified LD teachers. The officials reacted to this problem by applying pressure on state departments of education to initiate special temporary emergency certification programs. These programs licensed teachers for learning disabilities classrooms who had only minimal special training. Many such emergency programs were approved. The authors are acquainted with programs that licensed LD teachers after no more than two college courses in learning disabilities! And even though the shortage of certified LD teachers is no longer acute, many states with emergency certification programs have not revised their certification requirements to include more thorough preparation.

The phenomenal growth in numbers of children identified as learning disabled resulted in increasing amounts of supplemental monies being channeled to school districts. This increased spending soon came to the attention of state and federal lawmakers who quickly became disturbed about the rapidly growing budgets for learning disabilities. Their concerns intensified in light of complaints from professionals outside special education with regard to overidentification of learning disabled students and ill-prepared LD teachers.

The percentage of children identified as learning disabled continued to increase. Although two percent was an often-quoted estimate of the prevalence of learning disabilities, many school districts identified three percent, four percent, even six percent of their students. As of 1983-1984, 4.57 percent of America's children were identified as learning disabled. Currently, almost half (43 percent) of all children in special education are classified as learning disabled (Kirk & Gallagher, 1986). The authors recently worked in one Texas community in which over six percent of the students were labeled LD!

Because of these problems, lawmakers and state education agency officials turned their attention to the definition of learning disabilities. After all, if vast amounts of money were to be spent on LD, it was reasonable to demand a clear, objective, quantifiable definition of the condition. However, when officials began to examine the question of definition, they found the same confusion and lack of objectivity that characterized the rest of the field. When government hearings were held to consider the issue of definition and experts in learning disabilities were asked to give their opinions, the lack of consensus became painfully obvious. Lawmakers began to realize that they were funding special programs for children who were suffering from a disorder that had not yet been clearly and objectively defined.

Actually, this was to be expected. Problems of overidentification cannot exist in a field that has come to a consensus about the characteristics of a condition, produced a straightforward definition of that condition, and provided clear, objective, quantifiable ways to operationalize that definition. The field of learning disabilities did not then have, nor does it now have, such a definition or such operational policies and procedures. Learning disabilities experts have struggled with and have failed to reach consensus over definition since the field began.

## The Definition of Learning Disabilities

The field of learning disabilities came about because of almost universal recognition by experts that there were children who did not learn normally yet could not be considered mentally retarded, emotionally disturbed, partially sighted or blind, or otherwise handicapped. Although it was relatively easy to reach consensus that this problem existed, it has proven impossible to reach consensus on a formal definition of the condition. Kirk's definition was one of the earliest:

> A learning disability refers to a retardation, disorder, or delayed development in one or more of the processes of speech, language, reading, spelling, writing, or arithmetic resulting from a possible cerebral dysfunction and/or emotional or behavioral disturbance and not from mental retardation, sensory deprivation, or cultural or instructional factors. (Kirk, 1962. p. 263)

The definition that currently appears in the federal regulations follows:

> Specific learning disability means a disorder in one or more of the basic psychological processes involved in understanding or in using language, spoken or written, which may manifest itself in an imperfect ability to listen, think, speak, read, write, spell or do mathematical calculations. The term includes such conditions as perceptual handicaps, brain injury, minimal brain dysfunction, dyslexia, and developmental aphasia. The term does not include children who have learning problems which are primarily the result of visual, hearing, or motor handicaps, of mental retardation, or of environmental, cultural or economic disadvantage (Federal Register, August 23, 1977)

Notice that the term "learning disabilities" has been changed to "specific learning disabilities," but that the current definition is otherwise quite similar to Kirk's 1962 definition.

The definition may appear to be straightforward and objective at first glance. However, the utility of a definition depends on the ease with which it can be operationalized. In other words, its usefulness depends on the ease with which procedures can be provided to determine if a given child has the condition. In the field of learning disabilities, this objective has proven to be extremely difficult. In fact, problems of operationalizing certain aspects of the definition have been directly responsible for many additional problems, including the problem of overidentification.

## Operationalizing the Definition of Learning Disabilities

In the years from 1963 until 1975, three criteria were generally used for diagnosing learning disabilities. Typically, all three of the following criteria had to be met:

1. exclusion criterion
2. discrepancy criterion
3. deficits in basic psychological processes criterion

The *exclusion criterion* is met if it can be shown that the child's primary learning problem is not due to any other handicapping condition such as mental retardation, emotional disturbance, sensory deficits such as blindness or hearing problems, etc.

The *discrepancy criterion* is met if it can be shown that there is a severe discrepancy between what the child is capable of achieving and what the child is actually achieving. To document this criterion, the child is usually given an IQ test and any number of achievement tests or subtests in various subject matter areas. If the IQ score is significantly higher than the achievement test score, the criterion is considered met.

The *deficiency in basic psychological processes* criterion is met if it can be shown that the child is deficient in one or more of the basic psychological processes involved in understanding or in using spoken or written language. It is assumed that these deficits are a result of damage to the central nervous system, although such damage can rarely be proven. The state of the art in neurology is such that many minor neurological problems can only be inferred from behavior.

To document this criterion, the child is usually given any one of a number of standardized tests designed to tap abilities such as visual reception, association, closure, discrimination, and sequential memory, as well as these same abilities in the auditory modality. These tests are not intended to measure visual or auditory *acuity*. In other words, they are not intended to determine if the child is partially sighted or blind, or whether he has a hearing loss or is deaf. They are intended to measure whether the child is able to accurately *interpret* and *manipulate* what is seen and heard.

There are many practical problems with each of the above criteria. Interested readers are referred to Chalfant (1984) and to Cummings and Maddux (1985b) for more complete discussions of these problems. The problems connected with operationalizing the process deficit criterion is most relevant to the present discussion, and are the only ones that will be dealt with in this book. These problems are both scientific and political.

Scientific problems occur because, although there is general agreement that basic psychological processes exist, there is little agreement about exactly what constitutes such processes and how they should be measured. There is also disagreement as to whether or not such processes are related to academic tasks such as reading and writing, and whether or not they are conducive to remediation. Critics of a process approach to learning disabilities suggest that time and effort can be more productively spent on developing excellent ways to change more easily observable student behaviors, such as ability to solve math problems, read, or get along with peers. These issues have sparked a heated professional debate that has raged for nearly 25 years, and that has resulted in many of our current problems in the field of learning disabilities.

The political problems are both internal and external to the field. Internally, the controversy over processing is a reflection of a basic philosophical difference among professionals. It is ironic that the field of psychology was also once divided by this same difference in world views, although the schism in psychology took place years before the LD controversy. Psychology divided into two camps shortly after the turn of the century. One camp was dedicated to developing the discipline by attending to observable, quantifiable behavior. Another faction believed in pursuing introspection and attempting to describe the nature of human thought. Psychologists were classified as *behaviorists* or as *cognitivists* according to how they stood on this issue.

The controversy over processing in learning disabilities is really nothing more than a revival of the old schism in psychology between behaviorism and cognitivism. The behaviorists in learning disabilities reject psychological processes for the same reasons that earlier behavioral psychologists rejected introspection. They find the concept inexact, and they criticize instruments designed to measure psychological processes on the grounds that they lack reliability and validity. Similarly, the cognitivists in learning disabilities criticize the anti-processing camp on the same grounds that earlier cognitive psychologists rejected their behaviorist peers. Those supporting a process approach reject the academic approach as overly simplistic and assert that a science of learning disabilities cannot be built on a model of man as a machine. Such an approach, they assert, treats the symptom rather than the underlying cause.

Psychologists, however, unlike specialists in learning disabilities, kept their disagreement at a professional level, discussed and debated their differences, and were eventually able to turn the controversy into an asset rather than a deficit. Behaviorists worked on new and better ways of measuring and changing observable behavior while cognitivists continued to delve into the workings of the mind. The debate went on between the two schools of thought, but it was pursued at a professional level. Eventually, the fervor cooled and both camps profited from the debate. At the present time, there is even a movement within psychology to combine the two schools of thought into an approach known as *cognitive behaviorism*.

We believe in a similar course of action for antagonists in learning disabilities. Those who espouse a process approach should continue to work on improving instruments for measuring basic psychological process deficits and on methods for remediating and/or compensating for them. Those who take a more behavioral approach should refine existing methods for measuring and remediating behaviors critical to the learning disabled individual.

The debate in psychology turned out to be beneficial because it was an expression of an honest, scientific disagreement. The debate in learning disabilities has been destructive because it has degenerated into small-minded personal attacks sparked by petty jealousies and greed. We wrote about this problem in our 1985 book:

> While some critics of the process deficit approach were honest and scientific in their criticisms and were sincerely interested in strengthening the field, others used the temper of the times and the tentative nature of pioneer work in the field to build a career based on sarcasm and personal attacks. Some educators, the general public, and many policy-makers at federal, state, and local levels tend to listen most closely to those who speak loudest and with the most invective. While advocates of the process deficit approach were working to develop effective ways to assess and treat learning disabled children within the cognitive tradition, a small group of opportunists gained attention and built reputations through unqualified, authoritative statements about the ineffectiveness of such efforts. (Cummings & Maddux, 1985b, p. 11)

These conditions prevailed into the early seventies. The field was polarized into opposing camps, the number of public school classrooms for learning disabled children continued to increase at an alarming rate, and poorly trained teachers, many with emergency certification, were entering the field in increasing numbers. This was the state of affairs in 1975, when PL 94-142, the most significant special education legislation in the history of the country, became law.

## PL94-142

Whatever else they were, the sixties and early seventies were a time of increased social consciousness. Out of the civil rights fervor of the sixties came a new concern for the rights of all citizens particularly handicapped citizens. PL94-142, the Education for All Handicapped Children Act of 1975 guaranteed a free, appropriate public education to all handicapped children, including learning disabled children. In fact, this law made such an education a right in the same sense as freedom of speech, freedom of the press, and freedom of religion are rights.

This law and the regulations pertaining to it also included Federal definitions of all the handicapping conditions covered by the law. The definition for learning disabilities is the one which was quoted ealier in this chapter. As we have already stated, however, the really important provisions of law and regulation are those that set procedures for operationalizing a definition.

When the Federal Government began drafting proposed regulations for identifying learning disabled children, the officials in charge of these regulations were well aware of the chaos in the field. They knew about the processing controversy, and they were weary of the petty bickering about it among professionals. They knew about the problems of overidentification, and they were sensitive to the widespread concern that it would continue to be a serious financial drain on educational resources.

To deal with these problems, they took two decisive courses of action in the proposed regulations. Ironically, final decisions on these two actions resulted in a set of final regulations which exacerbated the very problems they were intended to relieve.

The first provision allowed each individual state to decide whether or not to include the deficits in basic psychological processes criterion when setting procedures for diagnosis of learning disabilities. The second provision proposed that the Federal Government would provide supplemental funding for programs for LD students for up to, but not exceeding, 2 percent of all children in a school district.

The proposed 2 percent cap on funding for LD students was opposed by practically all experts in learning disabilities as well as a number of influential advocacy organizations. In fact, the field of LD rose up in arms against the proposal. In the face of this overwhelming and well-organized opposition, the Government backed down and retracted the proposed cap. Although special education funding for all handicaps could not exceed 12 percent of the enrolled students, no cap was imposed on the percentage that could be classified as LD.

Although we were part of the opposition to the 2 percent cap, we are now sorry that we opposed it. If the cap had been included in the final regulations, it would have effectively blocked school districts from classifying unreasonably high percentages of their students as learning disabled. It may be that enactment of a similar cap in the future will be necessary to control the overidentification problem that presently afflicts the field of learning disabilities.

The provision in the proposed regulations that made it possible for states to eliminate a requirement to document deficits in basic psychological processes eventually became official. We believe this was a great error which has contributed substantially to the current problem of overidentification. Most state agencies elected not to include a processing requirement in their state regulations. In fact, as of 1984, only 17 states included a process criterion (Chalfant, 1984) (The states are Arkansas, Colorado, Connecticut, Florida, Hawaii, Idaho, Illinois, Michigan, Minnesota, Montana, New York, Ohio, Oklahoma, Utah, Vermont, Virginia, and Washington.) Furthermore, Mercer, Hughes, and Mercer (1985) assert that the current trend is for more and more states to eliminate the process criterion.

At first glance, elimination of a controversial criterion may seem an enlightened and thoughtful action. However, we must consider what remains of the operational definition after elimination of the process criterion. What is left are the other two criteria:

1. discrepancy
2. exclusion

That is, in order to qualify as learning disabled, it must be shown that a child (a) is capable of achieving more than he is achieving, and (b) is not primarily mentally retarded, emotionally disturbed, disadvantaged, or otherwise handicapped.

What this amounts to is covert redefinition of learning disabilities as mere underachievement. Using only these two of the original three criteria, any child who is an underachiever for any reason except mental retardation, emotional disturbance, etc., can qualify as learning disabled.

As any teacher knows, there are many diverse reasons for underachievement. Some of these are lack of motivation, poor teaching, frequent absences, and learning disabilities. Elimination of the process criterion has opened the door for classification of children as learning disabled who would never have qualified a few years ago. These are children who may need some special help in school, but who are not legitimate candidates for special education classes. As we said in our earlier book on the parenting of learning disabled children:

Although the concept may not be palatable to some educators, the fact remains that special education was conceived for and dedicated to the treatment of *abnormal* children. A child who does not learn because of poor teaching, low motivation, or other environmental influences is not abnormal and should remain the responsibility of regular education. We believe that, unless something is done to remedy the situation, overidentification and service will lead inevitably to the destruction of the learning disabilities movement. (Cummings & Maddux, 1985b, p. 14)

We wrote the above passage in mid-1984. Sad to say, nothing has occurred in the interim to cause us to revise that pessimistic assessment of the situation. In fact, if anything, things are worse now than then. When we wrote *Parenting the Learning Disabled,* we discovered that the number of children classified as LD in the U.S. had grown from 120,000 in 1969 to 1,745,865 in 1984 (Kirk & Chalfant, 1985). This represented an increase of 119 percent (Crawford, 1985). The most recent figures now show that the number of LD students has grown to 1,811,489 (Kirk & Gallagher, 1986).

We would support a return to the criterion requiring documentation of deficits in basic psychological processes. Although we recognize that tests designed to measure such deficits are flawed (as are all tests), and that much is unknown concerning these deficits, we do not believe that the baby should have been thrown out with the bath water. We believe that a combination of standardized tests and provision for the exercise of expert clinical judgment and teacher opinion could be used to do a better job of identifying the *truly* learning disabled.

Adelman and Taylor (1986) do a good job of identifying the problem:

Along with the frustration stemming from the prolonged debate over definition, there has been a shift in thinking about the breadth of the phenomenon the field is trying to define. As has been widely stressed, many early leaders in the field intended the term learning disabilities to be used for persons whose learning problems are caused by a central nervous system (CNS) dysfunction. That is, in the early stages of the field's development, learning disabilities were widely viewed as the result of minor neurological problems that interfered with effective perceptual or language processing. And it was though that those with such minor neurological problems were a relatively small group compared to the large number of learning problems seen in our society. As the legal definition is currently applied, however, the label is not restricted to those with such problems. (pp. 514-515)

These writers go on to reinforce our point that because diagnostic procedures are flawed does not mean that conceptualizations leading to them should be abandoned:

As we proceed, we must be careful that our efforts to develop a classification scheme are not limited by our current assessment capabilities. If we allow learning disabilities to be redefined and classified in terms of what can be validly measured at this time, we are likely to define the field out of existence. (p. 520)

With regard to overidentification they maintain:

Despite the difficulties and frustrations encountered in efforts to carefully delineate the population, the fact remains that many individuals labeled as LD should not be so designated; the field clearly cannot afford to ignore so much misdiagnosis. (p. 516)

Overidentification has damaged the field of LD in at least three different ways. First, it has started a backlash of opinion against the field by lawmakers, regular educators, and others who see an increasingly large percentage of the limited resources available to education being spent to fund classes for the learning disabled.

Second, and more seriously, it has stolen the special teacher's time and energy from truly learning disabled children. Overidentification has filled LD classrooms with large numbers of nonlearning disabled students who are underachievers for environmental reasons but who are not abnormal, or handicapped children, in the true sense of these terms.

Third, overidentification together with the misinterpretation of the mainstreaming component of PL94-142 has resulted in the erroneous belief among school administrators and others that learning disabled children can always be educated alongside normal children. This stems from the mistaken belief that PL94-142 is a mainstreaming law.

## The Abuse of Mainstreaming

Contrary to popular belief, PL94-142 *is not* a mainstreaming law. Such a law would require that handicapped children always be educated with nonhandicapped children. The belief that PL94-142 is such a law grew largely out of a widespread failure to read it. The term *mainstreaming* never appears in the Federal law or in the regulations that outline how the law is to be implemented.

PL94-142 is, instead, a *least restrictive environment* law. The law requires that all handicapped children be educated in the least restrictive environment that will work for them. What this means is that each child is to be evaluated on his or her capacity to learn alongside normal children. The child's educational placement is then to reflect that evaluation and is to make use of the normal program *to the extent that the regular program will meet his or her needs.* In other words, the least restrictive environment for any given child is a highly individual matter. For one child it might be a full-time residential setting, for a second it might be a self-contained special room in a regular school, and for a third it might be a regular education room with part-time tutoring in a special education resource room.

The Federal law and attending regulations do not state nor imply that the least restrictive environment for all handicapped children is the regular program, a resource room program, or any other single program. Instead, the least restrictive environment is a program that makes use of the regular program to the maximum extent practical according to the given child's abilities and disabilities.

Because of this requirement, the law requires that school districts provide a "continuum of placements." This means that many different special education placements must be available, each providing education alongside nonhandicapped children to a differing degree. Unfortunately, most school districts are not conforming to this requirement in their dealings with learning disabled children, and are offering only one placement for such students. Typically, this placement is the resource room. In this arrangement, the child is placed in the regular program for most of the day, and receives special help from a special education teacher for one or two class periods each day.

Resource rooms have become the sole choice in some districts because many school officials and some teachers believe that learning disabilities is such a mild condition that a resource room is the most extensive help needed by an LD student. However, automatically placing all LD students in resource room settings is clearly counter to the spirit and letter of the Federal law and regulations. As we have explained, the regulations require that determination of the least restrictive environment be dependent upon individual assessment of each child, and that placement be chosen from a continuum of placements depending on results of the assessment.

Many learning disabled children can be effectively treated using the resource room model. However, other, more severely handicapped learning disabled children cannot cope without more extensive help. The crucial point to remember is that learning disabilities exist on a continuum ranging from mild to severe just as do other handicapping conditions such as mental retardation. Although learning disabilities may be mild in comparison to severely retarded children, severe learning disabilities can have a dramatic impact on the lives of affected children and their families.

This failure to distinguish between the erroneous impression that PL94-142 is *a mainstreaming law,* and the fact that it is *at least restrictive environment law* has had several undesirable effects. As we have already described, it has caused many school districts to place all learning disabled students in resource room settings and to ignore the possibility of any other placements such as self-contained placements, part-time self-contained placements, etc.

A second undesirable effect of misunderstanding of mainstreaming is related to vocational education practices for learning disabled students. Many administrators of such programs assume that since learning disabled students can be taught academics in regular programs, they can profit from regular vocational education programs with no special provisions or modifications. Such is not the case, as we shall see when we discuss the vocational plight of the mildly handicapped later in this chapter.

## Learning Disabilities Summarized

Learning disabilities is the newest identified handicapping condition. The field grew out of the knowledge that there were a number of children who had learning problems but who had none of the previously defined handicaps of mental retardation, physical problems, etc.

The field of learning disabilities is at risk. It is torn from within by factionalism based on seemingly unresolvable philosophical differences. It is under attack from without by lawmakers and others who are alarmed by the overidentification and labeling of children as learning disabled. The problem of overidentification grew out of the problems of definition and related rules about how learning disabled children should be identified. Currently, classrooms for the learning disabled include many children who are underachievers, not because of a classic learning disability, but because of a number of problems such as poor teaching or lack of motivation.

A misunderstanding of PL94-142 and the term *mainstreaming* has led to a narrowing of school treatment options for LD students. Although the law requires that a continuum of placements be available, many districts have done away with all programs other than resource rooms. These programs do a good job with some mildly learning disabled children, but are insufficient for most of the more severe cases.

Proliferation of resource rooms and over-reliance on them has misled many administrators of vocational programs, who assume that vocational education for the learning disabled requires no modifications of existing regular vocational education programs. However, the poor employment record of the mildly handicapped, including the learning disabled, shows this assumption to be unwarranted.

## Mild Emotional Disturbance

Learning disabilities is the newest category to be recognized as a handicap by the public and by professionals. Emotional disturbance, on the other hand, is one of the oldest. The earliest recognition of the condition is buried in antiquity. Perhaps man has always recognized and reacted to the fact that some individuals differ markedly from the average in certain emotional and behavioral characteristics.

The fact that the field is not a new one might lead one to guess that there would be few unsettled controversies, or that the field has reached consensus on most important issues. Nothing could be further from the truth, as illustrated by this quotation:

> Currently, there is little agreement on the critical issues that pertain to the topic including: *definition*—what is emotional disturbance? *general perspectives*—what criteria establish an individual as emotionally disturbed? and *etiology*—what causes emotional disturbance? (Newcomer, 1980, p. 5)

A cursory reading of representative literature in the field reveals that there is great variance in the way individual experts choose to think about emotional disturbance. There are at least six different major approaches to the condition:

1. The Psychodynamic or Psychoeducational Approach
2. The Sociological Approach
3. The Ecological Approach
4. The Biological Approach
5. The Behavioral Approach
6. The Counter-theory Approach

Each of the above approaches leads to very different views concerning definition, etiology, and treatment of emotional disturbance.

### The Definition of Emotional Disturbance

The definition of the condition we are referring to is so controversial that not all experts in the field are even willing to acknowledge that "emotional disturbance" or "emotional illness" exists. Hewett and Taylor (1980) examined articles printed in *The Review of Educational Research* between 1941 and 1969 and report the following evolution of terms:

1941 Socially maladjusted
1944 Socially maladjusted
1953 Socially maladjusted
1959 Emotional factors and academic achievement
1963 Emotionally and socially handicapped
1966 Emotionally and socially handicapped
1969 Behavior disroders
(p. 10)

The 1960s saw a tendency for experts to abandon use of the term *emotional disturbance* and begin to use the term *behavior disorders*. This shift was probably due to the popularity of behavior modification techniques beginning in the 1960s (Hewett & Taylor, 1980).

The more popular term today is probably *behavior disorders*. Therefore, it was somewhat surprising that PL94-142, The Education for All Handicapped Children Act of 1975 uses the term *seriously emotionally disturbed* and does not refer to children with behavior disorders.

Perhaps that is because the framers of the law wanted to emphasize that the category was to be reserved for the more serious cases, and was not to include children with minor behavior problems. The PL94-142 definition of seriously emotionally disturbed is as follows:

> (i) The term means a condition exhibiting one or more of the following characteristics over a long period of time and to a marked degree, which adversely affects educational performance: (a) an inability to learn which cannot be explained by intellectual, sensory, or health factors; (b) an inability to build or maintain satisfactory interpersonal relationships with peers and teachers; (c) inappropriate types of behavior or feelings under normal circumstances; (d) a general pervasive mood of unhappiness or depression; or (e) a tendency to develop physical symptoms or fears associated with personal or school problems. (ii) The term includes children who are schizophrenic or autistic. The term does not include children who are socially maladjusted, unless it is determined that they are seriously emotionally disturbed. (*Federal Register,* Section 121a.5, 1977)

The exclusion of the socially malajusted was added to emphasize that children are ineligible who have simply learned a subcultural value system that is at odds with the mainstream value system. For example, juvenile gang members often fall into this group. There is nothing *abnormal* about many of these children. They have simply been exposed to, and learned, a different subculture. Within that subculture, their adjustment is quite normal and their behavior conforms to the internally prescribed and approved modes. Only those juvenile gang members who are *also* found to be seriously emotionally disturbed can qualify for special education services under this category.

It should be apparent that the definition of emotional disturbance will vary greatly according to the theoretical orientation of the person doing the defining. Of course this is also true of any of the handicapping conditions. However, there are so many diverse theories in emotional disturbance, that a discussion of definition scarcely makes sense if not carried out within the framework of these various approaches. Therefore, we will deal with definition in six sections, each dealing with one of the six major approaches enumerated above.

## The Psychodynamic or Psychoeducational Approach

This approach can be traced to Freud and his psychoanalytic approach to maladaptive behavior. Emotional disturbance is seen as the result of intrapsychic conflict among the id, the ego, and the superego. Briefly, the id represents the desire to satisfy instinctual desires such as sex and aggression. The ego is the logical, rational part of the personality and is capable of viewing the external world objectively. The superego contains the conscience and restricts the id from instant gratification of instinctual desires.

Freud called these structures the "psychic apparatus" and hypothesizes that abnormal behavior is a result of unconscious conflict related to experiences during childhood. Fear that the id might "win out" and dominate is regarded as an important source of neuroses, as is the presence of inordinate guilt from the superego. In either eventuality, the ego takes defensive steps to defend the personality. These defenses are often highly symbolic and sometimes bizarre. When the threat to the personality and the resulting ego defenses are sufficiently strong and sufficiently bizarre, the individual is judged to be emotionally disturbed.

To Freud and other devotees of this approach, the individual's past experiences are regarded as crucial. Sexual conflict and experiences are believed to be particularly important. A great deal of emphasis is placed on understanding the past cause of the behavior. In fact, the theory is that if the disturbed individual can be led to an understanding of the causes of the disturbance which are often rooted in infancy and childhood, the disturbance will disappear.

In this approach, the disorder is regarded as existing within the child, and the focus of treatment is on the child himself or herself. Carl Rogers (1969) is a modern therapist who operates from this theoretical perspective. Rogers places great emphasis on the importance of a good relationship between the teacher and the disturbed child. He recommends programmed instruction that proceeds at the child's own rate, the use of simulations in the classroom, and small group instruction. He rejects assigned readings, lectures, required examinations, and evaluation by the teacher.

Psychoanalytic theory has not been widely applied in school settings. It calls for a highly clinical approach as well as teachers who have been trained as therapists. The environment within which children would be educated would need to be highly permissive and would permit the expression of aggression and hostility. The problem of maintaining such an environment while keeping teachers and pupils physically safe, and parents and taxpayers satisfied, is difficult if not impossible. Therefore, the psychodynamic or psychoeducational approach is little used in public school settings with disturbed students.

## The Sociological Approach

The sociological approach to emotional disturbance deemphasizes the individual and emphasizes the role of the social forces that act on us (Newcomer, 1980). Disturbance is viewed as the breaking of social rules and the study of the behavior of groups of people rather than individuals is considered most important. Social change, for example, is often viewed as a cause of emotional disturbance. There is an emphasis on understanding and changing *roles* within the social system.

Farber (1968) is an articulate proponent of the sociological approach to understanding deviance. He suggests that handicapped individuals are part of the "surplus population" who cannot fill any of the available social niches. He further hypothesizes that there are various groups within the society in whose interest it is to ensure that surplus populations exist. For example, teachers, social workers, and employees of institutions for the mentally retarded or the emotionally disturbed depend on the maintenance of a surplus population for their very livelihood. Similarly, business needs a surplus population from which they can draw low-level workers when new niches are opened.

Labeling theory also evolved from a sociological approach to deviance. Briefly, this theory holds that labeling carries certain social expectations, and that once the label of "disturbed" is applied, persons so labeled will be affected by that label. They will be expected to behave in certain ways, and such behavior will be noted by those around them, while other types of behavior will be ignored.

Sociological theorists point out that not all rule-breakers are labeled and assigned the deviant role. Many people break rules, yet few are labeled. Some of the variables involved in detemining who will be labeled and assigned the deviant role include the amount of power held by the rule-breaker, the social distance between the rule breaker and agents of social control, and whether or not there is someone with a special interest in enforcing penalties against the rule breaker (Rhodes and Paul, 1978).

Proponents of this approach view the disturbance not as lying totally within the child, but as a product of societal roles and social pressure to conform to those roles (Newcomer, 1980). The sociological approach zeroes in on the relationship between the individual and societal roles, pressures, and expectations.

## The Ecological Approach

The ecological approach evolved from the sociological approach and from the science of biology. Briefly, it is concerned with the way an individual, particularly a "disturbed" individual relates to, and interacts with, the environment or the *ecosystem*.

Proponents of the ecological approach point out that man does not exist in a vacuum. Instead, he is a part of a complex system involving many interdependencies. Biologists refer to such interlocking dependencies as an *ecosystem,* and point out that if we change one component of such a system, we also change the whole system. Therefore, ecological theorists maintain that a disturbed individual cannot be viewed in an isolated fashion. In other words, it is a mistake to view that disturbance as lying entirely within the child. Ecological theorists insist on analyzing the entire ecosystem within which the child is experiencing difficulty. Disturbance is viewed as a problem of mutual adaption between the child and his *community* (Rhodes and Paul, 1978).

One of the earliest ecological definitions was the one set forth by Paul Graubard (1973). Graubard defined emotional disturbance or behavioral disability as:

> A variety of excessive, chronic, deviant behaviors ranging from impulsive and aggressive to depressive and withdrawal acts (1) which violate the perceiver's expectations of appropriateness, and (2) which the perceiver wishes to see stopped. (p. 246)

The critical element of ecological theory is that the child is never the sole concern. In order to understand emotional disturbance it is always necessary to consider at least two people: the child and the person or persons who view the child as a problem. Similarly, intervention efforts center on changing the child's behavior and on changing the expectations of whoever is reacting to the child.

Ecological theory attempts to construct a holistic science of human behavior in which all elements of the situation are analyzed. One of the best brief explanations of ecological theory and its relation to emotional disturbance is that by Rhodes and Paul (1978).

## The Biological Approach

The biological or biophysical approach holds that emotional disturbance is caused by biological malfunctioning of the organism. It is a medically oriented approach. Rimland (1969) defines emotional disturbance or behavior disorder from a strong biophysical orientation:

> A severe behavior disorder results solely from the effects of the physical-chemical environment. Biological factors may exert their effects prenatally, during labor and birth, and at any subsequent time. (p. 706)

Rimland takes an extremely radical biophysical approach, suggesting that *all* severe behavioral abnormalities are rooted in organic defects. He suggests that in those cases for which it is presently impossible to identify an underlying biological cause, it may be that our present expertise is too limited to identify the organic problem. He goes on to predict that science will eventually show the psycho-social factors have little if any role to play in the etiology of severe emotional disturbance.

Other biophysical theorists take the more moderate approach that organic variables provide only the predisposition for certain abnormal behaviors. These theorists hypothesize that the environment then provides the necessary catalyst to bring on the aberrant behavior.

Like psychodynamic theorists, the more radical proponents of the biophysical approach hold that the cause of emotional disturbance lies wholly within the child. Interventions thus focus on correcting the biological disturbances or defects thought to be the underlying cause of the problem.

Many educators and members of the general public find this approach more palatable than any of the other theoretical orientations to deviance. Special education professionals are particularly likely to find the biophysical approach attractive, perhaps because the history of special education is closely tied to medicine, a discipline that is itself principally biophysical in orientation.

## The Behavioral Approach

The behavioral approach to emotional disturbance is an American reaction against the early German cognitive orientation in general psychology. Early psychologists before the beginning of this century were interested in understanding the *internal workings of the mind.* Introspection was the method of inquiry, and knowledge so derived was, therefore, highly subjective.

The behaviorists, led by John Watson, took an applied approach by studying what people actually did. Observation of behavior was the method of inquiry, and the data studied were derived from quantifying and recording the behavior. The goal was to completely identify and describe the stimuli that elicits all behavioral responses.

Early behaviorists such as Watson and Edwin Guthrie are called *contiquity theorists,* because of their belief that learning depends on the closeness (contiguity) of stimulus and response. Later behaviorists such as Edward Thorndike and B. F. Skinner are *reinforcement theorists* because they focus on the importance of consequences such as rewards and punishments as determiners of behavior.

Behavioral theorists in emotional disturbance view deviant behavior as a product of past learning. The individual who is disturbed is seen as having been rewarded in the past for disturbed behavior. This resulted in the learning of inappropriate behavior. Treatment consists of identifying those rewards withholding them, and substituting rewards for desired behavior.

Behaviorists focus almost entirely on events outside the child's own body. The fault is not seen as lying within the child, but in an environment which has provided rewards for inappropriate behavior. The child's past is not seen as important (except that past rewards must be discovered and terminated) and the present is the focus of attention. Behaviorists have concentrated on developing highly accurate and efficient ways of measuring and recording behavior, and on investigating the relative effects of different schedules of delivering rewards.

## The Counter-Theory Approach

Counter-theory grew out of the social movements of the 1960s and is a rejection of traditional values and methods, including traditional views of *the scientific methods.* These theorists assert that the so-called scientific method has failed to yield knowledge and techniques useful in dealing with human beings.

Some counter-theorists assert that the existing educational system can be reformed while other, more radical theorists believe that the present system must be scrapped and a new system built in its place. All believe that human diversity is desirable, and that much of what is regarded as deviant behavior may actually be a normal response to an abnormal or sick environment.

Counter-theory in all its many forms has evolved from combining two very different philosophies: Marxism and existentialism. Interested readers are referred to an excellent analysis of the marriage of these two philosophies by Rhodes and Paul (1978).

Briefly, the movement incorporates from Marxist philosophy the concept of the danger of the domination of the common man by an industrialized and capitalistic society. It borrows from existential philosophy a concern for modern man alienated and dehumanized by the institutions by which he is surrounded and of which he is a member.

One of the criticisms of counter-theory is that it seems to be founded on a negative philosophy that opposes existing philosophies and methodologies but does not suggest alternatives. Although this criticism is not completely fair, it is true that writers sharing this philosophical orientation seem to be better at criticizing existing educational policies and procedures than they are at suggesting useful alternatives. Rhodes and Paul (1978) list four areas in which counter-theorists criticize existing educational efforts:

1. Counter-theorists oppose the idea that education's function is to disseminate a body of knowledge and skill that every generation must master.
2. Counter-theorists reject the traditional view of the teacher as knowledge dispenser and the student as passive knowledge consumer. Counter-theorists regard this as intellectual slavery and exploitation.
3. Counter-theorists reject the notion that literacy is an indispensible skill, and maintain that it is often merely a governmental device for keeping track of and propagandizing citizens.
4. Counter-theorists maintain that the institution of the school dehumanizes students. Some writers recommend the reform of existing educational institutions while others recommend the complete dismantling of modern education followed by the substitution of a new and more responsive educational system.

Counter-theorists also reject labeling, the concept of normality, grading by age, the lack of affective components in the curriculum, and the traditional teacher-student relationship. Private counter-theory schools have sprung up across the country, some in inner-city store fronts, others in affluent suburban neighborhoods. Although extremely diverse in their goals and procedures, all oppose the existing educational process, and all express dismay at the dehumanizing influence of that process.

A few examples of books based on counter-theoretical positions include *The Myth of Cultural Deprivation* (Keddie, 1973), *Hansels and Gretels* (Braginsky and Braginsky, 1971), *How Children Fail* (Holt, 1964), and *Teaching As a Subversive Activity* (Postman and Weingartner, 1969).

Although many educators find the writings of counter-theorists to be outrageously over-simplified and naively idealistic, we enjoy studying their positions. Perhaps their greatest contribution is their irreverance, and their willingness to question and reject a host of commonly-accepted educational beliefs and policies. Thus, they force us to examine our most treasured values and beliefs, a process we believe is always interesting and revealing, and which sometimes leads to positive changes in both attitude and action.

## The Prevalence of Emotional Disturbance

Most experts estimate the percentage of school age children with emotional disturbance to be about 2 to 3 percent. However, unlike the category of learning disabilities, the actual percentage of students identified as emotionally disturbed by the nation's school districts is far less than this. Kirk and Gallagher (1986) report that only .91 percent of children enrolled in public schools are currently identified as seriously emotionally disturbed.

These figures indicate that many emotionally disturbed children have not been identified and placed in appropriate special education programs. The reasons for underdiagnosis and placement are unknown, but there are a number of possible reasons or contributing factors that may be operating. First, it may be that school administrators, psychologists, and other school officials are reluctant to classify students as emotionally disturbed because of the stigma associated with such a diagnosis.

Second, it may be that the reluctance to classify students as emotionally disturbed occurs because of the high cost of many placements associated with a diagnosis of emotional disturbance. Many school districts do not offer services which are appropriate for the education of students with severe emotional disturbance, and are forced to contract with private agencies to obtain such services. These contractual arrangements can be extremely expensive when highly specialized residential schools are involved. It is not unusual for such services to cost 30 to 80 thousand dollars per year or more.

A third and related possible cause was investigated by Horner, Maddux, and Green (1986) who studied minority enrollments in regular and special education in a large metropolitan school district in Texas. The district studied had an enrollment of nearly 30,000 students with schools in both suburban and urban neighborhoods. There were .2 percent of students classified as mildly mentally retarded, .15 percent as emotionally disturbed, and 8.9 percent as learning disabled. The researchers compared the percentage of Black, Anglo, and Hispanic children classified as learning disabled, emotionally disturbed, and mildly mentally retarded to the percentages of Black, Anglo, and Hispanic children enrolled in the district (13.43, 55.2, and 31.4 percent respectively). Their results showed an overrepresentation of Black children classified mentally retarded and learning disabled, but no overrepresentation in the category of emotional disturbance. Hispanics were found to be overrepresented only in the LD sample, while Anglos were underrepresented in both the mildly retarded and learning disabled categories and overrepresented only in the emotionally disturbed category.

These data can be interpreted in many different ways and cannot be generalized to other parts of the country. However, it seems possible that the LD category is being used too extensively for students with poor English skills or poor academic skills in general due to cultural differences. Some Black and Hispanic emotionally disturbed children may be placed in LD classes because such a placement is often less expensive than a placement for emotional disturbance, because cultural or language differences are mistaken for learning disabilities, or because parents of minority children are sometimes less able to exert effective pressure on school districts to obtain an expensive placement in a program for emotionally disturbed students.

**Emotional Disturbance Summarized**

Although emotional disturbance has been recognized for many years as a handicapping condition, controversy in the field continues.

There is disagreement about many basic issues including definition, etiology, and treatment. The position one holds about these issues depends greatly on which of six philosophical schools one adheres to.

One of these approaches is the psychodynamic or psychoeducational approach which can be traced to Freud and his followers. Within this theoretical orientation, disturbance is believed to lie totally within the child and the cause is viewed as stemming from conflict among the psychic structures of id, ego, and superego. There is an emphasis on sexual conflicts during childhood, and understanding past experiences is believed to be essential to treatment. Psychodynamic theorists in schools reject autocratic discipline, teacher evaluation of students, lectures, and other traditional teaching practices. They advocate a good teacher-student relationship, the use of simulations, small-group instruction, programmed learning, non-graded settings, and permissive discipline.

The sociological approach views disturbance as the breaking of social rules. Sociological theorists do not believe that disturbance lies wholly within the child and place great emphasis on the effects of societal roles and pressures. These theorists reject labeling and emphasize the importance of bringing about changes in societal expectations concerning the disturbed child.

Ecological theorists define disturbed behavior as behavior that someone else wants to see stopped. Thus, emotional disturbance is not wholly within the child, and can be understood only in the context of the relationship between at least two people. These theorists emphasize the importance of changing not only the child's behavior, but also the expectations of those individuals in the child's environment.

Biological theorists believe that all deviant behavior will eventually be traced to physical defects. They point to what is known about the genetic predisposition to schizophrenia, for example, as evidence for this belief in more severe emotional disturbance. The more radical proponents of this approach suggest that physical causes will one day be found even for mild forms of emotional disturbance. This approach is grounded in the medical model, and intervention is frequently aimed at correcting the physical causes of behavioral abnormalities. Determining and describing the physical cause of emotional disturbance is emphasized heavily by proponents of this approach.

Not all experts in the field of emotional disturbance agree on the use of the term *emotional* disturbance. Many prefer use of the term *behavior disorders*. In some measure, preference for one term or the other is illustrative of the division of the field into a cognitive/behavioral dichotomy. The term *behavior disorder* is probably currently more popular than is *emotional disturbance.* Legislators, however, used *emotional disturbance* in Public Law 94-142, perhaps to emphasize that children so defined were to be those with more serious problems.

The field of emotional disturbance is characterized by underdiagnosis and placement. Although most authorities estimate that between 2 percent and 3 percent of school-age children are emotionally disturbed to the extent that special education services are required, less than 1 percent of the nation's students are currently receiving such services. Factors such as the high cost of supplying services as well as fear of the stigmatizing effect of the label may be responsible for underdiagnosis and placement of students with severe emotional disturbance.

It should be obvious that public school programs designed for emotionally disturbed students will vary greatly according to which theoretical model of disturbance is employed. As we have shown, there is a great diversity of approaches within the field. Unlike the area of learning disabilities, however, the differences of opinion have not been seriously destructive to progress in the field. This is probably because advocates of the various theoretical positions have behaved professionally by debating their ideas in a mature fashion, and by according each other the respect that professionalism demands of scholars with differences of opinion.

This book deals only with the mildly emotionally disturbed. Programs and services for severely emotionally disturbed individuals such as those diagnosed as autistic or schizophrenic are highly specialized and beyond the scope of this book.

## The Mildly Mentally Retarded

The field of mental retardation is much more stable than that of learning disabilities or emotional disturbance. Perhaps this is because there is a longer history of research in this field, or perhaps it is because the condition is slightly more straightforward and a bit easier to understand. Readers who are interested in a comprehensive early history of the field of mental retardation are referred to Kanner's *A History of the Care and Study of the Mentally Retarded* (Kanner, 1964). Information on the more recent history of the field is available in any good survey text on mental retardation.

## The Definition of Mental Retardation

There is no single definition or classification system acceptable to all disciplines interested in mental retardation. Perhaps this is so because each discipline has a different objective. Lawyers are mainly interested in where to put mentally retarded people, sociologists are concerned with understanding what role the retarded play in the social structure, physicians are interested in how the retarded can be physically changed, and psychologists seem interested in retarded populations primarily as a way to better understand *normality.* Educators, however, are primarily interested in accepting the individual as he is, and developing his potential to the fullest.

Throughout our discussion of learning disabilities and emotional disturbance, we have emphasized the importance of the way a condition is defined. Prevalence rates, classification systems, and even treatment programs and legislation can be traced to a definition. Indeed, it is possible to trace the changes in theory and practice relating to mental retardation by tracing the changes in definitions of retardation.

Currently, the generally accepted definition is found in the manual published by the American Association on Mental Deficiency (AAMD). This definition has also been incorporated into the regulations pertaining to Public Law 94-142:

> Mental retardation refers to significantly subaverage general intellectual functioning existing concurrently with deficits in adaptive behavior and manifested during the developmental period. (Grossman, 1983, p. 1)

A comprehensive history of the definition of mental retardation is beyond the scope of this book, although such a study is appropriate for serious students of the field of mental retardation. In this chapter, however, we will deal only with recent changes in the definition.

Grossman's definition quoted above is only a slight modification of the definition found in the AAMD manual in its 1961 version (Heber, 1961). However, the Grossman (1973) manual (which first appeared in a 1973 edition) did make very significant changes over the Heber manual pertaining to operationalizing the definition. In other words, there were changes in procedures used to *identify* mentally retarded individuals.

One of the most significant changes was in the way *subaverage general intellectual functioning* was to be determined. The Heber AAMD Manual had specified that, in order to qualify as mentally retarded, an individual must (among certain other criteria) score more than one standard deviation below the mean (the average score) on an individual intelligence test.

A *standard deviation* is a statistical term that refers to the way statisticians divide up the range of scores of a large group of people who have taken a standardized test. These scores are ranked from highest to lowest and the scores divided into six categories. Each of these categories is one standard deviation and each standard deviation on the most popular IQ test (the WISC-R) covers a range of 15 IQ points. The mean, or average score on this test is an IQ of 100. Therefore, a score that is more than one standard deviation below the mean on this test would be any score lower than 85 (100 minus one standard deviation, or 15 points, equals 85).

The problem with the Heber definition and the defining of the cutoff IQ score as 84 or below is in the numbers of individuals who can be considered retarded. The percentage of the population who score lower than one standard deviation below the mean is slightly in excess of 16 percent! Thus, the Heber manual took a very broad view of abnormality. In a nation of 200 million people, fully 32 million can be expected to score 84 or below on the WISC-R. Most people would not support the contention that there are 32 million retarded people in the country.

For this reason, the Grossman manuals redefined the cutoff point back to where it had been before the Heber manual was published. The Grossman manuals, like earlier criteria, stipulate that *subaverage intellectual functioning* is determined by an IQ score lower than *two* standard deviations below the mean. This returned the cutoff to include only those whose IQs fall below 70. Only about 3 percent of the population can be expected to score this low, a far more reasonable estimate of the prevalence of retardation than 16 percent.

The Grossman manuals also required that a diagnosis of mental retardation include documentation that the individual scored more than two standard deviations below the mean on a test of *adaptive behavior*. Additionally, the manual specified more components of adaptive behavior than had the Heber manual, and further specified that components of adaptive behavior are relative to the cultural group of the individual concerned.

The story of how the concept of adaptive behavior found its way into the definition of retardation is an interesting one that can be traced to the work of Jane Mercer, a California sociologist. Mercer was concerned with the disproportionate number of Black and Chicano children diagnosed as mentally retarded. She authored *Labeling the Mentally*

*Retarded* (Mercer, 1973), in which she reported on her study conducted in Riverside, California. She reported that the public schools are most often the agency which labels children as mentally retarded. She also found that the diagnosis was generally made on the basis of IQ score alone, regardless of how the child adapted to his environment away from school. She concluded that Heber's cutoff should be changed from one standard deviation below the mean to the bottom 3 percent (more than two standard deviations below the mean). She concluded that this would reduce ethnic imbalance. She further recommended that adaptive behavior should be an important aspect of diagnosis.

In her study, she found no Anglos with an IQ less than 69 who were "adapted" (not considered retarded outside of the school environment) and who were labeled retarded. She concluded that the schools do a good job of identifying Anglo retarded children. However, she found a large number of Black and Chicano children labeled retarded who had a measured IQ of less than 69, who were well adapted to their life outside of school, and who were not considered retarded by anyone who had contact with them in their everyday environment outside of school. This resulted in her conclusion that schools were overdiagnosing these minority children.

Mercer developed a series of 28 age-related scales to measure adaptive behavior, or adjustment to life outside of school. The scales made use of answers to questions asked of a respondent outside of school who was in close contact with the child being evaluated. When the label of retardation was applied only to those children who scored more than two standard deviations below the mean on both an IQ test and a test of adaptive behavior, the overrepresentation of minority group children among the retarded disappeared.

The Mercer study and others resulted in the widespread realization that schools were creating a *six-hour retarded child*. Such children are considered retarded only during the six hours they are in school. This realization, together with widespread disillusionment over the validity of standardized testing, particularly when used with minority students, led to the present requirement that a diagnosis of retardation include both assessment of general intellectual functioning and adaptive behavior.

## Levels of Retardation

Although deficient adaptive behavior must be evident, a useful rule of thumb is that children who score between IQ 50 or 55 and 70 can be considered mildly mentally retarded. Moderately retarded individuals include those scoring between IQ 35 or 40 and 50 or 55, and severely and profoundly retarded persons score below IQ 35. (Kirk & Gallagher, 1986)

This book deals with the vocational education of the mildly retarded, or those whose IQs fall in the range from 50 or 55 up to IQ 70. Kirk and Gallagher (1986) suggest that:

> A child who is mildly retarded because of delayed mental development has the capacity to develop in three areas: (1) in academic subjects at the primary and advanced elementary grade levels, (2) in social adjustment to the point at which the child can eventually adapt independently in the community, and (3) the occupational potential to be partially or totally self-supporting as an adult. (p. 119)

Drew, Logan and Hardman (1984) discuss the mildly retarded child in terms of Piagetian learning stages. Piaget, in discussing normal child development, suggests that children from 2 to 7 years of age go through the *preoperational* stage. During this period, perceptions are the primary learning method for the child. At approximately age 7, the *concrete operational* stage begins and continues through age 11. During this stage, perceptions are overshadowed by intellectual activity. Drew, et al. discuss how this progression is altered among mildly retarded children:

> Elementary-age mildly retarded children will be slower in progressing from the preoperational stage into concrete operations. Delay in development may be as much as 3 to 4 years. Even when the period of concrete operations is reached, only the lower stages may be attained during the elementary school years, with higher functioning in the period not attained until adolescence. (p. 222)

Mildly retarded children were once referred to as *educable mentally retarded*. The term was used since many mildly retarded children are capable of learning to read at least fourth grade level material, the level commonly associated with literacy. The term was eventually abandoned, however, since not all mildly retarded children were able to attain this level of reading proficiency, and since many moderately retarded children (formerly called *trainable mentally retarded*) could benefit from academic instruction. In other words, the terms *educable and trainable* set up stereotypic, and often unrealistic, expectations on the part of child service personnel.

The nation-wide trend in the treatment of individuals with mild mental retardation is toward normalization of environments including a strong trend toward deinstitutionalization. We support this movement.

However, we believe strongly that this trend can only be beneficial to mildly retarded individuals if strong community support is offered. Also, deinstitutionalization makes excellent prevocational and vocational training for the mildly retarded more important than ever.

## Mental Retardation Summarized

Although not without its controversies, the field of mental retardation is considerably less controversial than the fields of learning disabilities or emotional disturbance. Mental retardation has a longer history of research, and the condition may be somewhat more straightforward than is learning disabilities or emotional disturbance.

The definition of mental retardation has changed considerably over the years, although the current definition has been modified only slightly since about 1973. In 1973, the IQ score cutoff point for identification was lowered from scores below 85 to scores below 70 (more than two standard deviations below the mean). To qualify as mentally retarded today, an individual must also score more than two standard deviations below the mean on a test of his adjustment to life outside of school. Such tests are called tests of *adaptive behavior.*

Mildly retarded individuals generally have IQ scores between 50-55 and 70. These children have the potential to achieve some academic skills including reading at or approaching the fourth grade level. They are able to learn social skills to the point that most can adapt independently in the community, and they are able to learn job skills sufficiently to be partially or totally self-supporting if they are placed in adequate prevocational and vocational training programs.

This book deals only with the mildly retarded and their vocational needs. The moderately to severely or profoundly retarded have highly specialized needs beyond the scope of this book.

# WHY DO THE MILDLY HANDICAPPED NEED SPECIAL VOCATIONAL TRAINING?

We can answer the above question in a single sentence. Mildly handicapped students need special vocational training because many are not making a satisfactory career adjustment after they leave public school, and because they are capable of doing so if they receive adequate career and vocational training.

## Life After School for the Mildly Handicapped

More and more evidence indicates that handicapped adolescents and adults frequently are failing to make adequate postsecondary adjustment in terms of interpersonal skills, independent living, and work (Cox, 1977; Geib, Guzzardi, Genova, 1981; Gray, 1981).

Levitan and Taggart (1976) pointed out that only 40 percent of the adult handicapped population is employed as compared to 74 percent of the nonhandicapped population. Brolin and Elliott (1984) report that 7,800,000 handicapped adults in the United States have no income and 4,100,000 earn less than $3,000 per year. They calculate that approximately 9 million handicapped individuals do earn some money, but their average earnings are at least $2,000 less than that of nonhandicapped coworkers. Bowe (1978) estimates that two-thirds of all adults with handicaps are at or near the poverty level. Razeghi (1979) points out that the cost of dependency among unemployed disabled individuals currently exceeds $115 billion per year, and this figure is increasing.

These statistics are particularly discouraging in light of the knowledge that the poor vocational showing of handicapped individuals is not inevitable. Although much of the research is dated, we have evidence that mildly handicapped individuals, including those who are mildly retarded, can be partially or fully self-sufficient. A number of studies (Brolin, Durand, Kromer, & Muller (1975); Chaffin, Davison, Regan, & Spellman, 1971; Kidd, Cross, & Higginbotham, 1967; Kokaska, 1968; Strickland & Arrell, 1967) have shown that handicapped students provided with occupationally-oriented programs showed marked improvement in vocational and community adjustment.

Kirk and Gallagher (1986) sum up what research has revealed about employment of retarded adults:

> Mildly retarded adults can learn to do unskilled and semiskilled work. Failure in unskilled occupational tasks is generally related to personal, social or interpersonal characteristics rather than to an inability to execute the assigned task. (p. 159)

In a more recent study, Brickey and Campbell (1981) reported on a job-training program for mentally retarded adults which was so successful that the turnover rate was only 40 percent compared to 175 percent for regular employees and 300 to 400 percent for high school and college students. Brickey, Brauning, and Campbell (1982) reviewed the literature and reported a high rate of job placement success for mildly retarded students completing excellent vocational training programs.

Brimer and Rouse (1978) located those retarded students who had participated in a work-study program in high school and found that most were working and earning salaries above the minimum wage. Halpern (1973) found similar results in his follow-up of students who had attended work-study programs in high school. Additionally, he determined that full-time work study graduates were more often employed than those graduates who participated in part-time work study programs.

Research investigating efficacy of vocational and career education programs for learning disabled students is scarce, although there is ample evidence that these students are graduating from public school programs unprepared for life outside of school. Crimando and Nichols (1982) have shown that when post-secondary learning disabled individuals do find work, it is usually in dead-end jobs which are boring and do not make use of their full capabilities. We have referred to other research on the vocational plight of learning disabled individuals earlier in this chapter.

One of the few studies relating to the efficacy of vocational training programs for learning disabled students was conducted by Hasazi, Gordon, and Roe (1985). These researchers studied 462 Vermont special education students who had graduated, dropped, or left high school between 1979 and 1983. These students included 296 who had been classified learning disabled, emotionally disturbed, and mildly mentally retarded. These researchers found that those youth who had participated in high school vocational programs were more likely to be employed than those who had not been enrolled in vocational classes.

Because of widespread realization that learning disabled adults are not faring well after school, many experts in learning disabilities are calling for excellent career and vocational education programs for such students.

One problem with research into the efficacy of vocational programs is that most such studies compare handicapped students who were enrolled in vocational programs with students who were not. However, we should not expect poor, or inappropriate vocational programs to yield benefits to handicapped students. Therefore, future research on efficacy should be restricted to those programs that can be fully described and which are obviously of excellent quality.

Houck (1984) suggests that statistics on employment of learning disabled persons indicate that many fail to secure jobs or are underemployed, and suggests two actions:

First, at each stage of the educational program, professionals, parents, and the handicapped student must become more sensitive to the need for incorporating skills that will maximize future career options and the likelihood of success. And second, community members and employers must develop greater awareness of potential jobs for the handicapped and particularly the learning disabled worker. (p. 418)

Johnson and Morasky (1980) describe a special vocational and on-the-job training program for secondary learning disabled students in New York. This program resulted in improved self-concept and heightened motivational levels among participants.

Lerner (1985) emphasizes the need for career and vocational programs for learning disabled students:

Learning-disabled adolescents urgently need programs in career and vocational education, since their time remaining in school is usually limited. (p. 253)

Cummings and Maddux (1984) call for excellent career and vocational programs for learning disabled students, and discuss the need for convincing parents of the importance of such programs.

One problem with evaluating the effectiveness of existing programs for learning disabled students is that many of these vocational programs are inappropriate in their organization and implementation. Too frequently, learning disabled students have only two choices. One is to enroll in regular vocational courses. This is frequently disastrous, since the teachers of these courses often do not know how to modify their programs for LD students and often use the same teaching methods used in academic courses. Extensive reading assignments, long term papers, and other such assignments frequently cause learning disabled students to fail or drop out of vocational courses for the same reasons they fail or drop out of academic courses.

The other choice for many LD students is to enroll in special education vocational courses, most of which were originally intended for retarded students. Teachers of these courses frequently do know how to modify teaching methods to accommodate students with deficient academic skills, but the focus of these programs is frequently on developing low-level skills in preparation for placement in jobs that are far below the capability of many LD students. Because LD students find these programs boring and demeaning, they may drop out or, if they complete the program, they may find themselves placed in jobs that are tedious, boring, and below the level that is appropriate for them. Thus, when research is conducted on efficacy of vocational training for LD students, researchers should determine whether or not the programs being tested were appropriate for the students enrolled. Only then will efficacy studies show whether vocational training results in improved career adjustment.

Research on efficacy of vocational programs for mildly emotionally disturbed children is also scarce. Brolin (1982) calls the literature on the vocational adjustment of emotionally disturbed people *negligible*. He suggests some possible reasons for this scarcity:

> They are probably one of the most difficult groups to rehabilitate; many of them have complex needs that continue even if and after they gain employment; they are a very diverse group; and there is difficulty finding them after placement. (p. 64)

The only efficacy study found was the Hasazi, Gordon, and Roe (1985) study discussed above. Career and vocational programming for emotionally disturbed students appears to be a grossly neglected topic. The majority of books on the education of emotionally disturbed students do not list *vocational education* or *career education* as topics in their indices. This seems puzzling in light of the fact that emotionally disturbed students may have a particularly difficult time gaining and keeping employment. Levinson (1984) calls attention to this fact:

> Among the handicapped, emotionally disturbed students may be at a particular disadvantage in regard to securing and maintaining long term employment. It has been said that individuals lose their jobs not because of technical incompetence, but because of skill deficiencies wihin the affective and social domain. Because emotionally disturbed students by definition lack "an ability to build or maintain interpersonal relationships," display "inappropriate types of behaviors or feelings under normal circumstances" or display "a generally pervasive mood of unhappiness or depression," their chances of maintaining employment once it is secured, is diminished. (p. 77)

Brolin (1982) asserts that the emotionally disturbed group is the largest served by vocational rehabilitation. He adds, however, that they have the least probability of success before and after rehabilitation services.

Levinson (1984) suggests:

> To provide for the needs of secondary school emotionally disturbed students, programs must focus on academic, behavioral, social and emotional, and vocational functioning. A vocational emphasis provides a practical basis upon which academic, behavioral and social and emotional skills may be integrated and taught. If the goal of special education is to provide students with the skills necessary to become independent and productive members of society, then a vocational orientation for the emotionally disturbed at the secondary school level may be a most appropriate form of programming. (p. 80)

# BARRIERS TO SPECIAL CAREER/VOCATIONAL
# EDUCATION PROGRAMS

Since experts agree on the need for excellent career and vocational programs for handicapped students, it may seem puzzling that so few special vocational programs exist, or that so few regular programs enroll handicapped students. As seen above, what little progress that has been made has been in the area of mental retardation. Very little progress has been made in instituting effective programs for learning disabled and emotionally disturbed students (Sitlington, 1981), and much remains to be done in development of programs for mildly mentally retarded students.

We have already examined the scarcity of special career and vocational education programs for these groups. Additionally, even though legal mandates exist for the inclusion of handicapped students in regular career and vocational programs, this is rarely occurring. Although handicapped individuals constitute 10 to 12 percent of the general population, they account for only 2.56 percent of the total enrollment in vocational education programs (Office of Civil Rights, 1979).

There are many possible explanations for the scarcity of career and vocational treatment options for mildly handicapped students. One reason is that since elementary schools were the first to institute special education programs, secondary schools instituting such programs used the elementary program as a model. Since the elementary program focused almost entirely on the academic skills of reading, writing, and arithmetic, secondary programs did the same thing. Secondary programs became academically oriented rather than career and vocationally oriented.

Another reason for the scarcity of career and vocational placement options for mildly handicapped children in public school is related to parental attitudes. Parents of mildly handicapped children, particularly parents of learning disabled students, frequently insist on an academic focus for their children, and resist advice that the child should receive career and vocational education services as well. Sometimes this is because of poor communication by school counselors, psychologists, and other professionals who mistakenly give the impression that all learning disabled students are capable of success in college (Cummings & Maddux, 1984). Although some mildly learning disabled children can, with great dedication and effort, succeed in college, most severely learning disabled children cannot.

Kokaska and Brolin (1985) provide a list of problems related to career and vocational education for handicapped students. They include a lack of administrative support, lack of cooperation among many professional disciplines and agencies, poorly conceived career and vocational assessment practices, stereotyping of handicapped people's needs and abilities by professional workers, and unresponsive teacher training programs.

Another reason for inattention to career and vocational programs is related to the temper of the times. The 1980s have seen a *back-to-basics* movement sweep the country. In this atmosphere, career and vocational education is often viewed as a watered-down curriculum, a relaxation of standards, and a generally less-than-rigorous approach to education. The back-to-basics movement frequently emphasizes academics to the exclusion of all else. In such a climate, legislators are hesitant to fund career and vocational programs and risk alienating powerful pressure groups who view the nation's children as a weapon to use against other countries or as an economic resource to exploit to ensure scientific, technological, and economic ascendancy in the world market.

Cegelka (1985) lists a number of factors contributing to handicapped underrepresentation in vocational education programs. These include: (a) high dropout rates of handicapped secondary students; (b) the focus on mainstreaming handicapped students in the regular curriculum; (c) secondary special education teachers who have "little realistic understanding of the realities of the world of work and who have their strongest preparation in elementary level methodologies and curriculum" (p. 605); and (d) the resistance of vocational education teachers to include handicapped students in their programs. This resistance exists partially because of the view that including handicapped students would lower the status of vocational programs and jeopardize their existence since these programs are evaluated on the basis of job layoffs of former participants.

We believe that the attitude of vocational teachers is frequently a barrier to providing excellent career and vocational programs for mildly handicapped students. This is not surprising in light of the fact that only 3 percent of all vocational education teachers in the U.S. have completed courses on the special needs of handicapped students. In addition, McDaniel (1982) reports that vocational instructors are often reluctant to accept handicapped students in regular classroom settings, even when special accommodations are not needed. McDaniel concludes that "The teachers' lack of training could account for their generally negative attitudes toward handicapped students" (p. 377).

Similarly, Minner (1982) found that vocational teachers held unrealistically negative academic and behavioral expectations concerning handicapped children, especially those labeled learning disabled. Minner recommended further research on methods of altering and improving vocational teacher attitudes toward handicapped children.

## SUMMARY

We have attempted to answer two questions in this chapter:

1. Who are the mildly handicapped?
2. Why do the mildly handicapped need a special vocational program.

We have briefly defined each of the handicapping conditions including learning disablities, mild mental retardation, and mild emotional disturbance.

We then discussed the career adjustment plight of individuals who suffer from these conditions, and presented evidence that proper career and vocational training can prevent many of the problems experienced by the handicapped.

We will go on in future chapters to explore specific problems and solutions related to the issues raised in this chapter.

## Chapter Two

# CAREER EDUCATION: AN OVERVIEW

## HISTORICAL DEVELOPMENT OF CAREER EDUCATION

KOKASKA (1983) states that the roots of career education can be traced to the work of Richard Hungerford in the New York City school system in the 1940s and to the work-study programs developed by Kolstoe and Frey (1965). However, the concept of career education was first officially introduced to American educators in 1971 by the U. S. Commissioner of Education, Sidney P. Marland, Jr., at a national conference of secondary school principals. At that time, educators were concerned with the large numbers of students who were either dropping out of school or who were graduating without being adequately prepared for work. In his address, Marland (1971) pointed out that nearly 2.5 million students were leaving school each year without the necessary skills to enter the world of work.

In response to these discouraging statistics, many educators voiced the need for a more practical and meaningful approach to education. Career education was introduced as the means by which this approach could be provided (Brolin, 1978). According to Brolin, Elliott, and Corcoran (1984), it was believed that the introduction of career education would result in greater school relevance and meaning, and that students would become more aware of themselves, their potentials, and the type of careers they could assume in the future as responsible adults.

In an effort to make education more relevant to current economic and employment realities, the concept of career education emphasized (a) relating academic subject matter to various careers and occupations, (b) developing work skills appropriate for current occupational demands, (c) emphasizing the respectability of all work, and (d) stressing

41

the value of avocational work (Cegelka, 1985). According to Cegelka, career education "sought to increase the life satisfaction of workers, restore the work ethic, and increase national productivity" (p. 575).

From the early 1970s to the early 1980s, career education progressed rapidly (Kokaska & Brolin, 1985). In 1976, Dr. Marland returned to Houston to keynote the first National Commissioner's Conference on Career Education. He commented on the fact that never in the educational history of the United States had there been such an enormous reform movement in such a brief span of time. At the Helen Keller Centennial Conference, Hoyt (1980) noted that the concept of career education had survived for a full decade — three times as long as the typical educational reform movement.

Unfortunately, however, not all goals of career education have been achieved. Many of the early concerns of proponents of career education continue to be voiced today. Findings of the National Assessment of Educational Progress (1978a; 1978b) revealed that only 2 percent of 34,000 surveyed high school students considered public education effective in preparing them for work. Also, these students had not acquired necessary skills such as measuring, computing costs, filling out job applications, and thinking critically. Investigators also judged their occupational aspirations to be unrealistic.

According to Siccone (1983), American schools are graduating students with all-time low achievement levels at the same time that society is moving into an information-based age of high technology. In addition, the Carnegie Council of Policy Studies in Higher Education (Kerr, 1979) reported that nearly one-third of high school-aged individuals were ill-employed, poorly educated, and incapable of functioning in society. In some communities, school dropout rates were as high as 23 percent for Caucasians, 35 percent for Blacks, and 45 percent for Hispanics. Irrelevant school curricula was cited as the primary cause for the high rates of student dropout.

## CAREER EDUCATION DEFINED

According to Cegelka (1981), when the concept of career education was first introduced by Marland, he declined to offer an official definition of the concept. Marland preferred to *describe* the new concept rather than *define* it. Thus, scholars and practitioners would be free to debate, define, and implement the concept as they wished and in a manner that best suited their needs. Marland felt that an operational definition of the new concept would come about after national debate, research, scientific analyses, and testing of assumptions in real schools and classrooms. Marland also hesitated to define the new concept because of his desire to give it a grass-roots flavor.

Over the years, many definitions for career education have appeared. Some of the differences in definitional approaches are partly a function of the differing needs of various groups (Cegelka, 1981). For example, a definition suitable for a school superintendent may not be appropriate for use by a teacher or a college professor. Cegelka also notes that some of the more substantial differences in definition reflect differences between definitions that have a restricted, vocational focus and those that reflect a more universal, *all of education* approach. To give the reader an idea of the diversity of career education definitions, we would like to present some that have been proposed over the past decade.

In 1975, the official U. S. Office of Education defined career education as "the totality of experience through which one learns about and prepares to engage in work as part of his or her way of living" (Hoyt, 1975, p. 4). While some people interpret this definition to include voluntary work, productive use of leisure time, and the unpaid work of homemakers and students (Kokaska, 1983), others interpret it as emphasizing preparation for *paid* employment (Brolin & D'Alonzo, 1983).

Other definitions take a broader view of career education (Gysbers & Moore, 1975; Hanson, 1977; Super, 1976). These specify that a career encompasses many different roles including occupational, social, leisure, and interpersonal. Others describe a job as only one part of a person's career. Goldhammer (1972) discusses several "careers" in which individuals become engaged. These include (a) producer of goods and renderer of services; (b) member of a family group; (c) participant in social and political life; (d) participant in avocational pursuits; and (e) participant in the regulatory functions involved in aesthetic, moral, and religious concerns.

A more recent definition provided by Hoyt (1977) recognizes broader roles in one's career pattern. According to this definition, career education is defined as follows:

> An effort aimed at refocusing American education and the actions of the broader community in ways that will help individuals acquire and utilize the knowledge, skills, and attitudes necessary for each to make work a meaningful, productive, and satisfying part of his or her way of living. (p. 5)

Another definition of career education is provided in the official statement of the Council for Exceptional Children:

> The totality of experiences through which one learns to live a meaningful life . . . providing the opportunity for children to learn, in the least restrictive environment possible, the academic, daily living, personal-social and occupational knowledge and skills necessary for attaining their highest level of economic, personal, and social fulfillment. The individual can obtain this fulfillment through work (both paid and unpaid) and in a variety of other societal roles and personal lifestyles.

In 1980, at the Helen Keller Centennial Conference, Hoyt further refined his definition when he stated that career education is:

> . . . making *work* a personally meaningful and productive part of the total lifestyle of all persons . . . that *work* as used in career education, is defined as "conscious effort, other than that aimed at coping or relaxation, to produce benefits for oneself and/or for oneself and others." Furthermore, the word "career" as used in career education, is defined as "the totality of work one does in his/her lifetime." (p. 2)

Brolin, Elliott, and Corcoran (1984) comment on the above definition pointing out two important concepts about career education that are included: (a) career education is a focus on productive work activity, and (b) one's career is more than an occupation; it is all the various kinds of work activity engaged in throughout a lifetime. They go on to say that while career education should not be the only education students receive, it should be a substantial part. While career education should not replace what educators do, it should re-direct existing public school curriculum around a career development theme for more relevant and meaningful learning.

Brolin, et al. (1984) describe the major components of a comprehensive educational program as consisting of (a) *general and continuing education* which consists of learning about the world in which we live, basic academic skills, aesthetic appreciation, physical education, and so on; (b) *specific vocational programming* which consists of vocational counseling, vocational assessment, vocational education and training; job placement, and follow-up; and (c) *career education* which adds a third dimension often missing in a comprehensive educational program. The authors state that these three components should not be thought of as discrete entities to be taught separately, but should be integrated components existing throughout an individual's public school career.

In conclusion, Brolin et al. (1984) state that career education is a total educational concept that includes the following major tenets:

1. It begins in early childhood and continues through the retirement years.
2. It encompasses the total curriculum of the school and provides a unified approach to education for life.
3. It focuses on the various life roles, settings, and events that are important in the productive work life of the individual.
4. It encourages all members of the community to have a shared responsibility and a mutual cooperative relationship among various disciplines.
5. It includes learning in the home, private-public agencies, and the employment community, as well as in the school.
6. It encourages all teachers to relate their subject matter to its career implications.
7. It recognizes the need for basic education, citizenship, family responsibility, and other important educational objectives.
8. It provides for career awareness, career exploration, and skills development at all levels and ages.
9. It provides a balance of content and experiential learning with substantial hands-on activities.
10. It provides a personal framework to help individuals plan their lives through carefully conceived career decision-making.
11. It promotes the opportunity for students to acquire a saleable entry-level occupational skill before leaving school.
12. It actively involves the parents in all phases of education.
13. It actively involves the community in all phases of education.
14. It requires a lifelong education based on principles related to total individual development.

## VOCATIONAL VS. CAREER EDUCATION

One commonly-held misconception is that vocational education and career education are identical. Kokaska (1983) points out the difference in the two concepts by defining vocational education as including training in a wide variety of *specific technical skills* essential in performing work roles. He states that:

> This training is supervised by specialists who qualify for such occupational areas as accountant, secretary, or electrician. Training begins at the secondary level and is defined in terms of courses within an instructional program. (p. 194)

Kokaska goes on to say that career education, as opposed to vocational education, encompasses all levels of the school system, involves all teachers, and promotes cognitive, affective, and psychomotor skill development.

Cegelka (1985) also defines career education as being broader than vocational education. She explains that career education encompasses vocational education, work attitudes, and skills at the secondary and post-secondary levels while the purpose of vocational education is to provide specific vocational skill training and vocational adjustment. She stresses that "career education is concerned with the quality of the individual's total life adjustment." (p. 601)

In summary, the concept of career education was introduced in 1971 to meet the educational needs of large numbers of students who were dropping out of school because of what they considered to be a lack of relevancy in education. Since that time, many individuals and groups have endorsed the concept. However, just as many others have resisted including career education in the public school curriculum. That resistance has intensified in the last few years with the recent emphasis on upgrading the quality of education and stressing the teaching of academics. However, as Brolin and D'Alonzo (1983) point out:

> Career education is a total educational concept. It is not intended to replace present educational practices, as some seem to believe, but rather to help make all instructional material personally relevant by restructuring it around a career development theme . . . Career education brings meaning to the curriculum by making individuals more aware of themselves, their potentials, and their educational needs. (p. 97)

## LEGISLATION AND CAREER/VOCATIONAL EDUCATION

During the late nineteenth and early twentieth centuries, industrialization, increased immigration, and greater numbers of students in secondary schools resulted in demands for public school vocational education programs (Cagelka, 1985). Because of these demands, laws were passed for vocational education in the secondary schools.

The first of these laws was the *Smith-Hughes Act of 1917,* which was the first law to make federal monies available for vocational education. *The Vocational Education Act of 1963* extended vocational education services to include individuals who had left school, who needed vocational training to gain entry into the job market or to maintain or advance in present jobs, and who had academic, socioeconomic, or other handicaps that prevented them from succeeding in regular vocational education programs. According to Cegelka (1979):

> This emphasis on the needs of individuals represents a fundamental philosophical shift in the approach of Congress to vocational education. While the Smith-Hughes Act of 1917 focused on the needs of employers, the Vocational Act of 1963 emphasized the importance of vocational skills to workers as a means of insuring their own welfares. (p. 163)

The 1968 Amendments to the Vocational Act of 1963 specified that monies be set aside for the provision of vocational education programs for handicapped and disadvantaged students. The 1968 Amendments also defined the term *handicapped* for vocational education purposes. Most categories of handicapped students were included with the exception of learning disabilities. The 1976 Amendments to the Vocational Act of 1963 included learning disabled students among those eligible for services. These amendments also specified that handicapped children be included in regular vocational education programs with special assistance and equipment being provided as needed.

Federal legislation has also addressed the need for vocational guidance. In 1962, the Economic Assistance Act specified the need for effective career counseling as part of its various programs including Job Corps, VISTA, etc. The 1964 Amendments to the National Defense Education Act encouraged educational agencies to provide counseling and guidance to assist students in achieving appropriate career development. Finally, the 1968 Higher Education Act Amendments provided for the training for school guidance counselors.

## Career/Vocational Legislation and Handicapped Populations

A variety of federal legislation favorably affected career education efforts for handicapped individuals (Cegelka, 1981). The Education for All Handicapped Children Act of 1975 (PL94-142) mandated that handicapped students be provided an appropriate public school education in the least restrictive educational environment. This implied that career/vocational education experiences could be mandated if they were considered those most appropriate for achieving the objectives of a handicapped student's Individual Education Plan (IEP).

As we have already stated, the 1968 and 1976 Amendments to the Vocational Education Act of 1963 required that states set aside 10 percent of their federal vocational education monies for use with handicapped students. Also, the Comprehensive Employment and Training Act (CETA) of 1973 was amended with additional regulations that extended CETA training and employment efforts to include all handicapped individuals whose handicaps presented substantial barriers to employment, regardless of income.

The Vocational Rehabilitation Act of 1973 contained important implications for career education efforts for handicapped persons. Section 504 prohibited the exclusion of handicapped individuals, solely on the basis of their handicaps, from participation in, or from any of the benefits of, any program or activity receiving federal assistance. Section 503 required any business receiving more than $2,500 in federal monies to take affirmative action to hire the handicapped. Another important feature of the Vocational Rehabilitation Act was to make services to the severely disabled a priority objective. According to Cegelka (1981), this was particularly timely because of recent demonstrations of severely handicapped individuals' ability to perform highly complex work tasks.

Cegelka (1981) comments that the sweeping mandates of Section 504 and of PL94-142 resulted in some confusion as to which program, agency or profession was primarily responsible for providing which types of career preparation programming for handicapped groups. She states that an important solution to these problems occurred in 1977 when the Rehabilitation Services Administration and the U. S. Office of Education issued a *memorandum of understanding*. This official declaration of cooperation provided for collaboration and coordination in the delivery of career preparation services to handicapped individuals.

Two recent pieces of legislation have further mandated the inclusion of handicapped groups in career/vocational planning and program development. The Job Training Partnership Act (JTPA) took effect in October, 1983. The purpose of the Act was to establish programs to prepare youth and unskilled adults for entry into the labor force and to afford job training to economically disadvantaged and other individuals facing serious barriers to employment.

Finally, the Carl Perkins Vocational Education Act of 1984 focused on providing quality vocational education to groups traditionally underrepresented in vocational programs. One of its stated purposes was to provide access and quality programs for underserved students, especially the disadvantaged, the handicapped, men and women entering nontraditional occupations, adults in need of training and retraining, single parents and homemakers, the incarcerated and individuals with limited English proficiency. Two themes were important to this law: (a) the emphasis on providing supplemental services for special students within the mainstream, and (b) the emphasis on building programs and relationships with community-based organizations and the private sector.

In summary, career/vocational education programs have been mandated through legislation since 1917. However, not until the middle 1960s have such programs been available to handicapped individuals. Although great strides have been made to prepare handicapped students for adult life, there is still much to be done. For the remainder of this chapter we will consider existing problems in career/vocational preparation of handicapped groups, look at various attempts to solve those problems, and discuss future directions of career/vocational education for handicapped individuals.

## CAREER/VOCATIONAL EDUCATION FOR HANDICAPPED POPULATIONS

If mildly handicapped students are to profit from career/vocational education programs, those who design them should be aware of and understand the historical development and philosophies of traditional career/vocational education programs for handicapped students. Such knowledge will allow program designers to incorporate relevant elements of both approaches into a career/vocational education model uniquely suited for mildly handicapped students. Thus, the purpose of the following discussion is to describe the historical development, philosophies, and descriptions of traditional career/vocational education programs for handicapped students.

### Historical Development

Traditionally, the focus of occupational programming for handicapped students has been on *vocational* education, and emphasis has been on the teaching of specific job skills. Until recently, career education, in terms of helping the handicapped individual obtain personal fulfillment through work, has been neglected. However, recent legislation and professional attitudes are paving the way for a more comprehensive approach toward providing handicapped students with a comprehensive career/vocational education program.

In 1978, the U. S. Office of Education took the position that an appropriate comprehensive vocational education should be made available to every handicapped student (*Federal Register*, Sept. 25, 1978). This statement was developed jointly by the Bureau of Education for the Handicapped (now Office of Special Education) and the Bureau of Occupational and Adult Education. It emphasized that handicapped individuals encounter major barriers in obtaining employment and job-related training, and are more frequently unemployed and underemployed than are nonhandicapped individuals (Phelps & McCarty, 1984).

These concerns are justified in light of recent employment statistics pertaining to handicapped individuals. Levitan and Taggart (1977) noted that only 40 percent of all handicapped adults are employed, compared to 74 percent of the nonhandicapped population. In his study of the employment patterns of mentally retarded persons, Hightower (1975) reported that only 21 percent are fully employed when they finish school, while 40 percent are underemployed, and 26 percent are unemployed. In another discouraging report, Poplin (1981) noted that of the 30 million disabled persons in the United States, only 4.1 million are employed. Finally, Brolin and Elliott (1984) reviewed national income figures and determined that 7,800,000 handicapped adults have no income and 4,100,000 earn less than $3,000 per year. Razeghi (1979) estimates that the cost of dependency among handicapped individuals exceeds $115 billion per year.

We have already mentioned legislation that has been enacted in an attempt to combat the employment problems of handicapped individuals and lay the foundations for career education for handicapped students. While passage of these laws has resulted in national efforts to improve secondary vocational programs for handicapped students, Heller (1981) has referred to these efforts as minimal. The impact of legislation is yet to be felt to any degree. Brolin and Elliott (1984) assert that many of the 500,000 special education students who leave the educational system each year continue to do so "woefully unprepared to acquire satisfactory societal roles in occupational, avocational, and daily living activities" (p. 12). Sitlington (1981) maintains that handicapped students who graduate from high school have acquired entry level skills at best, and Levinson (1984) reports that over one million students currently lack the career and vocational skills needed to compete for jobs in their communities. Finally, Hoyt (1975) has commented on the tendency of society to act as though a handicapped person should be satisfied with and grateful for any kind of work society provides. He states that it is wrongly assumed that handicapped persons are incapable of becoming bored on the job. In addition, we are often shocked if a handicapped person is anything less than eternally grateful when provided with a job, regardless of how menial or boring that job is.

As we have described in a previous chapter, several possibilities exist to explain public schools' failure to prepare adolescent students for work. One contributing factor has been the tendency to institute secondary special education programs modeled after elementary counterparts. These programs focus on academic skills such as reading and arithmetic, and neglect career or vocational components (Cummings & Maddux, 1984; D'Alonzo, Marino, & Kauss, 1984; Heller, 1981). Hohenshil (1984) has commented:

> In the past, the goals of most secondary special education programs were similar to those provided in the elementary schools. Many special educators seemed to believe that if their students didn't learn to read, write, and do arithmetic in elementary school, then they should get another 6 to 8 years of the same. (p. 51)

Heller (1981) discusses other associated problems including subject-matter orientation of secondary school teachers and emphasis on elementary practicum experiences for special education teachers-in-training.

Another contributing factor to public school failure to provide appropriate career/vocational education has been the lack of professionals specially trained to provide vocational and career education services to handicapped learners (Levinson, 1984). Educators trained in special education who traditionally have been responsible for educating handicapped students often lack knowledge and skills in vocational and career education (Cummings & Maddux, 1984; Levinson, 1984). Consequently, they have emphasized academic rather than vocational preparation of handicapped learners (Kokaska & Kolstoe, 1977). Vocational educators, on the other hand, while knowledgeable about career/vocational development and programming, know little about educating handicapped students (Cummings & Maddux, 1984; Levinson, 1984).

Another problem is related to the difficulty faced by many handicapped students who attempt to enroll in regular vocational education programs. According to Marino (1981), career education and vocational training usually provided in the secondary school for nondisabled students is also available but often elusive for disabled students. This type of training and education is ordinarily offered as an elective at the secondary level. Nondisabled students who register for these elective programs are usually accepted. However, handicapped students who register for these same programs are frequently screened out because they lack the prerequisites and background to qualify for the courses (D'Alonzo, Marino, & Kauss, 1984).

The same problem exists in terms of career exploration and guidance for handicapped students. Hohenshil and Warder (1978) note that vocational educators express an urgent need for diagnostic services to identify, plan, and evaluate educational programs for handicapped students. However, school counselors are usually not trained to work with handicapped students and lack the diagnostic skills needed to develop appropriate programs for them. On the other hand, vocational rehabilitation counselors lack knowledge of public school vocational education programs, and are unable to contribute to the vocational programming of the handicapped in the public schools (Levinson, 1984).

Heller (1981) places the blame on American secondary schools and concludes that "The fact is undeniable — secondary education remains a vast wasteland for the potential that handicapped individuals hold" (p. 583).

A final, major factor underlying all of these difficulties may be that career/vocational theory-builders have developed their theoretical assumptions with normal, nonpathological populations, and have been little concerned with handicapped groups (Conte, 1983).

Whatever the reasons, the fact is that career education programs suited to the unique educational needs of handicapped learners have not yet been developed. More is needed in terms of both theoretical bases and educational programs. As previously mentioned, the only options usually available to handicapped students are special education programs and vocational education programs.

## Traditional Special Education Vocational Programs

In the past, career education programs for handicapped learners have been delivered through special education work-study programs (Brolin & D'Alonzo, 1983; Sitlington, 1981). These programs were initiated in the 1950s and the 1960s because of the concern that academically-oriented curricula were not meeting the vocational and social needs of handicapped students leaving the school system (Brolin & D'Alonzo, 1983). Research on community adjustment of mildly handicapped students revealed that a majority had major difficulties after leaving public school (Brolin, 1972; Brolin, Durand, Kromer, & Muller, 1975; Tobias, 1970). However, a number of other studies (Brolin, et al., 1975; Chaffin, Davison, Regan, &

Spellman, 1971; Kidd, Cross, & Higginbotham, 1967; Kokaska, 1968; Strickland & Arrell, 1967) reported that handicapped students provided with occupationally-oriented programs showed marked improvement in vocational and community adjustment.

The emphasis of these programs has traditionally focused on development of work attitudes and general work behaviors, rather than on specific skill training. From the beginning, these programs have been designed primarily for mentally retarded adolescents. Little has been done for other handicapped groups, particularly learning disabled and behavior disordered students (Sitlington, 1981).

The basic purpose of these programs has been to coordinate classroom activities with on-the-job experiences. According to Sitlington (1981), work-study programs closely resemble the cooperative education model employed by regular vocational education, although the classroom experience emphasizes general work habits and attitudes rather than specific instruction in occupational areas. The work-study model is used almost exclusively in self-contained classroom settings.

Thompson and Wimmer (1976) have identified five primary components of the work experience sequence: (a) prevocational experience, (b) job analysis; (c) in-school work experiences, (d) community placement, (e) after graduation placement and follow-up.

## Regular Vocational Education

The inclusion of handicapped students in regular vocational education programs is mandated by for major pieces of legislation: (a) The Rehabilitation Act of 1973, Section 504; (b) The Education for All Handicapped Children Act of 1975 (PL94-142); (c) The Education Amendments of 1976, Title II (PL94-482); and (d) The Carl D. Perkins Vocational Education Act of 1984 (PL98-524).

As with career education, a number of definitions of vocational education exist (Sitlington, 1981). The Education Amendments of 1976 use the following definition:

> Vocational education means organized educational programs which are directly related to the preparations of individuals for paid or unpaid employment or for additional preparation for a career requiring other than a baccalaureate or advanced degree . . . (p. 53865).

According to Sitlington (1981), vocational education has much to offer handicapped students in specific skill training for semi-skilled and skilled occupations.

Unfortunately, even though legal mandates exist for the inclusion of handicapped students in regular vocational programs, this is rarely occurring. According to the Office of Civil Rights in 1979, handicapped individuals constituted 10 to 12 percent of the general student population, yet they accounted for only 2.56 percent of the total enrollment in vocational education programs, with one-third of these students receiving their training in segregated vocational programs for the handicapped. Apprenticeship programs had the lowest percentage of handicapped student enrollments (0.37%) with work-study programs having the highest percentage (4.48%). This data led to the Office of Civil Rights' (1980) conclusion that handicapped students are clustered in vocational education programs that prepare them for lower-level occupations. Other career preparation programs also show underrepresentation of handicapped participants: 3 percent of total CETA clients; 3 percent of community college enrollments; and 2 percent of enrollments in four-year colleges (Cegelka, 1985).

According to Cegelka (1985), a number of factors contribute to handicapped underrepresentation in vocational education programs. These include: (a) high dropout rates of handicapped secondary students that may be as much as five to six times higher than those for non-handicapped students; (b) the focus on mainstreaming handicapped students in the regular curriculum; (c) secondary special education teachers who have "little realistic understanding of the realities of the world of work and who have their strongest preparation in elementary level methodologies and curriculum" (p. 605); and (d) the resistance of vocational education teachers to include handicapped students in their programs. This resistance exists because of the view that including handicapped students would lower the status of vocational programs and jeopardize their existence since these programs are evaluated on the basis of job layoffs of former participants.

To conclude, career education and vocational training are necessary if mildly handicapped individuals are to become independent of parents and community social and welfare agencies. According to D'Alonzo, et al. (1984):

> Career education and vocational training hold the key to unlocking the "ports of entry" into the world of work for the disabled student. Educators, industrialists, and manufacturers, as well as political agencies, are well aware of the potential manpower and human resources of the disabled available in all communities. They know that, if properly trained through career and vocational education, disabled persons can be assets and valuable employees. (pp. 24-25)

Even though legislation has mandated that handicapped students be included in public school career/vocational programs, such participation is rare. According to Cegelka (1985), it is impossible to legislate "emotions, attitudes, or a sense of commitment" (p. 606). She emphasizes the need to allay the fears and concerns of vocational educators by assuring them that inclusion of handicapped students will not displace nonhandicapped students in vocational programs. She also stresses that:

> The focus of vocational education must be broadened to provide greater emphasis on the development of general work skills and attitudes. In-service education must provide vocational education teachers with the needed instructional skills for working with students with disabilities, and program entrance requirements must be changed to reflect the competencies needed to perform the jobs targeted on the IEPs rather than the aptitudes required to complete an entire training program. Finally, program evaluation should be broadened to include the provision of services to special needs students and not limited to labor market layoffs. (p. 606)

## Future Trends

We have presented an historical overview of the development of career/vocational education programs for handicapped youth in the public schools. In light of recent legislation, particularly the Carl D. Perkins Vocational Education Act of 1984, it appears that more mildly handicapped youngsters will be served in regular vocational education programs. However, if these students are going to be appropriately served, innovative programs must be designed which focus on the labor market and include appropriate support services. In addition, every career/vocational education program must develop employability and job skills, positive attitudes, and the knowledge essential for entering the workforce (Phelps, 1985).

Phelps (1985) lists several innovations that must occur if career/ vocational programs are going to be effective for handicapped participants.

1. In the past, career/vocational programs for special needs students have been developed in public school secondary classrooms. However, as the average age of the population continues to rise and efforts are expanded to identify handicapped adults, postsecondary institutions will be challenged to respond to their needs. If quality programs are going to be provided for handicapped adults, vocational administrators and program coordinators will need to work closely with

JTPA service delivery agencies; community-based organizations; business, industry, and labor groups; rehabilitation agencies; and many other human service agencies.

2. Public school teachers and administrators face very different challenges in terms of providing appropriate career/vocational services to special populations. To make sure that various special populations are enrolled in adequate numbers, administrators must think in terms of categories and labels. However, if these students are going to be effectively served once they are enrolled, teachers and guidance counselors must do just the opposite—ignore the labels and focus on the students as individuals.

3. For most mildly handicapped students and adults, mainstreaming is the approach of choice. Employability and occupational skills are best developed in regular vocational classrooms, and in programs that integrate cooperative vocational education and vocational student organization experiences. Also, the social benefits of mainstreaming are important for most mildly handicapped students. Handicapped students learn to cope and interact with their nonhandicapped peers, and nonhandicapped students learn to value the contributions of special needs students.

4. Small group, cooperative learning activities are the most effective methods for teaching handicapped students in regular vocational classrooms, particularly when the activities involve group rewards for team member achievement.

5. Individualized functional skills assessments are essential for handicapped learners. They identify each student's interests, abilities, strengths and deficiencies. In addition, they enable teachers to avoid the pitfalls of labeling. Assessment information should be used to pinpoint appropriate learning activities, not to limit students' experiences.

6. A broad range of support services should be available to enhance the possibility for success for handicapped learners. These include basic skills instruction, equipment modification, language interpreters, special instructional materials, modified vocational instruction by special education and other staff, employability skills instruction, and career information and counseling. It is important to recognize that the need for these services will vary from one special needs learner to another. In addition, different students within the same population group may require distinctly different services.

7. To ensure provision of adequate support services, there must be careful collaboration among the various professionals and agencies that assist handicapped individuals. Thus, special and vocational teachers must develop a close working relationsip with counselors, special education personnel, social workers, and teachers of basic skills.

8. To be effective, IEPs must be continuously monitored by everyone involved in a particular student's educational program. It is imperative that instructors and support staff be familiar with weekly instructional objectives and learning activities.

9. Finally, as vocational educators expand their efforts to appropriately serve handicapped individuals, a broad perspective on the subject must be developed. This can be done by adopting an operational definition that emphasizes examining the needs of individuals, and places the responsibility for collectively addressing these needs on special educators, vocational educators, and other professionals who work with handicapped populations.

## SUMMARY

In this chapter we have provided an overview of the development of the concept of career education. We have also discussed the relevancy of providing excellent career/vocational education programs for handicapped populations. Finally, we described some of the future implications of career/vocational education for handicapped individuals.

To date, handicapped youth are still lacking in career/vocational skills necessary for successful entry into the competitive work world, and life as adults. There is yet much to be done. Phelps (1985) sums it up nicely with the following statements:

> At a time when resources are scarce and the excellence in education movement seems to have largely overlooked the diverse needs and learning styles of students, providing individualized planning and services for all will be a significant challenge. But ultimately that is the direction in which vocational education must move. (p. 26)

## Chapter Three

# CAREER DEVELOPMENT THEORY AND
# HANDICAPPED POPULATIONS

A MAJOR problem with the traditional career development approaches with handicapped populations stems from the fact that none of these are based on any theoretical model. In reviewing the literature in preparation for the writing of this book, we found nothing to indicate that any theoretical approaches have been given major consideration in the design and implementation of career/vocational programs for handicapped populations.

This concern is echoed by other writers as well. Phillips, Strohmer, Berthaume, and O'Leary (1983) point out that "no clear picture exists of the nature of career development for members of special populations" (p. 13), and Conte (1983) reports the absence of writings concerning the application of vocational development theories to disabled individuals.

One reason for the lack of career development theory with regard to handicapped populations may be that there is no underlying *philosophical* structure in career education for the handicapped. Has anyone asked the question — Why do we do what we do with regard to planning career/vocational programs for handicapped populations? It seems that the more typical course of action is (a) to administer vocational assessment batteries made up of instruments that frequently suffer from a lack of reliability and validity and that are seldom, if ever, based on any theoretical structure; and (b) to develop a curriculum that is usually some combination of traditional approaches such as training in daily living skills, teaching of appropriate work behaviors, job development, and on-the-job training.

Lately, *transition from school to work* and *integration of handicapped students* into the *regular vocational programs* are the trendy new phrases in career/vocational education programs for handicapped individuals. Our

59

concern is that programs developed for handicapped students are based on traditional and stereotypic views of their capabilities rather than on any philosophical viewpoint.

For example, in their book, *Career Education for Handicapped Individuals*, Kokaska and Brolin (1985) express the need to establish efficacy for career education for handicapped individuals, and they even talk about the paucity of available empirical research on the topic. However, the 15 top priority research topics they identify deal with topics like attitudes impeding employment opportunities for handicapped persons; teacher motivation; teaching technologies; personnel development; effective parent training; effect of handicapping conditions on career potentials; effective counseling techniques; and so on. While these are all important topics, if no theoretical or philosophical base exists on which to test hypotheses, then any research results in these areas will be meaningless. For example, it is easy to say that a topic for research will be "effective counseling techniques" or "critical incidents or factors that lead to maintenance, improvement, or loss of jobs" (Kokaska and Brolin, 1985, p. 380). However, how can effective counseling techniques be empirically tested unless those techniques are based on a systematic theory?

Osipow (1983) states that career counselors who work without theoretical orientations have difficulty integrating the many disjointed research findings into some "meaningfully organized body of knowledge" (p. 5). He describes eclectic counselors as those who work intuitively and listen sympathetically, and then he cautions that professional counseling should be more than sympathetic listening. Thus, it becomes pointless to investigate effective career counseling techniques used with handicapped persons if no theoretically-based counseling techniques are being used. Perhaps the first question that should be asked is: What kind of techniques are being used to counsel handicapped persons? The next question should be whether *any* of these techniques are philosophically-derived and/or based on career development theory. It is one thing to place a mentally retarded student in a traditional high school work-study program because that is traditionally what is done for such students. It is quite another thing to use highly-researched, theory-based assessment instruments as guides to determine students' interests, work personalities, and career development levels, and then to design an individualized career/vocational education program based on results from such assessment. When such programs are implemented, *then* their effectiveness can be investigated through empirical studies. There will be structure on which to develop research questions such as: What was the program? On what theoretical foundation was the program developed? Was the program effective over the long-term? For what handicapped groups was the program most effective? Perhaps one theoretical approach works best with some handicapped populations, and other approaches with different populations. Obviously, before such counseling approaches can be tested, career/vocational counselors who work with handicapped populations must be cognizant of various career development theories and understand the importance of developing their own theoretical views. While career counselors trained in psychology are usually cognizant of various career development theories, most special educators are not. Thus, discussion of such theories should be included as important components in teacher training programs in career/ vocational education of the handicapped.

Kokaska and Brolin (1985) also state that "critical incidents or factors that lead to maintenance, improvement, or loss of jobs" (p. 380) should also be a top priority research topic. Again, if such research is to be conducted, there must be some starting point. Do we just pull what we think are *critical incidents* out of the air, or do we go to the literature to determine what researchers have already derived to be *critical incidents or factors?*

It is our contention that studies already exist that have looked at these variables empirically, especially with regard to nonhandicapped populations. At the risk of overstating our case, career development theories have been developed that take into account the many variables that contribute to job stability or the lack of it, and many empirical studies have been done to validate these theories. Thus, instead of grasping at straws in an effort to determine what *critical factors lead to maintenance, improvement or loss of jobs for handicapped individuals,* it makes more sense to go to the existing research and determine if results can be replicated with handicapped populations.

What we may discover is that existing career development theories may not apply to handicapped populations without modification, or that new theories may need to be developed. Even so, by going to existing research as a starting point, structure is built into our investigations, and findings will validate or disprove the usefulness of an existing career development theory for handicapped groups. According to Osipow (1983), "all theory is imperfect" and "it should properly be assumed that theories will eventually die and be replaced by newer theories that deal with observed events in a more general and useful way than their predecessors" (p. 3) Perhaps research structured around existing career development theories will result in redefining these theories to include assumptions appropriate for handicapped as well as for nonhandicapped individuals.

The remainder of this chapter will discuss existing theories of career development and the application of such theories to special populations.

## THEORIES OF CAREER DEVELOPMENT

Perhaps the best source for a discussion of career development theory can be found in Osipow's book, *Theories of Career Development* (Osipow, 1983). Osipow discusses career development in terms of four theoretical approaches: (a) personality approaches; (b) developmental/self-concept approaches; (c) social systems approaches; and (d) trait-factor approaches. We will discuss each of these approaches, providing specific examples of each. We will also attempt to relate the relevance of each approach to handicapped populations.

### Personality Approaches

Personality theorists are concerned with the particular personality factors involved in career choice and career satisfaction. Related research projects have investigated the personality characteristics of people in different occupations, individual lifestyles that relate to certain vocations, psychopathology that is associated with certain professional activities, and specific needs of workers in particular occupations (Osipow, 1983). The general hypothesis of these studies is that individuals select jobs to satisfy personal needs.

**Roe's Personality Theory of Choice.** One theorist who discusses career development from the personality perspective is Anne Roe. Roe takes the position that there is a relationship between early experiences and attitudes, abilities, interests and other personality variables and the ultimate vocational selection of an individual (Roe, 1957).

Roe's theory grew out of investigations into the developmental backgrounds and personalities of research scientists. She discovered that there were major personality differences between physical-biological scientists and social scientists, particularly in the interactions these individuals had with people and things. Roe concluded that these personality differences reflected early individual experiences with parents and had a significant impact on their later choice of vocation.

Another component of Roe's theory is the contention that each individual is genetically predisposed to expend psychic energy. Thus, this genetic predisposition combined with an individual's childhood experiences determines a developing pattern of need satisfaction. Finally, an individual's pattern of satisfying personal needs is relevant to the total life pattern of the individual, including the person's choice of vocation (Roe, 1957).

According to Osipow (1975), Roe takes the position that career choice is a reflection of personality and personality development. According to Roe (1957), the crucial periods of personality development occur in early childhood. Thus, certain parent-child interactions, in combination with various genetic differences, influence the development of certain need hierarchies. These need hierarchies, in turn, result in two basic interpersonal orientations: either toward or not toward people. Careers reflecting an orientation toward people are those of service, business contact, organizations, arts and entertainment, and general cultural areas. Occupations reflecting an orientation that is not toward people includes scientific, technological, and outdoor careers.

What specifically does Roe say about child-rearing practices as they relate to needs satisfaction? Roe (1957) describes differences in parental handling of children as the *child being the center of attention, the child being avoided,* or *the child being accepted.* She states that the specific behaviors of the parents are less important than their attitudes towards the child. Finally, she specified how each parental style affects the satisfaction of the child's needs.

1. **The Child as the Center of Attention.** Parental behavior may be overprotective or overdemanding. According to Roe (1957), the *overprotective* parent babies the child, encourages dependence, and restricts any exploratory behavior. Parents concentrate on physical characteristics and real or imagined talents of the child.

These parents maintain primary emotional ties with the child. The overprotective parent provides full satisfaction of lower-order physiological and safety needs. However, they are less prompt to attend to higher-order needs for love, self-esteem, and a sense of belonging. When these needs are met, they are usually done so on the condition that the child remain dependent and conform to socially desirable behavior. In such homes, self-actualization is often discouraged. Overprotective parents also teach the child to place much emphasis on the immediacy with which needs are gratified.

Like overprotective parents, *overdemanding* parents promptly and adequately satisfy the child's physical needs, and impose conditions on the love they offer to the child. In these homes, love is offered in return for social conformity and high achievement in school and work. The child's needs for information, understanding, and self-actualization may be encouraged, but only within prescribed areas seen as important by the parents.

2. **Avoidance of the Child.** Parents in this category tend to either reject or neglect the child. According to Roe (1957), parents who *reject* the child may provide safety and adequate gratification of physiological needs, but deliberately refrain from love and esteem gratification. Roe states that unless rejected children see others treated in a different way from themselves, they are likely to suffer from stunted, although not necessarily distorted, development.

On the other hand, *neglectful* parents who only minimally meet physiological and safety needs of the child, may not injure their children as much as parents who withhold love and self-esteem. Parents who neglect the child do not generally do so intentionally.

3. **Acceptance of the Child.** According to Roe (1957), children in this group are "full-fledged members of the family circle, neither concentrated upon, nor overlooked" (p. 215). Accepting parents are undemanding, nonrestrictive, and encourage independence in their children. The breakdown in this group of parents is on the basis of the warmth or coldness of the family climate. Parents in this group are either *casually* or *lovingly* accepting of their children. Noninterference of casually accepting parents is usually by default. For parents who exhibit loving acceptance of their children, noninterference with and encouragement of the child's own resources and independence may be either intentional and planned or a natural reflection of parents' general attitudes towards others. Accepting parents offer reasonable gratification of all their childrens' needs. Gratifications will not be deliberately delayed, and any delay will not be disturbing to the child.

What do these parental attitudes and practices have to do with eventual adult behavior patterns, particularly with regard to eventual selection of careers? According to Roe (1957), each situation described will have a specific impact on the development of basic attitudes, interests and capacities that will be given expression in the general pattern of the individual's life, including emotional reactions, activities, and vocational choice. Roe states that occupation, more than any other aspect of life, reflects most clearly the combination of genetic and experiential variables. These variables then determine the degree to which an individual is oriented toward or not toward persons.

Adults from child-centered overprotective or overdemanding families will continue to derive their self-esteem and sense of who they are from the opinions and attitudes of other persons toward themselves. Therefore, these individuals will likely go to work in service occupations that are primarily oriented toward people. On the other hand, adults raised in rejecting homes may strongly reject people as adults and turn to occupations with a major orientation that is not people-oriented. Finally, individuals from accepting homes may or may not have primary interests in people. However, these interests will not be defensive in either case, and they will not carry the kind of uncertainty shown by those in the first two groups (Roe, 1957).

Roe has organized the world of work into eight groups and six levels. This classification has two dimensions: *focus of activity* and *level at which the activity is pursued* (Roe, 1957). It is important to understand that while the early home atmosphere influences the *type* of vocational activity, genetic factors such as intelligence combined with socioeconomic background influence the occupational *level* the worker achieves. Thus, according to Osipow (1983), "the theory attends to every important aspect of vocational selection" (p. 19). The development of needs has an influence on whether or not the individual selects a vocational context that is toward others or not toward others. On the other hand, the level of occupation results from genetic differences in people including differences in intelligence and the ability to manipulate various aspects of the environment. Thus, according to the tenets of the theory, investigation of an individual's childhood experiences combined with an accurate assessment of the child's aptitudes should result in fairly accurate predictions of what occupational class the child will pursue. Also, in retrospect, people working in different occupations that are on the same level, should report childhood environments that differ.

## Developmental/Self-Concept Theory of Career Development

According to Osipow (1983), this approach fuses two models into one, and can be called either the *developmental* or the *self-concept theory*. This approach grew out of the early work of Buehler (1933) on the one hand, and out of the work of Carl Rogers and client-centered counselors on the other hand. The main tenets of this approach are (a) people develop more clearly defined self-concepts as they grow older; (b) people make career decisions based on a comparison of their view of the occupational world and their own self-image; and (c) the adequacy of the eventual career decision depends on whether or not the individual's image of the chosen occupation is similar to that person's self concept.

**Super's Developmental Self-Concept Theory of Vocational Behavior.** One theorist whose work is built around the developmental/self-concept theory of vocational behavior is Donald Super (1976). According to Osipow, Super's work came under two strong influences. The first of these was self-concept theory as illustrated in the writings of Carl Rogers (1942; 1951), Carter (1940), and Bordin (1943). According to these writers, individuals respond to vocational interest inventories based on how they view themselves in terms of stereotypes held about occupations. Also, a person selects or rejects a particular occupation based on whether or not it corresponds with that individual's self-view.

The second major influence on Super's work was Buehler's (1943) work in developmental psychology. Buehler holds that life consists of several, distinct stages with each stage initiating a different life task. The first stage is a growth state that starts at birth and ends around the age of 14. Second is the exploratory stage that occurs between the ages of 15 and 25. The third stage is maintenance, beginning at age 25 and lasting until about age 65. The final stage, which Bueler calls decline, begins at age 65.

Super uses this concept of life-stages to develop his theory of career development. Each of these life stages are characterized by specific tasks which must be completed successfully before success can occur in the next stage.

Super proposes that people choose occupations that are most likely to permit them self-expression. He suggests that vocational choices depend on the life-stage in which an individual finds himself and that different vocational behaviors can be better understood if they are viewed within the changing demands of the life cycle (Osipow, 1983). For example, there is likely to be more changing of occupations during the *exploratory* stage than during the *maintenance* stage of development.

Super believes that most individuals possess the potential for finding success and satisfaction within a variety of occupational environments. He states that different occupations reflect certain patterns of interests and abilities, and people are more likely to be satisfied if they are in occupations that reflect a pattern of interests and abilities that correspond to their own.

Super also proposes that vocational self-concepts develop when children observe and identify with working adults. Finally, in accordance with his view of life-stages, Super suggests that an individual's vocational adjustment at one period of life is likely to be predictive of techniques that person will use to adjust during a later life-stage.

In other words, career behavior follows regular and predictable patterns that can be recognized through careful study and observation of the individual. These patterns are seen as the accumulated results of various psychological, physical, situational, and societal factors which combine to form the entirety of an individual's life. These patterns include: (a) the *stable* pattern, in which an individual enters an occupation early and remains in the occupation permanently. This pattern is followed by most of those who enter the field of medicine; (b) the *conventional* pattern in which several jobs are explored, with one finally becoming stable; (c) the *unstable* pattern in which the individual tries a series of jobs yet only finds temporary stability that is soon disrupted; and (d) the *multiple trial* pattern in which the individual moves from one stable entry-level job to another, exemplified by those in domestic service careers (Super, et al., 1957).

Super's concept of career-pattern suggests that individuals are presented with different vocational tasks depending on the various stages of their life cycle. Thus, the tendency to pressure individuals to make binding career decisions during adolescence is naive since the period of adolescence is only a segment of the vocational life of an individual. According to Super (1957), the individual's entire life cycle must be observed to fully understand that person's vocational life.

Finally, Super also states that environment and heredity have an impact on vocational maturation. By manipulating certain aspects of the environment, greater facilitation of vocational maturity can occur.

**Super's Five Career Stages of Life (Biller, 1985).** According to Super (1957), there are five career life-stages. Each life-stage is characterized by specific tasks that must be faced by the individual in that stage, and which are considered prerequisite for success in the next stage. Following are descriptions of these five career life-stages.

1. **Growth Stage (0-14 years).** The primary task of the first stage is for the young child to develop an awareness of self. According to Super (1957), the infant possesses an awareness of self at birth beginning with primary self-percepts that deal with raw sensations of hunger, pain, and temperature. As the child matures, secondary percepts develop, and initial sensations become ordered. As the child matures further, the self-percepts become more complex and abstract and develop into systems of self-concepts. Among the systems of self-concepts is the vocational self-concept. During the Growth Stage, the individual becomes aware of his or her own distinctiveness, yet at the same time recognizes similarities

with others. As children grow, they develop a self-concept based on a combination of self-perceptions and the perceptions that others have of them. During this period, young children role-play, imagining themselves to be firemen, nurses, or cowboys and cowgirls. Thus, initial career thinking is in the form of fantasy. Later career thought during this stage focuses on likes and dislikes, and toward the end of the growth stage, the child thinks about careers in terms of his or her own abilities.

2. **Exploration Stage (15-24 years).** The primary task during this stage is to explore the world of work in order to crystallize, specify, and implement a vocational preference. During the first substage of this period, the individual makes tentative occupational decisions based on needs, interests, capacities, values, and opportunities. Next, those decisions are refined or rejected based on reality-testing. For example, an aspiring physician must be capable of making good grades, and the student who wishes to be a musician must have some measure of talent. Finally, it is during this stage that the individual makes an initial career commitment and enters the first trial job.

3. **Establishment Stage (25-44 years).** During this stage, the individual desires to enter a permanent occupation. Initially, there is a period of occupational changes due to unsatisfactory choices. Finally, from the ages of 31-44, the individual enters into a period of stable work in a given occupational field.

4. **Maintenance Stage (45-65 years).** During this period, the vocationally mature individual continues and progresses in the chosen occupation.

5. **Decline Stage (65-death).** During this stage, there is a period of declining vocational activity until around age 70, followed by a cessation of vocational activity.

In summary, Super's theory proposes that individuals move through life stages, each requiring specific vocational behaviors. The young child develops an awareness of and fantasizes about the world of work; the adolescent explores different career opportunities; the young adult enters a period of job training and seeking; the mature adult settles into a vocation, seeking improvement in position within that occupation; the older adult gradually declines in vocational activity. During each stage of development, certain behaviors are more likely to result in growth than others. The success with which an individual accomplishes the specific vocational tasks of each stage is dependent on the successful performance of the tasks in the preceding stage (Osipow, 1983).

**The Ginzberg, Ginsburg, Axelrad, and Herma Theory.** Another developmental career theory is that of Ginzberg, Ginsburg, Axelrad, and Herma (1951). The authors see vocational choice as a irreversible process that occurs within clearly marked periods and that is characterized by a series of compromises the individual makes between aspirations and possibilities (Osipow, 1983). The three major periods of this process are the Fantasy period, the Tentative period, and the Realistic period. We will discuss each of these periods.

1. **The Fantasy Period.** During this period, the child exhibits a lack of reality orientation that is reflected in the occupational preferences expressed at this time. Maturational development during this period requires the child to change from a play orientation to a work orientation. At the beginning of this period, the child's vocational preferences are reflected through play. During this time, the child engages in activities simply for the sake of the characteristics intrinsic in the activities (Osipow, 1983). As the child grows older, he or she expresses a preference for vocational activities that have potential for extrinsic rewards such as parental approval, money, or achievement.

Ginzberg and his associates hypothesize that young children are frustrated by a sense of inadequacy and impotence resulting from their small size and relative ineffectiveness when compared with adults. One way to relieve this frustration is by identifying with and emulating the adults around them (Osipow, 1983). Since adult roles are most clearly manifested in work, children play at working, assuming make-believe identities. This allows them to reduce their feelings of inadequacy and internalize the values of the adult world.

During the Fantasy period children ignore reality, their abilities and potentials, and the perspective of time. However, these play activities are important and help promote the child's readiness for the next period in vocational selection.

2. **The Tentative Period.** This period occurs between the ages of 11 and 18, and is divided into four substages: Interest, Capacity, Value, and Transition. The *Interest Stage* is the time (around ages 11 and 12) when the child begins to consider the need to identify a career direction. The child becomes increasingly aware of likes and dislikes, and makes choices in terms of the potential they hold for intrinsic enjoyment. However, children in this period are aware of their instability, and accept the need to defer final selections until they are older.

During the *Capacity Stage,* which occurs between the ages of 12 to 14, the child begins to think about ability in terms of vocational thinking.

He or she not only identifies an area of interest, but begins to think in terms of ability to perform well in those interest areas. During the Interest stage, the child's career choices reflects an identity with parents. During the Capacity stage there is a decrease in parent identity and the child is influenced by other adult models.

During the *Value Stage* that occurs during the 15th and 16th years, adolescents experience a dramatic change in their approach to vocational choice. They become aware of the idea of service to society, and begin to think of choosing careers on the basis of humanitarian reasons. During this period, young persons begin to associate certain lifestyles with different occupations. They also have a clearer understanding of their own strengths and limitations, and begin to think about occupations that will allow them to put their special abilities to use. Finally, it is during this period that children begin to develop a broader perspective of time. They begin to understand that a career involves years of day-in and day-out activities that will eventually become a life pattern. Also during this period, youth become sensitive to the fact that they must soon make a vocational commitment.

The *Transition Stage* closes the Tentative Period of vocational development. This stage occurs at about age 17 or 18, and is calmer than preceding stages of this period. At this time, the young person realizes the necessity to make realistic vocational decisions and to accept responsibility for consequences of those decisions. By this time, the individual is becoming less dependent on parents, and has more independence of action than in earlier stages. Greater freedom allows the youth to search out new surroundings in which to try out skills and abilities. During this period, there is increased awareness of amount and kind of preparation necessary for various occupations, financial rewards associated with different occupations become clear, and greater understanding occurs with regard to lifestyles associated with different work. Finally, sexual maturity and marriage possibilities conflict with the need to delay marriage for the purpose of pursuing a career.

3. **The Realistic Period.** This period follows the last stage of the Tentative Period and occurs between the ages of 18 and 22 until as late as the age of 24. The age ranges of this period fluctuate more than previous periods because of the different preparation and training required by different occupations. This period is characterized by three substages: Exploration, Crystallization, and Specification. The *Exploration Stage* is the first stage of the Realistic Period and is marked by a more narrow focus of vocational goals than earlier periods. However, a good

deal of vocational flexibility is characteristic of this period. Although young adults experience a good deal of independence during this period, they continue to experience much indecisiveness. Their interests continue to change, and their circumstances generally don't demand a specific decision to be made. The main task of this period is for individuals to choose from among two or three strong interests. However, this decision produces some anxiety because of the fear of making the wrong career choice, both in terms of job satisfaction and financial reward. Also, the pressure of time left to make a decision is felt more acutely during this period.

The *Crystallization Stage* follows the Exploration Stage. By the time the young person enters this stage, there is a clear idea of what occupational tasks should be avoided and of the time by which decisions have to be made. By this time, decisions become firm and degree of commitment to a choice becomes strong. Ginzberg and his associates also talk about a stage of pseudocrystallization during which the student thinks and acts as though career crystallization has taken place, though later events indicate otherwise. According to Osipow (1983), Ginzberg and his associates do not explain how to tell pseudocrystallization from true crystallization. Osipow further comments that "the concept of crystallization becomes a loophole to explain the behavior of a certain (unspecified) class of students who make late and unpredicted changes in their plans" (p. 197).

The last stage of the Realistic Period is the *Specification Stage*. For some individuals, this stage never truly arrives. It is the final stage of career development. At this point, the individual refines the career choice by selecting a specific job or graduate school subspecialty. Ginzberg and his colleagues suggest the possibility of a pseudospecification, but do not distinguish it from the real specification.

According to Ginzberg and his associates, variations in this pattern of vocational development will occur for biological, psychological, and environmental reasons. These variations will occur in two realms. First, individuals will vary with regard to the range of choices they express over time. Some people will choose an occupation early in their lives and never change careers. Others may try a variety of occupations before finally choosing a permanent one. The difference has to do with the nature of a person's abilities. For example, a person who possesses a highly-developed occupational skill that emerges early in life, is likely to exhibit a narrow range of occupational choice.

The second cause of variability has to do with the timing of the Crystallization Stage. For some people, crystallization occurs toward the end of the Tentative Period, while for others crystallization does not occur until they are well into their twenties.

There are also certain conditions that differ from normal variations. Ginzberg and his associates consider these conditions to be deviant patterns. These patterns occur because the individual does not conform to age mates in some significant aspect of vocational development. For example, a person might pursue an unrealistic choice far beyond the time when age-mates have discarded such choices. Or an individual may not be close to achieving a crystallized choice by the end of the Realistic period. Ginzberg and his associates explain various reasons for deviant patterns, including severe emotional disorders or unusual personal financial circumstances such as excessive affluence.

## Social Systems Approaches

The sociological model of career development has as its central theme the idea that societal circumstances beyond the control of the individual have a significant impact on career choice. According to this view, chance plays a major role in career decisions, the individual's self-expectations are not independent of society's expectations, and career opportunities are related to class membership (Osipow, 1983). Thus, systematic career planning and counseling may not be as relevant to eventual career decisions as "being in the right place at the right time." Several variables impact a person's eventual career choice. First of all, social class membership both influences and is influenced by occupational membership (Havighurst, 1964; Hollingshead, 1949; Osipow, 1983). According to Hollingshead, individual life styles result from such variables as values in the home, the adult models one identifies with, differential rewards for work versus play and for enterprise versus academic achievement.

Another variable that sometimes influences an individual's occupation is heredity. In American society, inheritance of occupation usually occurs in the form of inheritance of family-owned businesses such as retail stores and farms. Occupation also may be inherited in a situation where the parent's occupation requires isolation from other people. This isolation may be physical or psychological. Physical isolation occurs in careers in farming, lumbering, fishing and other similar occupations. Psychological isolation occurs when an occupation sets members apart from the comunity at large or requires frequent moves from location to location. Such occupations include medicine, the military, religion, and the like.

A person's education has a major effect on occupational mobility. However, an individual's academic goals are a function of a particular set of experiences. For instance, according to Osipow (1983): "to the degree that parents influence the educational decisions of their offspring and to the degree that social class influences parental attitudes toward and capability of providing educational opportunities, social class factors are highly important in educational-vocational decisions" (p. 228). Osipow provides an example of parental influences on education when he states that there will not be a heavy emphasis on academic training in a low socioeconomic neighborhood where the norm is hard physical work, and people are admired for their physical abilities.

Social class also influences the occupational choices of adolescents. According to Sewell and Shah (1968), higher-class adolescents make career decisions at a later age than lower-class youth, and different careers are chosen by each group. Upper-class parents tend to offer or withhold rewards based on academic achievement, and may encourage their offspring to put off work until after college graduation. On the other hand, parents in lower socio-economic classes may see a college education as frivolous, and insist that their children go to work as soon as they graduate from high school.

Another variable that seems to affect occupational choice is family size. Blau and Duncan (1967) found that individuals from small families began working at a higher occupational level than did individuals from larger families. Family size effect on occupational level is even more positive for only children.

Other related findings suggest that fathers' income is highly related to childrens' occupational choices (Rosenberg, 1957); children generally follow careers that resemble those of their fathers (Porter, 1954; Clark, 1967; Hollingshead, 1949; Miller & Form, 1951); socioeconomic status may have an effect on development of occupational interests (Hewer, 1965; Hyman (1956); Pierce-Jones, 1959); and lower-class youth are less likely than youth in middle-and upper-classes to express vocational interests (Stephenson, 1957).

While no specific theory has been developed based on the sociological approach to career development, several schemes exist that attempt to place occupational choice within a social and/or cultural context. Blau, Gustad, Jessor, Parnes, and Wilcox (1956) state that social structure impacts vocational choice because of its influence on the individual's personality development and on economic and social conditions that determine individual occupational decisions. Blau and his colleagues believe that individual characteristics, including biological and psychological factors, combine with environmental conditions, such as geography, social resources, opportunities for mobility and so on, to shape a person's eventual occupational choice. The individual then makes the choice based on an apprisal of the most highly-valued career that realistically can be attained. Sound occupational information is crucial to making the best decision. Thus, Blau and his associates believe that information about occupational organizations of American culture and sociological elements of various careers, is more effective for describing various careers than information about education, income, and ability requirements for certain occupations.

**A Developmental Theory of Occupational Aspirations.** Another sociological perspective on occupational choice is put forth by Gottfredson (1981). Gottfredson calls her approach a developmental theory of occupational aspirations which appears to combine both development and social systems views about careers (Osipow, 1983). She believes that social groups share occupational images and preferences. Variables that work together to shape these images include (a) one's perception of how successful an occupation is; (b) which occupational alternatives seem to be accessible and acceptable; (c) the range of occupational alternatives available; (d) perceptions of whether the job is more suited for males or for females; and (d) perceptions of personality traits of individuals working in a particular occupation.

According to Gottfredson (1981), occupational preferences develop as part of one's developing self-concept, and they develop in four stages. The first stage, *orientation to size and power*, occurs in children aged 3 to 5; the second stage is *orientation to sex roles*, ages 6 to 8; the third stage is *orientation to social evaluation*, ages 9 to 13; and finally, the fourth stage is *orientation to the internal unique self* which develops around the age of 14.

Gottfredson believes that social class membership has an effect on one's perception of an occupation's attractiveness. For example, lower-level jobs are seen more positively by individuals in lower-class groups than by individuals from a higher social strata. Although parents from all classes aspire for their children to obtain high-level jobs, lower-class parents are less affected than higher-class parents if their offspring do not meet their aspirations.

Gottfredson says that individuals ultimately have to compromise between aspiration and reality when making career choices. She suggests three principles that govern the compromise process: (a) more central aspects of self-esteem will take priority when an individual compromises occupational goals; (b) individuals usually stop exploring job options when they become engaged in a satisfactory, rather than the most optimal, occupation; (c) people accommodate psychologically to compromises they make.

Osipow (1983) describes Gottfredson's work as a valid attempt to integrate the social systems and the developmental approaches to career development. Although the theory is still too new to present new data and lacking in instrumentation to test its assertions, assumptions, and hypotheses, it does provide a new stimulus for research.

**Environmental Press.** The idea of environmental press emphasizes situational influences on behavior. The society dictates the development and timing of vocational behavior, requiring the individual to make career decisions within the structure of the social system. Included within the social system are cultural subsystems, the community, and personal sources of influence such as home, family, school, church and the like. Thus, an individual's occupational choice is the result of a compromise between the self and the requirements of the social system (Osipow, 1983; Super & Bachrach, 1957). According to Osipow, the emphasis of the environmental press approach to career choice is on the compromise between individual inclinations and societal influences. To date, little research has been conducted looking at the effects of environmental press on individual career choices.

**Industrial Organization.** This approach considers the effect of industrial organizations on vocational behavior. According to Gross (1964; 1967), organizations affect career behavior in four ways.

1. Most people adjust to the particular problems of life in large organizations. These problems include knowing how to deal with authority, accommodating to routine work, resolving the conflict for the organization's need for creativity and its demand for conformity, and dealing with the fact that at retirement, social mobility is downward rather than upward.
2. The particular organizational environment in which an individual is employed largely determines the character of the people with whom that individual interacts.
3. The organization in which an individual is employed plays a major occupational role, influences income, and impacts the individual's

material lifestyle. In other words, the organization has a dramatic impact on an individual's behavior outside the workplace.

4. Within the organization, an individual's career pattern may require several job changes as the career matures. Thus, organizational life limits its workers from becoming too well-suited for one job, since organization requirements change frequently.

## Trait-Factor Approaches

The trait-factor theoretical approach assumes that a straightforward matching of individual abilities and interests with an appropriate vocational environment is possible, and once such a match is made, the individual's problems of vocational choice are solved (Osipow, 1981). According to Osipow, the vocational testing movement grew out of the trait-factor approach resulting in the development of various instruments to test vocational interests and aptitudes. These include the Strong-Campbell Interest Inventory (Campbell, 1974; Campbell & Hansen, 1981), the Kuder Occupational Interest Survey (Kuder, 1966; Kudar & Diamond, 1979), the Differential Aptitude Tests (Bennet, Seashore, & Wesman, 1969), and the Guilford-Zimmerman Aptitude Survey. Osipow states that the trait-factor model has been absorbed into other career-counseling approaches, and that not many present-day career counselors are pure trait-factor adherents.

Two trait-factor approaches are particularly relevant to the content of this chapter. One of these is the *Work Adjustment Theory* of Lofquist and Dawis (1969), and the other is Holland's (1985a) *Theory of Vocational Personalities and Work Environments*. Following is a discussion of each of these approaches.

**A Theory of Work Adjustment.** This approach is the result of work done by Lofquist and his associates in the Work Adjustment Project at the University of Minnesota. According to Dawis (1973), the program consists of a series of research studies on the general problem of adjustment to work. These studies had as their primary objectives (a) to develop tools for the prediction of work adjustment; and (b) to explore the process of adjustment to work.

According to Dawis (1973), the *Theory of Work Adjustment* is based on the assumption that each individual has as a basic human motive the need to achieve and maintain correspondence with his or her environment. When correspondence occurs between the individual and the enrivonment, there is a harmonious relationship between the individual and the environment, the individual and the enrivonment are suited to each other, consonance exists between individual and environment, and there is a reciprocal and complementary relationship between individual and environment. The individual has certain requirements of the environment, and the environment makes certain requirements of the individual.

In the work situation, the individual brings certain skills to the environment, and the work environment provides certain rewards in the form of wages, prestige, personal relationships, and the like. When the requirements of the individual and the work environment are mutually fulfilled, the individual seeks to maintain that mutuality or balance. According to the theory, the process of seeking to achieve and maintain correspondence with the work environment is *work adjustment.*

Another component of the theory is that of *tenure.* Tenure on the job is the result of correspondence between the individual and the work environment. As correspondence increases, the probability of tenure and the projected length of tenure increase. On the other hand, as correspondence decreases, the probability of tenure and the projected length of tenure decrease. According to Dawis (1973), tenure is the most basic indicator of correspondence between the individual and the work environment.

If an individual has substantial tenure, it can be assumed that the requirements of the individual and the requirements of the work envioment are mutually fulfilling. The individual who fulfills the requirements of the work environment is defined as a *satisfactory* worker, and if the work environment fulfills the requirements of the individual, then the individual is defined as a *satisfied* worker. According to the theory, *satisfactoriness* and *satisfaction* are basic indicators of how successful the individual has been in maintaining correspondence with the work environment. Satisfactoriness is an *external* indicator of correspondence, and is derived from such environmental sources as the organization, the supervisor, and co-workers. Satisfaction is an *internal* indicator of correspondence, and is represented by the individual's expression of the extent to which the work environment satisfies personal needs and requirements.

Although levels of satisfactoriness and satisfaction may fluctuate both with the individual and with the work environment, minimum levels of satisfactoriness are required *of* the individual, and minimum levels of satisfaction are required *by* the individual. These levels can be determined by observing groups of individuals with substantial tenure in a specific work environment. Once these levels are determined, then tenure can be predicted for other individuals in the same work environment.

According to Lofquist and Dawis (1969), satisfactoriness and satisfaction can be used along with measures of work personalities to predict work adjustment. For example, for a given work environment, the work personalities of individuals who are both satisfactory and satisfied can be assumed to be *correspondent* with the work environment. Thus, certain personality traits required for successful adjustment to a specific work environment can be identified. Personality traits corresponding to a specific job can be used as measures to estimate the correspondence of other individuals to that job, thus predicting the future work adjustment of those individuals.

Also, work-personality/work-environment correspondence can be used to predict satisfactoriness and satisfaction. According to Dawis (1973), since satisfactoriness and satisfaction, when taken together, can be used as measures to predict tenure, then work-personality/work-environment correspondence can be used to predict tenure as well. Therefore, according to the theory, the key to the prediction of work adjustment outcomes such as satisfactoriness, satisfaction and tenure, lies in determination of work-personality/work-environment correspondence. To make this determination, expression of work personality and work environment must be in the same terms. Dawis (1973) states that in the *Theory of Work Adjustment*, the work environment is expressed in work personality terms, "specifically in ability and need (reinforcer) terms" (p. 55). The choice of work personality terms is based on concepts derived from differential psychology, the branch of psychology concerned with the study of individual differences.

> The individual starts life with unique response potentials derived from his genetic inheritance. As he interacts with the environment, he experiences a variety of stimulus conditions, many of which he finds reinforcing. The individual matures and his experience broadens. He develops abilities and needs. Abilities are basic dimensions of response capability generally utilized by the individual. Needs are basic preferences for responding in certain stimulus conditions which have been experienced as reinforcing. Abilities and needs, according to the *Theory of Work Adjustment*, are the major concepts that define the work personality.
>
> The individual's abilities and needs undergo further development principally through social and educational experiences. This process of development (individuation of the work personality) continues to a point of relative stability. The *Theory of Work Adjustment* is premised on the existence of a relatively stable work personality (Dawis, 1973, p. 55).

According to Dawis (1973), the theory describes the work environment in work personality terms — in terms of ability requirements and reinforcer systems. Ability requirements and systems of reinforcement are determined from the study of satisfactory workers who have substantial tenure.

Dawis (1973) describes ways to increase correspondence, should an individual become discorrespondent with the work environment. First of all, the individual may *act on* the work environment to change it so that it will be more correspondent with that individual's work personality. A second way to increase correspondence is for the individual to *react* to the work environment. This is done by changing the manner in which the worker expresses his or her work personality to make it more correspondent with the work environment. Thus, according to Dawis, two modes of work adjustment exist—the *active* mode and the *reactive* mode. Thus, individuals working to maintain correspondence with the work environment may be described as *active* or *reactive*.

Another dimension of the work adjustment process has to do with the degree of discorrespondence an individual will tolerate before that person is motivated to initiate a change. The person who can tolerate a relatively *loose* correspondence with the work environment is described as *flexible*. An individual who cannot tolerate anything but a *tight* correspondence with the work environment is described as *rigid*. According to Dawis (1973), *looseness* or *tightness* of correspondence can be determined objectively through measures of work personality and work environment. Degree of tolerance can be derived from the level of satisfaction expressed by the individual.

A third dimension of the work adjustment process has to do with the speed with which an individual attempts to instigate change once that person becomes discorrespondent with the work environment. The words *fast* and *slow* can be used to describe the speed with which the individual achieves correspondence from an initial state of discorrespondence. Thus, workers are seen as fast adjusters or slow adjusters.

According to the theory, these three dimensions of work adjustment can be used to determine *styles* of work adjustment. Individuals can be described in dichotomies of active or reactive, flexible or rigid, fast adjusting or slow adjusting. Thus, according to the theory, there are eight possible styles of work adjustment, including active-flexible-fast adjusting, active-rigid-slow adjusting, and so on. These same terms can be used to describe work environments. So, the concept of correspondence between work personality and work environment—in terms of work adjustment *style*—can be used to predict the degree of work adjustment.

In summary, the complexity of work adjustment is seen in the variety of cross relationships including those occurring between abilities and needs, structures and styles, and personalities and environments (Dawis, 1973).

To enable testing and application of the theory, Lofquist and his associates in the Work Adjustment Project at the University of Minnesota have developed instruments to measure the major theoretical concepts of satisfaction, satisfactoriness, needs, abilities, reinforcer systems, and ability requirements. These instruments include the following:

1. The Minnesota Importance Questionnaire (MIQ) to measure individuals' vocationally relevant needs.
2. The Minnesota Job Description Questionnaire (MJDQ), to measure the reinforcers available in specific jobs and the levels at which they exist. Through use of the MJDQ, Occupational Reinforcer Patterns (ORPs) have been developed for about 150 jobs.
3. The Minnesota Satisfactoriness Scales (MSS), to measure how satisfactorily individuals perform on their jobs.
4. The Minnesota Satisfaction Questionnaire (MSQ), to measure the satisfaction of individuals' needs through work.

According to Dawis (1973), considerable research has been conducted with these instruments, and findings lend support to the theory. The instruments are described and their development documented in research monographs of the *Minnesota Studies in Vocational Rehabilitation* series.

**Holland's Theory of Vocational Personalities and Work Environments (Holland, 1985a).** According to Osipow (1983), Holland's theory assumes that career choices are an extension of an individual's personality and represent that person's attempt to implement broad personal behavioral styles in the context of one's work. One dimension of Holland's theory is that people project their views of themselves and of the world of work onto occupational titles. Thus, by allowing individuals to express their preference for, or feelings against, a particular list of occupational titles, Holland assigns people to personal categories that have theoretical implications for personality and vocational choice.

Another concept of the theory is the idea that there are six personal orientations to the world and six matching work environments. These include: (a) Realistic (R), (b) Investigative (I), (c) Artistic (A), (d) Social (S), (e) Enterprising (E), and (f) Conventional (C). An individual's predominant personality type is determined by assessment of vocational interests using the *Self-Directed Search*, an instrument developed by Holland (1985b).

After interests are assessed, a three-letter occupational code is obtained. The three letters represent that individual's predominant personal orientations based on Holland's six categories of personality and work environments. For example, if a three-letter code of RIS is obtained, then the individual is considered as having a predominant Realistic personality orientation to the world combined with secondary Investigative and Social characteristics. According to Holland (1985a), the three-letter code represents the three types a person resembles most, allows for complexity of personality, and reduces some of the problems that might result from categorizing a person as a single type.

Instruments developed by Holland to assess occupational interests include the Vocational Preference Inventory (VPI) (Holland, 1977), the Self-Directed Search (SDS) (Holland, 1985b), and the Self-Directed Search Form Easy (SDS-E) (Holland, 1985b). According to Holland (1985a), vocational interests are an expression of personality, therefore interest inventories are personality inventories.

Holland illustrates the relationships among the six types with a hexagon. Each type is depicted at one of the corners of the hexagon as shown in Figure 1.

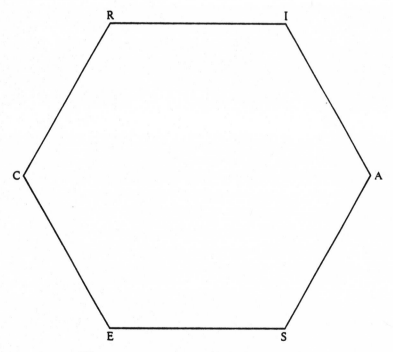

**Figure 1.** Adapted from Holland, 1985b.

The hexagon first occurred to Holland when he studied the intercorrelation matrix of scores on one of his interest inventories. Distances between the points are inversely proportional to the size of the correlations between them (Holland, 1985a). Several studies have investigated the appropriateness of the hexagon, and support usually has been found (Prediger, 1982).

According to the theory, individuals in occupational environments suited to their personality types are more likely to be satisfied with their jobs, be better employees, and are less likely to change jobs. The converse is true for individuals working in environments not suited to their personality types. Implications for vocational counseling following assessment and classification of personality type are obvious. Following is a description of each of the six Holland categories.

1. The *Realistic* personality is characterized by aggressive, antisocial, and masculine behaviors. Emphasis is on physical, highly concrete activities, and abstract problem situations are avoided. A Realistic environment is one requiring manual abilities, and in which there is little contact with other people. Such occupations might include heavy machinery operation, outdoor work such as farming, manual labor, and so on.

2. Like the Realistic individual, the *Investigative* personality avoids interpersonal contact. However, unlike the Realistic type, the Investigative person enjoys abstract problem-solving and prefers activities requiring organizing and analyzing rather than those requiring dominating and persuading traits. The Investigative environment requires the ability to solve abstract problems and a scientific curiosity. Scientists and mathematicians fit well into the Investigative environment.

3. The *Artistic* personality is similar to the Investigative in terms of dealing with abstractions. This individual also tends to be asocial except for the need to use people as an audience for creative performance. However, unlike the Investigative type, the Artistic individual is more feminine than masculine, shows relatively little self-control, and expresses emotion more readily than most people. Other characteristics include a dislike of structure, difficulty dealing with authority, and rebelliousness. Artistic environments include the theater, dance companies, art studios, and the like.

4. Individuals with a *Social* orientation prefer close interpersonal situations, enjoy helping others, and have good interpersonal skills. They

avoid situations requiring intellectual problem-solving and tend to dislike physical activities. Social occupations include teaching, counseling, and social work.

5. *Enterprising* personalities also have strong interpersonal skills. However, instead of using these skills to help and support other people, they use them to manipulate and dominate. Enterprising individuals respect and desire wealth, power, and status. They achieve these goals by manipulating others. Enterprising environments include sales occupations, corporations, and politics.

6. *Conventional* types respect rules and regulations; they practice self-control; and they have a desire for order, both of things and people. These individuals often subordinate their personal needs, and they have strong respect for others who have power and status. These types enjoy working in structured occupations such as accounting, clerical work, bookkeeping, and such.

**Congruence, Consistency, and Differentiation.** Three concepts relative to the Holland types are those of (a) congruence, (b) consistency, and (c) differentiation.

*Congruence* is best defined as the match between the personality type and the occupational environment. For example, a person with a *Realistic* personality should be happiest in a Realistic occupation such as that of auto mechanic or engineer, depending on the individual's needs and abilities. Conversely, the incongruent individual is more likely to be dissatisifed, unhappy, and unsuccessful in his or her occupation.

The term *consistency* applies to the interrelationship among the personality types within an individual. Consistency can best be understood through examination of Holland's hexagon. Consistency occurs when the predominant types within the individual are close to one another on the hexagon. For example, the Investigative-Artistic personality is more consistent than the Artistic-Conventional personality. The consistent individual finds it easier to evaluate personal characteristics in terms of making appropriate career choices. The inconsistent personality, on the other hand, may find it difficult to select an appropriate work environment, and may frequently change from one occupation to another.

Finally, *differentiation* can be defined as how strongly the predominant Holland type is predominant within the individual. According to Holland (1985a), each individual personality consists of a mix of all six types. However, some types are more predominant than others. Individuals taking the SDS list the three types with the highest score as their three-letter code. For example, a listing of IAS would indicate that the person scored highest on Investigative items, followed by high scores on Artistic and Social items. On the other hand, a highly differentiated personality may score extremely high in one category, and fail to score at all in the other five. This individual is then described as highly differentiated. According to Holland, the more highly differentiated a person is, the easier it is for that person to evaluate his or her personality and job interests. In contrast, the undifferentiated personality may have many skills and interests, and will find evaluation of self and job interests more difficult. However, once the undifferentiated person finds an occupational niche, that individual may be happier than the differentiated personality since it will be easier to develop interests outside the work environment.

**The Effects of Self-Evaluations and Early Experience.** Some other interesting components of Holland's theory include the concept of effective self-evaluation and the influence of early experiences (Osipow, 1983). According to Holland, appropriate self-evaluation is dependent on several variables including intelligence, social status, economic condition, educational level, and health. If these variables exert a negative influence upon the individual, the result may be a "flat" profile of types. Should this occur, the individual will encounter difficulty in selecting an occupational environment, and may constantly change from one work situation to another.

Holland also says that vocational self-evaluation is dependent on the adequacy of self-knowledge and occupational knowledge. The more information a person has about each of these, the more effective and appropriate the occupational choice.

Finally, Holland hypothesizes that social pressures in childhood and early adolescence, and experiences with parents may have a significant effect on determining an individual's personality type.

# IMPLICATIONS OF CAREER DEVELOPMENT THEORIES FOR HANDICAPPED INDIVIDUALS

At the beginning of this chapter, we commented that, in our view, one of the major problems with traditional career development approaches with handicapped individuals is that none of these approaches are firmly based on theory. Obviously, this has not been the case in career development approaches for nonhandicapped groups, as evidenced by the existence of several well-developed and researched theories of career development. Vocational theory-builders have limited their research to testing their theoretical assumptions with nonhandicapped populations. Thus, they often hesitate to apply these assumptions to handicapped populations (Conte, 1983). However, although career-development research with handicapped groups is lacking, some writers believe that career development of handicapped individuals may not be different from career development of people in general (Kapes & Parrish, 1983). Conte (1983) agrees, and states that:

> What is called for is not a separate theory of vocational development for disabled persons, but rather a reexamination of current theories in light of the observation that these theories may not in fact fit the data of exceptional or minority groups, of which the case of disabled persons is only one. Thus, renewed efforts to integrate thinking about disabled persons and vocational development are clearly needed, and a greater understanding of the differences in life experiences encountered by many disabled persons is necessary if vocational practitioners are to be successful in helping persons who are disabled to fulfill their vocational aspirations (p. 327).

As we have already stated, career development research and theory has typically omitted discussion of the career needs of disabled persons. In their review of vocational guidance research, Holcomb and Anderson (1977) point out that less than 6 percent of articles appearing in major professional journals during the period from 1971-1975 addressed the concerns of special populations. Conte (1983) gives several reasons for the failure to apply career development theories to disabled individuals:

1. Writers and researchers may consider disabled persons as being subject to the same developmental forces and experiences as nondisabled persons, thus they don't need any special consideration.
2. Writers and researchers may assume that life experiences of disabled individuals or the nature of the disability make this population so different from the rest of society that theories of career development cannot and should no be applied to them.
3. Career development theorists may consider their work too recent or theoretical to apply to career development issues of handicapped populations.
4. Writers and researchers may be unfamiliar with the lives and experiences of disabled populations.

Conte also makes the point that while some attempts have been made to apply career development theories to handicapped groups, these ordinarily suffer from some inherent weaknesses including the following:

1. Much of the theoretical writing on career development of disabled persons focuses on models of work adjustment rather than on patterns of career development of the relationship among various jobs held by an individual throughout his or her lifetime.

2. Much of the theory that has been developed with handicapped persons focuses on traumatically disabled individuals rather than on congenitally disabled persons. One consequence of such an emphasis is a "strong tendency for the literature to be dominated by discussions of psychological variables affecting career behavior, often to the exclusion of variables external to but nonetheless influential on the individual" (Conte, 1983, p. 317).

3. There seems to be a considerable degree of conceptual overlap and ambiguity between theories of career development, career choice, and work adjustment.

Thus, it seems apparent that there is a lack of adequate career development theory to explain and predict career/vocational behavior of handicapped populations. This may be one reason that public school career/vocational education programs have not been appropriate for mildly handicapped students. Thus far, most of the few attempts to develop such theories have been made with physically handicapped and mentally retarded populations, groups who traditionally have received vocational preparation and training. Yet even these theories are considered inappropriate and ill-conceived.

Also, it is not likely that a need will be seen to develop career development theories applicable for mildly handicapped individuals as long as the teaching of academics continues to take priority in their educational program. Consequently, if appropriate career/vocational education programs are to be developed for this group, such programs will likely have to use existing theories as their foundation. Therefore, for the remainder of this chapter, we would like to suggest some possibilities for applying each of the previously discussed theories to the needs of handicapped populations.

## Roe's Personality Theory of Choice

There is some relevance of Roe's theory to career development of handicapped persons, especially with regard to the impact of early experiences on future career development and occupational choice. According to Roe's theory, children from overprotective home environments tend to develop images of themselves that are dependent on other people's opinions of them. Also, children from such homes are characterized as placing much emphasis on the immediacy with which needs are gratified.

It is Roe's hypothesis that when such children become adults, they will seek occupations that are primarily oriented toward people. Since it is a well-known fact that many parents of handicapped children are overprotective of those children, there are some interesting correlates that one might draw when applying the theory to handicapped individuals. For example, studies looking into locus of control often conclude that handicapped youth frequently are more dependent on their teachers for feedback on academic performance than are nonhandicapped students.

We also know that one of the major problems of handicapped adults is that of desiring immediate gratification of their needs. This is especially true in the area of money management. One of the most frequent complaints of those who work with handicapped adults is that their clients often spend their paychecks on frivolous items, with nothing left over to take care of essentials like rent and utility bills. Another related problem is the tendency for handicapped workers to fail to attend work if something more desirable is in the offing such as a ski trip or a day of shopping. Not only do they fail to come to work, they usually make no attempt to notify employers of their decision.

Finally, with regard to the tendency of individuals from overprotective homes to work in people-oriented professions, we do know that many handicapped individuals choose people-oriented occupations as adults. In a study conducted by the authors (Cummings & Maddux, in press), it was found that a large number of learning disabled high school students preferred to work in social occupations, and that more learning disabled than nonlearning disabled students preferred these occupations. Although it is risky to state with any certainty that these students chose such occupations because they came from overprotective homes, it would be interesting to investigate whether or not such a correlation might exist.

Roe also talks about the impact of rejecting parents on future career needs of individuals. Children from such homes are likely to suffer from stunted career development, and are likely to choose occupations with a major orientation that is not towards people. Again, we know that parents of handicapped children sometimes have a tendency to reject such children (Cummings & Maddux, 1985b). We also know of the vocational difficulties suffered by many mildly handicapped adults

(Cummings & Maddux, 1985a; 1985b; in press) both in finding a job, and in keeping a job once it is obtained. Interestingly, in the previously-mentioned study conducted by the authors (Cummings & Maddux, in press), almost as many learning disabled high school students chose occupations that required little contact with people as those who chose social occupations. Again, it would be interesting to look into the family background of these students to determine if their parents were more rejecting than accepting of their disability.

Although Roe's assumptions are interesting when they are applied to career development problems of handicapped individuals, there are some serious flaws to the theory. We would refer the interested reader to Osipow's (1983) discussion of these flaws rather than go into detail about them ourselves. However, Roe's theory does suggest some interesting implications for career planning and counseling for handicapped youth. Roe's insistence of the impact of early experience on future occupational choice seems to support the notion of the importance of early intervention in preventing future problems with handicapped individuals. Perhaps if parents could be made aware early of the problems associated with either overprotecting or rejecting their handicapped children, with the help of knowledgeable professionals, they could work to avoid such attitudes. Also, career counselors who work with handicapped youth could use information about early childhood experiences to help young people prepare for careers that have potential for satisfying needs that were neglected in their childhood.

In light of the cautions put forth by Osipow, we hesitate to say with any assurance that Roe's theory is operational. One of Osipow's main concerns is that Roe's theory is lacking in providing counseling goals and recommendations, and does not present any remedial measures to use to correct deviant vocational patterns. In fact, Osipow (1983) warns that the theory has few applied implications and little empirical support in its current state. He says that "without a major revision it is not likely to have a growing impact on vocational counseling" (p. 34).

## Super's Developmental Self-Concept Theory of Vocational Behavior

Super believes that career choice is the result of a developmental sequence of vocational tasks that corresponds with various stages of the life-cycle. The accomplishment of the specific vocational task in each life stage is dependent upon successful performance of the tasks in the preceding stages. He proposes that people develop more clearly defined self-concepts as they grow older; people make career decisions based on a comparison of their stereotypes of various occupations with their own self-image; and the adequacy of a person's vocational choice is dependent on whether or not that individual's image of the chosen occupation is consistent with his or her self-concept. In a nutshell, to make an adequate vocational choice, an individual must be provided opportunity to gain knowledge about various occupations in the world, while at the same time being provided with plenty of experiences with people and life-events so as to develop an adequate concept of himself or herself as an individual.

While Super's theory appears to be valuable for nonhandicapped individuals, there are some interesting complications for use with handicapped persons. First of all, for an individual to make an appropriate vocational choice, that person should have developed clearly-defined self-concepts. One way that clearly-defined self-concepts are developed is through interactions with other people. From such interactions, we become sensitive to the effect of our behaviors on others and others' subsequent responses to those behaviors. We modify our behavior according to others' negative and positive responses to it. Thus, the more experiences we have with others, the more sensitive we become to their responses to us, and the more often we modify our behavior in the direction of social appropriateness.

What implication is there here for handicapped persons? First of all, the handicapping condition itself often prevents the social interactions that are commonly available to most nonhandicapped persons. Consequently, fewer interpersonal opportunities are available for handicapped persons. Secondly, even if handicapped persons were provided with as many social opportunities as nonhandicapped people, they are not as likely to develop sensitivity to others' reactions to them. The literature is full of research findings that indicate social perception deficits among even mildly handicapped youngsters. Also, because of their more limited experiences, handicapped persons may not have the same knowledge as nonhandicapped individuals about the variety of occupations that exist. Thus, because handicapped individuals are less likely than nonhandicapped persons to have clearly-defined self-concepts, and since they have a more limited view of various occupations, they may not be capable of making adequate career decisions.

Super also makes the assumption that the adequacy of one's career. decision is dependent on whether or not one's view of the chosen occupation is similar to one's self-concept. What are the implications here? One possibility may be that if the handicapped person's self-concept is not well-developed, then that individual may have unrealistically high or low expectations in matters of career choice. For a more thorough discussion of the specific application of Super's theory to the career development of adolescents and young adults with learning disabilities, we would refer the interested reader to Ernest Biller's work, including his book entitled *Understanding the Career Development of Adolescents and Young Adults with Learning Disabilities* (Biller, 1985a; 1985b).

What interventions are implied in Super's work? Since the successful completion of vocational tasks must occur in each stage of the individual's development, early intervention is important in the case of handicapped individuals. Super talks about the unique problems of *late bloomers* and *untalented* individuals, descriptors that could easily apply to many emotionally and mentally handicapped persons. He states that late bloomers probably have not identified with the adult world to a sufficient degree. As a consequence, these individuals need an accepting relationship with an adult who can serve as a model, and from whom the student can learn acceptable adult outlets for interests and talents (Osipow, 1983). Super describes untalented individuals as persons who have no special vocational preferences and who drift from one job to another. Super suggests that these people should learn to harness what talents they may have through some training to provide them with some occupational structure.

In conclusion, Super's theory suggests the importance of early intervention in career development planning for handicapped populations. Super emphasizes the need for career education that emphasizes continual exposure to the concepts of self and work throughout the curriculum. Osipow (1983) reiterates this approach and suggests that the goal of career education should be to continuously provide students with information about themselves and the educational/vocational world, so that they can make intelligent decisions throughout their development.

## The Ginzberg, Ginsburg, Axelrad, and Herma Theory

This theory, like Super's, sees vocational choice as an irreversible developmental process. According to the theory, four significant variables are involved in career choice (Osipow, 1983) including environmental impact, educational impact, emotional and personality factors, and individual values.

Although the theory was developed with nonhandicapped populations in mind, the theory makes an attempt to explain deviant patterns of career development such as might occur with many handicapped youth. Ginzberg and his associates attribute these deviant patterns to an individual's lack of conformity to agemates in some significant aspect of development. Osipow (1983) comments that the theory permits a counselor to develop certain expectations of problems in career development when confronted with an individual with a deviant vocational pattern. However, according to Osipow, the theory does not suggest corrective measures when deviant patterns are observed, nor does it specify what counseling techniques should be used to facilitate vocational development.

There are also other limitations to the theory (Osipow, 1983). There is an absence of data on older students; studies testing the theory are mostly limited to samples of upper-income male-only populations; and there is a complete absence of test data from which to validate assumptions of the theory. Thus, we would advise caution in applying hypotheses to handicapped populations.

## Sociology and Career Choice

For many *school-identified* handicapped youth, socioeconomic status plays a major role in their academic difficulties. Obviously, children from low-income families whose major concern is providing food and shelter will not perform as successfully in school as children from higher social strata. Likewise, their vocational development is apt to suffer. However, for young people whose learning problems stem from some organic difficulty, socioeconomic status becomes secondary to the handicap itself. Thus, handicapped children from higher socioeconomic levels are likely to experience vocational development that is just as stunted as that of handicapped youth from lower social classes. For example, the upper-class handicapped youth is just as likely as the lower-class handicapped youth to have difficulty making appropriate career decisions and obtaining jobs in higher-level occupations. Thus, in our opinion, the sociological model of career development has less relevance for handicapped individuals than do other models.

## Trait-Factor Approaches

Trait-factor theories of career development make the assumption that individuals are likely to be most satisfied in their occupations if the work environment matches, or is congruent with their personal traits and characteristics. We have already discussed implications of the developmental/self-concept theory for handicapped populations. That is, one explanation for the unsuccessful vocational experiences of many handicapped individuals may be attributable to their failure to successfully complete certain vocational tasks during critical life-stages.

However, we believe that another viable explanation for vocational failure of handicapped persons stems from society's tendency to occupationally stereotype handicapped persons in terms of their interests and capabilities. Typically, handicapped persons are considered capable of performing only tedious menial, entry-level jobs. Jobs fitting this stereotype include manual labor, food service occupations, janitorial services, and the like. Because of these stereotypic views, many career/vocational education programs for handicapped youth train participants to work in such jobs, regardless of whether or not students are interested in them. Thus, the possibility exists that many handicapped adults are working in occupations that are not suited to their personalities and interests. The result of such mismatching may be job dissatisfaction and instability among many handicapped workers, particularly those with higher levels of intelligence. Therefore, we believe that trait-factor approaches are as relevant as developmental approaches in explaining occupational behavior of handicapped persons.

**Theory of Work Adjustment.** This approach is based on the idea of the importance of the correspondence between the individual and the work environment. According to the theory, once the individual achieves correspondence with his or her work environment, tenure is achieved. Conversely, if the individual does not achieve correspondence, then that individual is likely to be dissatisfied, be an unsatisfactory employee, and have short-lived tenure. Several instruments have been developed to measure (a) individual interests; (b) characteristics of a variety of work environments; (c) whether an individual is satisfied in a particular job; and (d) whether an individual is satisfactory as an employee.

According to Osipow (1983), this theory seems well-instrumented, has propositions that are open to testing, and is relatively straightforward and simple. Data from the few studies that have been conducted with the theory are encouraging, and the instrumentation seems valid and accessible to investigators. Researchers are encouraged to conduct investigations in order to further elaborate what appears to be a substantive approach for explaining vocational behavior.

**Holland's Theory of Vocational Personalities and Work Environments.** Another personality/trait theorist whose work shows promise for use with handicapped populations is that of John Holland (1985a). Holland proposes that an individual's career choice reflects to some extent that person's personality and behavioral styles. He also proposes that individuals will be most satisfied if they are employed in occupational environments that are congruent with their personalities. Well-validated instrumentation has been developed to test the theory both in terms of measuring individual interests and of determining characteristics of a variety of occupations.

Although Holland's work has been primarily with nonhandicapped populations, there are some components that are applicable for individuals who are vocationally nonfunctional, as are many handicapped groups. According to Holland (1985a), effective self-evaluation results in easier identification of occupational interests. However, appropriate self-evaluation is dependent on several variables including intelligence, social status, economic condition, educational level, and health. If these variables exert a negative influence on the individual, that person is likely to have difficulty selecting an appropriate occupational environment and may constantly change from one environment to another.

Holland (1985a) also states that vocational self-evaluation is dependent on the adequacy of self- and occupational knowledge. The more information the individual has about each of these, the more effective and appropriate the occupational choice will be.

Finally, Holland (1985a) hypothesizes that social pressures in childhood and early adolescence, and experiences with parents probably have a significant effect on determining the personality type. There are obvious implications here for handicapped persons.

Holland's theory has stood the scrutiny of research and appears to be one viable explanation of vocational choice and career patterns. Investigators continue to apply the theory to a variety of populations. It is possible that application of Holland's theory to handicapped populations will be useful in terms of understanding their occupational characteristics and in helping them attain job satisfaction and personal achievement. The authors have conducted research (Cummings & Maddux, in press) to determine if learning disabled high school students have vocational interests and personalities as varied as those of nonhandicapped high school students. Holland's Self-Directed Search (SDS) was used to measure personality and occupational interests. Results indicated that there was no difference between the groups in terms of occupational interests. If such is the case, then career/vocational programs for learning disabled students, at least, should focus on preparing them for occupational roles as varied as those filled by nonhandicapped persons.

In conclusion, one advantage of trait-factor approaches over developmental approaches to explain vocational behavior is that investigators and counselors don't have to be as concerned about early life experiences and developmental patterns. Much information can be gained from administering instruments to determine an individual's occupational interests. Measured interests, in turn, can be helpful in two ways: (a) counselors can use outcomes of interest measures to guide individuals to make appropriate career choices; or (b) they can be used to determine if individuals are working in suitable occupations. Such instrumentation should prove valuable in determining if handicapped workers exhibit as much variety of occupational interests as nonhandicapped workers, and if handicapped workers are overrepresented in certain occupations that fit stereotypic views of those workers' interests and abilities.

## SUMMARY

In this chapter, we have attempted to present a rationale for the importance of basing career education approaches for handicapped populations on some philosophical structures that can be developed into theoretical models. We have presented several existing theoretical models developed for nonhandicapped populations that might have application for handicapped groups as well. These theories have included Personality approaches including Roe's Personality Theory of Choice; Developmental approaches including those of Super and the Ginzberg, Ginsburg, Axelrad, and Herma theory; Social Systems approaches such as that described by Gottfredson; and Trait-Factor approaches including those of Lofquist and Dawis, and John Holland. Finally, we have presented possible applications and implications of these theories for handicapped groups.

Hopefully, readers will use information provided in this chapter as motivation for considering the importance of modifying existing theories or of developing new theories of career development that consider the specific career needs of handicapped groups in their assumptions.

Chapter Four

# CAREER/VOCATIONAL ASSESSMENT
# AND EVALUATION

THE AREA OF career/vocational assessment is crucial to the implementation of quality career/vocational education programs. This is especially true since the passage of the Education for All Handicapped Children Act (PL94-142); Title II of the Education Amendments of 1976 (PL94-482); and the Carl Perkins Vocational Education Act of 1984 (PL98-524). All of these laws mandate that handicapped students are entitled to an appropriate career/vocational education. Lately, the process of vocational assessment is receiving increased attention (Stodden & Boone, 1986). One of the main reasons for this increased attention is the fact that the Perkins Act of 1984 states that each special needs student in vocational education must receive vocational assessment and career/vocational counseling services. Specifically, the law states:

> Each student that enrolls in vocational education programs and to whom subsection (b) applies shall receive — (1) assessment of interest, abilities and special needs of such student with respect to completing successfully the vocational education program. (Title II Basic State Grants for Vocational Education; Part A Vocational Education Opportunities; Section 204(c) Criteria for Services and Activities for the Handicapped and Disadvantaged).

However, the Federal rules and regulations for the Perkins Act (*Federal Register*, August 18, 1985, p. 33233) do not delineate specific guidelines on how services should be provided (Ianacone & Leconte, 1986). Therefore, even though there is a mandate to include career/vocational assessment and evaluation as a part of handicapped students' program, no clear understanding or agreement exists to define the nature of career/vocational assessment.

In fact, the entire field of career/vocational special education is presently in a state of transition. Traditional methods of providing handicapped students' preparation for the world of work are currently giving way to new approaches aimed at integrating handicapped students into vocational programs designed for nonhandicapped students. We agree with the concept that handicapped students should be prepared for competitive employment (such preparation is especially relevant for mildly handicapped students). However, we are concerned that vocational education is likely to share many of the problems faced by regular education because of the PL94-142 mandate that handicapped students be educated in regular classrooms. PL94-142s mandates have resulted in positive gains for moderate and severely handicapped individuals, both in societal attitudes and in availability of appropriate educational programming. However, this has not always been true with mildly handicapped students. All too often in the past, these students have been placed in the regular classroom as a matter of course, not as a result of individualized educational planning. Consequently, many students who could have benefitted from more special help in academics were often placed in the regular classroom with teachers who did not have the expertise to teach them. Too often, the outcome for these students has been many years of school failure, high drop-out rates, and unsuccessful entrance into the adult world.

Thus, we would warn against integration of handicapped students into regular vocational education classroom *without careful attention to planning and implementation*. Such a movement will be catastrophic for some students unless both special educators and vocational educators pay careful attention to make sure that the best possible match is made between the handicapped student and the student's educational program and eventual occupational placement. Each handicapped student's vocational program must be suited to the individual's unique needs, regardless of whether the primary educational arrangement is the special or the regular vocational education classroom. One way to ensure an appropriate, individual career/vocational education pogram for handicapped students is through quality career/vocational assessment.

The purpose of this chapter is to emphasize the importance of career/vocational assessment and evaluation as it relates to the development of appropriate educational programs for this population. We will begin the chapter with a definition of career/vocational assessment and evaluation for special populations. Next, we will discuss traditional approaches and the appropriateness of these approaches for mildly handicapped students. The remainder of the chapter will be devoted to discussions of assessment approaches that are relevant to the career/vocational needs of mildly handicapped youth. We will conclude by presenting examples of some of the newer approaches to providing career/vocational assessment in the public schools.

## CAREER/VOCATIONAL ASSESSMENT AND EVALUATION: A DEFINITION

The terms career/vocational assessment, vocational assessment, and vocational evaluation are often used interchangeably, although the literature sometimes makes slight distinctions among them. The most common distinctions made are between the terms *vocational assessment* and *vocational evaluation.*

Several writers have attempted to define *vocational assessment.* Sitlington and Wimmer (1978) describe it as "A continuous process of obtaining information about student performance in areas related to the world of work" (p. 85); Botterbusch (1976) calls it "The process of assessing a person to determine the specific nature of his or her aptitudes, skills, characteristics, and work-related behaviors (p. 2); and the Tenth Institute on Rehabilitation Services (1972) identifies vocational assessment as a comprehensive process that systematically uses work, real or simulated, as the focal point for vocational exploration to assist individuals in vocational development.

Other writers attempt to define vocational evaluation as being different from vocational assessment. According to Kapes and Parrish (1983), both the term *vocational evaluation* and many of its techniques were developed by professionals who worked with adults in the field of vocational rehabilitation. Vocational evaluation has been defined as the process of identifying a person's physical, mental, and emotional abilities; and limitations and tolerances for the purpose of predicting current and future employment potential and adjustment (Virginia Commonwealth University, 1966). Peterson (1982) considers vocational evaluation as a subcomponent of the more comprehensive process of vocational assessment. Finally, Kiernan and Petzy (1982) see evaluation as a process used to make specific decisions based on the analysis of data or information derived from an assessment.

For our purposes in this chapter, we like two different interpretations of the career/vocational assessment/evaluation process. The first was suggested by Cobb and Larkin (1985) and the Division on Career Development (DCD) and the second by the Council for Exceptional Children (Sitlington, Brolin, Clark, & Vacanti, 1985).

Cobb and Larkin believe it is counterproductive to distinguish between the two terms as they relate to student assessment. They would prefer to make a distinction among the many purposes for which vocational assessments are conducted rather than distinguish between the terms *assessment* and *evaluation*. Their preference is to eliminate the term *vocational evaluation* when it pertains to the entire range of assessment activities associated with educational placement and programming. Instead, these authors prefer to use the term *vocational assessment* to apply to individuals, and *vocational evaluation* to assess merit or worth of state and local service delivery at the programmatic level. In the authors' words, "we believe one should *assess individuals* (and their match with curriculum and instructional delivery) and *evaluate programs*" (p. 3). We agree with these writers, and will distinguish between the terms in the like manner.

We also like the operational definition and purpose of assessment put forth by the Division of Career Development (Sitlington et al., 1985) because, as the authors state, "it determines to a great extent the methods and process to be used and the personnel to be used in the assessment process" (p. 3). DCD recommends that the term *career assessment* be used to define a developmental process that begins in elementary school and continues through adulthood. Thus, *career assessment* is a broad term that includes *vocational assessment* or *vocational evaluation,* just as career education encompasses vocational education. According to the authors, the career assessment process should address all aspects of career education including preparation for employment, for the roles of family member, citizen, and for leisure, recreational, and avocational activities. Areas to be included in the career assessment process should be specific to the components of the career education model being implemented.

According to Sitlington et al. (1985), results of the career assessment process should be included in the Individualized Educational Plan (IEP), and the process should have the following goals: (a) to assess interests, strengths, and needs as they apply to all future adult roles; (b) to assess educational strengths and weaknesses; (c) to provide data to determine appropriate career/vocational educational placement; and (d) to provide information pertaining to appropriate post-school preparation and placement.

In conclusion, although distinctions are made between career/vocational assessment and evaluation, we consider *vocational assessment* to be the most appropriate term when discussing the use of specific instruments with individuals. However, we believe *career assessment* is appropriate as the broader term to define the ongoing evaluation of an individual's career education program as it develops from childhood through adulthood.

## TRADITIONAL VOCATIONAL ASSESSMENT APPROACHES

In 1978, the U. S. Office of Education took the position that an appropriate comprehensive vocational educational program should be available to every handicapped person (Sitlington, 1981). Also, laws were passed in the middle 1970s to put teeth into the federal commitments to provide career/vocational education programs for handicapped youngsters. PL93-112 (the Rehabilitation Act of 1973); PL94-142 (the Education for All Handicapped Children Act); and PL94-482 (the Education Amendments of 1976, Title II) all mandated that public schools provide appropriate vocational programming for handicapped students in the least restrictive environment. Until these mandates, public schools offered only traditional vocational education programs designed for nonhandicapped students. Handicapped students frequently were denied access to these programs for several reasons: (a) they were unable to pass required safety tests, (b) they were not able to keep up with course content, and/or (c) instructors did not want to or were not able to individualize course content for handicapped students. In addition, regular vocational education programs received federal and state funding based on post-school employment success of former student participants. Vocational education program administrators feared that enrolling handicapped students in vocational education classes would result in reduced numbers of graduates who would successfully enter the job market upon graduation, resulting in reduced funding levels.

However, laws passed in the mid-1970s mandated that handicapped students be given vocational options. Until that time, the only vocational assessment implemented in schools were the safety tests students were required to take prior to entering a specific program. Therefore, there were no educational precedents for vocational assessment of handicapped students. However, laws mandated that schools assess handicapped students in all areas of their disabilities, including vocational assessments. As a result, school systems adopted models of vocational assessment from the field of vocational rehabilitation (McCaray, 1982; Nadolsky, 1981; Neubert, 1986). Thus, the vocational rehabilitation model became the basis for career/vocational assessment of handicapped students. However, because of the differences between vocational rehabilitation service delivery systems and those of public education, these models have been controversial in terms of the objectives of the model, the personnel who conduct the assessments, and the usefulness of reports and recommendations made to public education personnel (Neubert, 1986).

We recognize the legitimate concerns expressed above, and acknowledge the transition that is occurring in the field of career/vocational assessment from the rehabilitation model to models that are more relevant to the public school setting. However, if the reader is to have a point of comparison, we consider it important to describe traditional models of vocational assessment before moving to a description of newer, more relevant approaches to career/vocational assessment. Also, while the newer approaches are certainly more appropriate for mildly handicapped youngsters, the traditional approaches continue to have some relevance for more severely handicapped students. Therefore, we will present the reader with some of the traditional models of vocational assessment, followed by recent criticisms of those approaches.

In his book, *Vocational Preparation of Persons with Handicaps,* Brolin (1982) describes vocational assessment as having three components: clinical assessment, work evaluation, and work adjustment. Kapes and Parrish (1983) similarly divide vocational assessment into three levels: (a) Level I includes psychological, social, physical, and academic assessment; (b) Level II deals with information on aptitudes, basic skills, interests and work value; (c) Level III includes work samples, situational assessment, and job tryout. However, levels II and III in the Kapes and Parrish model more closely approximate Brolin's Work Evaluation component. Thus, in our attempt to combine elements from both approaches, we will consider traditional assessment as consisting of three components which we will designate as Educational and Behavioral Assessment, Aptitude and Ability Assessment, and Work Adjustment.

## Educational and Behavioral Assessment

The first assessment component includes medical, social, educational, and psychological assessment. This is the only level of career/ vocational assessment that does not include vocational assessment specialists. Relevant data consists of information pertaining to langage, emotional and behavioral development; intelligence scores; academic achievement scores; and information pertaining to physical development including speech, vision, and audiology reports.

A second type of data might include observational information derived from interviews with students, parents, and teachers. Kapes and Parrish (1983) state that students can offer helpful information regarding their career expectations, attitudes toward vocational education, and attitudes toward work in general. Parents can offer additional information about interests and work habits at home. Finally, academic and vocational teachers can provide additional information regarding work-related attitudes and employability skills as well as student abilities and interests.

School records can also reveal information about intelligence tests results, attendance patterns, grades, and disciplinary problems.

## Relevant Instrumentation

1. Academic achievement tests such as the Wide Range Achievement Test (WRAT), Key Math Diagnostic Arithmetic Test; the Peabody Individual Achievement Test (PIAT), or the Woodcock Reading Mastery Tests can be used to measure educational performance.
2. Social and developmental characteristics can be measured by the Vineland Social Maturity Scale, the Brigance Test of Essential Skills, and the American Association of Mental Deficiencies (AAMD) Adaptive Behavioral Scales.
3. Physical strength and manual dexterity can be assessed by tests such as the Purdue Pegboard or the Minnesota Rate of Manipulation Tests.
4. Tests to measure intelligence include individual intelligence tests such as the Stanford-Binet, the Wechsler Test Series (the WISC-R for students from 6- to 16-years-old or the WAIS for students over the age of 16), the Kaufman Assessment Battery, or the Slosson Intelligence Test. We strongly recommend against using IQ scores obtained from group IQ tests, since these instruments are much inferior to instruments that are administered individually.
5. Some instruments to measure social or affective characteristics include the Nowicki-Strickland Locus of Control Scale (Nowicki & Strickland, 1973), or the Tennessee Self-Concept Scale.

According to Kapes and Parrish (1983), if a vocational placement cannot be made after examining all of Level I data, then additional information can be obtained through the second and third levels of assessment, which Brolin (1982) calls the Work Evaluation Assessment component.

## Attitude and Ability Assessment

This component of vocational assessment includes information on aptitudes and basic skills and information on interests and work values (Kapes and Parrish, 1983). The emphasis here is on work, either simulated or real, and some writers believe this approach is more useful in planning career/vocational education programs than psychological and achievement tests (Brolin, 1982; Peterson, 1986). According to Brolin, four types of assessment activities are included in this component. These include intake and counseling interviews, standardized vocational testing, work and job samples, and situational assessment.

**Intakes and interviews.** These are an important first step in the vocational assessment process because they can provide information about an individual's interests, work history, and future occupational goals. They can also make professionals aware of an individual's home environment including the kind and amount of parental support the handicapped individual will receive in any vocational endeavors.

**Standardized Vocational Tests.** These instruments include both measures of aptitude and interests. They provide examiners with the opportunity to watch the manner in which the student solves problems, handles frustrations, perseveres, concentrates, follows directions, and the like. Several textbooks provide extensive lists of these instruments (Brolin, 1982; Kokaska & Brolin, 1985; Swanson & Watson, 1982).

**Work and Job Samples.** These assessment procedures are considered by some writers to be the most valid method of vocational assessment (Brolin, 1982; Peterson, 1986). Brolin describes *Job samples* as being models or reproductions of a job that actually exists in an industrial, business, or other setting. Those involved in job sample assessment use actual tools representative of the job being modeled. Performance is measured according to standards and norms associated with that job.

**Work Samples.** These are described as simulated tasks or work activities for which there is no industrial, business, or other counterpart. According to Brolin (1982), work samples can be classified into five major categories: (a) Indigenous Work Samples which represent the major elements of a job or occupation as it exists in the community; (b) Job

Samples which are entire replications of jobs or occupations from industry; (c) Cluster Trait Work Samples which are used to determine a group of worker traits related to a series of jobs; (d) Simulated Work Samples which are replicas of segments of related work factors and tools of an industrial job; and (e) Single-Trait Work Samples which evaluate an isolated characteristic of a specific job or family of jobs.

According to Kokaska and Brolin (1985), work and job samples appear like real-life jobs and can be motivating to the person taking them. Although administration is somewhat time-consuming, and they are expensive to develop, work and job samples can be designed using local work environments as models.

**Situational Assessment.** These assessment techniques are probably the most frequently used work evaluation approach. This assessment approach focuses on the individual's work personality rather than on specific vocational skills. It involves providing a group of persons with a real or simulated work environment, and then observing and recording specific behaviors that are exhibited during the assessment period. Later, inappropriate behaviors are identified and attempts are made to modify such behaviors. The work situation can be simulated in the classroom, tied to an existing job, or created in a sheltered workshop or work-activity center. The success of the assessment depends heavily on the effectiveness of those observing the work behavior (Brolin, 1982).

## Measures of Work Adjustment

This assessment approach relates to the "purposeful behavioral change process by which individuals can learn acceptable work behaviors and employability skills" (Kokaska & Brolin, 1985, p. 291). The emphasis here is on developing the actual work personality and potential of the worker. According to Brolin (1982) work adjustment has three objectives:

1. To orient individuals with little or no work experience to the world of work.
2. To develop prevocational skills.
3. To change specific work deficiencies that will hinder a person from securing employment.

According to Kokaska and Brolin (1985), educators can assess work adjustment through several approaches. These approaches include: the engineering approach, the counseling approach, the instructional approach, and the situational work approach.

**The Engineering Approach.** This approach focuses on modifying the worker and the work place. This includes the following:

1. *Modifying the environment* through changing the physical layout or location of the work environment, and providing assistive devices to enable the handicapped worker to perform work-related tasks.
2. *Modifying the process* by restructuring job procedures. This includes analyzing the work task; determining whether or not the task can be performed by the handicapped worker; and, if necessary, redesigning the task to accommodate the handicapped worker.
3. *Modifying the machine* involves modification and adaptation of equipment to permit access to handicapped workers.
4. *Modifying the person* by using medical or engineering technology to design prosthetic devices to enable handicapped workers to successfully engage in work tasks.

**The Counseling Approach.** Counseling is used as a technique for encouraging individuals to see themselves, their relationships with others, and their behavior in relation to the world of work. Individual counseling focuses on an individual's personal adjustment to work, while the group counseling approach focuses on interpersonal adjustment. Brolin (1982) reports that both processes may be necessary to work adjustment counseling.

**Instructional Work Adjustment.** This is a process in which a professional such as a vocational counselor, an adjustment specialist, or a teacher, meets with a small group of students on a regular basis. The purpose of the group meeting is to teach participants better work attitudes and to enhance work personality characteristics. Small group discussion, instructional materials, and audiovisual aids are used to motivate clients to participate.

**The Situational Work Approach.** This approach is similar to situational assessment, except that the purpose and outcome differ (Brolin, 1982). The focus of this approach is on the modification of specific work behavior within the context of an actual work environment. The work can be real work performed in a work environment such as a sheltered workshop, or simulated work can be performed in a job laboratory within a public school or rehabilitation facility. According to Kokaska and Brolin (1985), the situational work approach allows for work conditioning to occur. Thus work requirements relative to quantity, quality, and speed can be increased gradually, and work tasks can progress from simple to more complex tasks.

## Criticisms of Traditional Vocational Assessment Approaches

As we said at the beginning of this chapter, traditional vocational assessment approaches have come under recent criticism for several reasons.

1. Traditional concepts, instrumentation, and assessment strategies are not relevant for educational program development (Cobb & Larkin, 1985; Meehan & Hodell, 1986; Porter & Stodden, 1986). The public school vocational instructor may not know how to use assessment information to make program decisions, or educational program options that relate to vocational assessment information may not be available (Meehan & Hodell, 1986).

2. Vocational information may be inappropriate for the student or educational setting (Meehan & Hodell, 1986).

3. The teacher may not know how to interpret vocational assessment data (Meehan & Hodell, 1986).

4. Assessment decisions have often been made by individual professionals, rather than by interdisciplinary teams. Consequently, vocational assessment has often consisted of unrelated activities and commercial work sampling systems that reflect the needs of traditional rehabilitation evaluation settings rather than those of the school or community work site (Stodden & Boone, 1986).

5. Handicapped students frequently receive vocational assessment in rehabilitation centers that are typically isolated from actual vocational training programs and that rarely include vocational education personnel in the assessment process (Stodden & Boone, 1986).

6. Assessment activities are oriented more to retraining and placement of persons with acquired handicaps than to career/vocational exploration, planning and programming, and training needs of educational settings (Ianacone & Leconte, 1986).

7. Commercial assessment systems are often used that are not reflective of the local labor market, not appropriate for diverse handicapping conditions, and use norms that are not reflective of student performance (Ianacone & Leconte, 1986).

8. The cost of transporting students from school to the vocational assessment center is often prohibitive.

9. Assessment personnel frequently have no training in vocational/special education (Ianacone & Leconte, 1986).

10. There has been a lack of communication and understanding about the need for and integration of vocational assessment services in the

educational setting. Special educators have failed to understand the need for and benefits of the vocational assessment process (Ianacone & Leconte, 1986).

11. Teachers are reluctant to sacrifice blocks of instructional time so that students can complete the assessment process (Ianacone & Leconte, 1986).

12. Vocational educators have concerns regarding the relevancy of available work samples to the content and structure of the educational training program (Ianacone & Leconte).

13. Administrators have expressed concerns about justifying the heavy expenditures in terms of equipment, personnel, transportation needed to establish assessment centers when compared to the limited numbers of students served (Ianacone & Leconte, 1986).

These concerns echo those of our own. We have also been concerned about the relevance of applying the vocational rehabilitation model to developmentally handicapped persons (Cummings & Maddux, 1985b). Obviously, the term *rehabilitation* itself indicates an orientation to retrain a once-intact individual. In fact, one of the evaluation criteria used in vocational rehabilitation settings is the length of time that passes between onset of rehabilitation training and successful re-entry into the world of work. It is our belief that most vocational rehabilitation professionals do not have the training and/ or skills necessary to successfully prepare for eventual work those individuals who have been handicapped from birth. Unlike those with acquired disabilities, congenitally disabled persons will require *habilitation* rather than *rehabilitation,* and the process is likely to be lengthy and difficult. Consequently, these individuals are likely to receive inappropriate services when such services are administered by professionals who have been trained to move clients as quickly as possible through the rehabilitation process. Thus, we agree with those who advocate shifting to a new model of vocational assessment more relevant to the needs of the public schools, that accommodates for individual needs of handicapped learners, and that better reflects the vocational training opportunities and the local labor market (Cobb & Larkin, 1985; Ianacone & Leconte, 1986; Meehan & Hodell, 1986; Neubert, 1986; Porter & Stodden, 1986; Stodden & Boone, 1986). Therefore, the remainder of this chapter will describe some of the more recent approaches to career/vocational assessment for handicapped individuals.

# CURRICULUM-BASED VOCATIONAL ASSESSMENT (CBVA)

As we have already stated, traditional vocational assessment procedures have followed the vocational rehabilitation model. Although this model has been quite successful in training adults with acquired handicaps for re-entry into the work world, it has not been as successful when implemented with developmentally handicapped students in the public schools. Problems with the model have occurred for several reasons: (a) it has been expensive for public schools to implement; (b) assessment is usually a one-shot procedure lacking follow-up procedures; (c) assessment is usually conducted by an independent evaluator in a location far removed from the educational setting of the student; (d) assessment procedures sometimes require students to be away from the classroom for as long as two weeks, taking time away from educational instruction; (e) special and vocational educators often fail to see the relevance of such assessment to educational goals and objectives; (f) outcomes are nebulous and difficult to evaluate especially in terms of educational programming. The unfortuate outcome of inappropriate vocational assessment frequently has been inadequate vocational education programs that have failed in their efforts to prepare handicapped youth for successful entry into the world of work and adult life. Ianacone and Leconte (1986) sum up the problem when they state that "an analysis of past experience and research cautions against reliance on existing models that have been marginally effective and do not provide the outcomes we expect" (p. 119). Cobb and Larkin (1985) reiterate these concerns and report that the rehabilitation assessment model is not educationally relevant and that "vocational assessment processes in our schools have evolved attempting to make predictions about employment suitability, but not very often about the curricular ecology" (p. 3).

In light of these problems, and in response to recent mandates resulting from passage of the Carl D. Perkins Vocational Act of 1984 (PL98-524), the need to combine quality vocational assessment with appropriate vocational education programs for handicapped students has become a major concern of career/vocational professionals. Thus, in recent years, professionals in the field have begun to stress the need to develop vocational assessment procedures that are tailored to meet the particular needs of local education agencies (Ianacone & Leconte, 1986); that accommodate for the developmental levels of students (Ianacone & Leconte, 1986); that adequately reflect the vocational training opportunities and the local labor market (Cobb, 1985); that is dynamic and continuous as opposed to a static, one-shot program (Ianacone & Leconte, 1986); and that is cost-effective.

In recognition of this need, professionals are considering the development and implementation of curriculum-based vocational assessment (CBVA) within the public school setting (Porter & Stodden, 1986). Just what is curriculum-based vocational assessment? It has been defined as a process for determining students' career development, vocational needs, and instructional/growth needs based on their ongoing performance within existing course content and other educational activities (Ianacone & Leconte, 1986; Porter & Stodden, 1986). It is described as a data collection, decision-making, and program-planning process. Its purpose is two-fold: (a) to increase the handicapped student's understanding of self in relation to work; and (b) to collect developmental information pertaining to career/vocational programming decisions throughout an individual student's educational career.

Several advantages are cited as reasons for schools to move from traditional methods of vocational assessment to the curriculum-based model (Cobb & Larkin, 1985; Ianacone & Leconte, 1986; Porter & Stodden, 1986; Stodden & Boone, 1986; Tucker, 1985):

1. It is appropriate for students with mildly handicapping conditions.
2. It relates activities to instructionally relevant purposes.
3. It emphasizes a multidisciplinary team approach to assessment.
4. It stresses integration of assessment information in career planning and vocational and educational programming for handicapped students.
5. It is appropriate and adaptable to any school system.
6. It relies on the use of existing school and community resources to gain vocational assessment data about individual students.
7. It is structured, and depends on cooperative planning and implementation, ongoing administrative support, and constant monitoring.
8. It reflects the needs, training options, and employment opportunities available in individual local education agencies and communities.
9. It provides a means of matching student interests and strengths to instruction. The result is increased learning outcomes and reduced limited access to vocational programs, low achievement, and behavior problems.
10. It fits well within the goals and objectives of the IEP process.

One of the most important components of the curriculum-based vocational assessment process is that of planning. Specific steps are outlined in detail elsewhere (Ianacone & Leconte, 1986; Stodden & Boone, 1986). However, some of the key elements in planning include (a) identify key development personnel; (b) review existing models and relevant research; (c) develop program tenets based on previous research; (d) determine specific roles for assessment planning team members; (e) develop principles for guiding assessment activities; (f) develop the assessment model; (g) establish an operational plan to implement the process; (h) evaluate activities; (i) implement, evaluate, and expand options.

Ianacone and Leconte (1986) present several benefits that result from the curriculum-based vocational assessment process:

1. It maximizes the impact on curriculum and instruction.
2. It allows for ongoing collection of data during the career development of a student.
3. It internalizes the process with all staff and helps focus on career and vocational outcomes.
4. It generates an ongoing career and vocational assessment base that affects and guides the development of a student's individualized educational program.
5. It gathers information at various stages of career orientation, exploration, and preparation.
6. It uses an ongoing source of assessment data for career/vocational planning and decision-making.
7. It allows for continual development of self-awareness and realistic goal-setting for students.
8. It is cost effective.

Now that we have pointed out the advantages of curriculum-based vocational assessment over more traditional rehabilitation models, we would like to briefly describe two CBVA models that appear to be relevant for public-school career/vocational education settings. One of these models was developed by Cobb and Larkin (1985), and the other by Porter and Stodden (1986).

## A Paradigm of Vocational Assessment (Cobb & Larkin, 1985)

A fundamental assumption of this model is a team approach to vocational assessment in normalized settings that includes vocational, special and regular educators. In this model, the vocational assessment process is assigned five chronological steps, each of which relates to ongoing instructional delivery and fits well within the IEP model. These procedures include screening, placement, program planning, monitoring of individual progress, and individual program evaluation. Each of these will be discussed in turn.

**Screening.** This procedure deals with the question of whether or not vocational education is the appropriate curriculum option for a given student. To determine an answer to this question, assessment data is gathered that includes parent input, student input, relevant student records, teacher interviews, and review of available program alternatives.

**Placement.** Once a student has been screened and vocational education has been determined to be the appropriate curriculum option, a decision must be made with regard to the specific vocational program that best suits the needs of the student. Typically, vocational education curriculum consists of nine different divisions including agriculture, trades and industrial, business and office occupations, distributive, technical, home economics, health occupations, industrial arts, and cooperative education. However, larger or smaller numbers of options may be available in individual schools.

Assessment information to determine placement can be obtained (a) through parent interviews; (b) from the student through interviews, informal interest inventories, and tours of different programs; (c) through observation of the vocational teacher's teaching styles and strategies; (d) physical location of the specific program; and (e) whether or not there is a work-study component to the program.

Finally, these authors warn against placing too much emphasis on local job availability as an assessment technique for determining program selection. They emphasize that *little* emphasis should be placed on making program selection decisions based on existing community employment opportunities. They warn against the stereotypic response of over-enrolling handicapped students in programs that provide training for work in "least-preferred" occupations such as the fast-food industry or food service programs. They state that "mildly handicapped students are no more in need of *job-specific training* for these positions than are nonhandicapped students" (p. 7). Finally, they emphasize that the entire range of vocational education programs should be as available for mildly handicapped students as they are for nonhandicapped students.

**Program Planning.** Assessment for the purpose of program planning should include data to determine the support services that must be provided for an individual student to ensure success in the assigned vocational placement. This data is collected through observational assessment of the student's interaction with the curriculum, with teachers, with other students, with facilities and equipment, within the home and community. According to the authors, such assessment results in the development of annual goals and short-term instructional objectives that directly relate student deficits to curriculum and to a specification of necessary supportive services.

**Monitoring Individual Progress.** The authors stress that assessment for the purpose of monitoring student progress has typically been ignored. They recommend curriculum-based, direct, frequent, and informal measures be used for this activity. They also stress that direct, performance-based measurement is preferable to indirect written assessment. A problem exists when handicapped students in vocational preparation programs are taught performance-based skills such as correctly taking blood pressure or installing brake shoes, but are required to demonstrate competence through written measures. Vocational teachers should be encouraged to use more direct measures to evaluate handicapped students' competencies in performing specific skills.

**Program Evaluation.** According to the authors, assessment for individual program success occurs at semester's or year's end, and should seek answers to two questions: "How well has the supportive service structure served this student?" and "Is a curriculum change warranted?" (p. 11) If it is determined that a curriculum placement has not succeeded, then assessment data should provide information that suggests a specific cause and gives direction for change.

In addition to their five-step model, Cobb and Larkin suggest two fundamental shifts in assessment service delivery. First of all, they encourage school districts that operate, or are considering operating, formal vocational evaluation laboratories to closely examine benefits associated with such laboratories and how well outcomes match teacher and student assessment needs. When consideration is taken of high start-up costs, need for substantial staff, and space requirements of such laboratories, the authors caution school districts to consider other alternatives. Preliminary research looking into the efficacy of such laboratories has failed to provide evidence of results of formal vocational assessment processes being used to assist vocational and special educators in program planning, monitoring, or evaluation. Also, there is little evidence to suggest that assessment results are ever translated into IEP goals and objectives.

The authors also advocate a shift in the role and competencies of the vocational assessment specialist. It is their belief that this individual should (a) be able to function as part of a team made up of regular, vocational, special, and rehabilitation personnel who are responsible for synthesizing information from diverse sources and translating it into useful vocational programming procedures for students; (b) have the ability to train vocational, special, and regular educators to effectively monitor student progress; (c) be able to interview parents, teachers, and students themselves to obtain information regarding student interests and abilities; (d) be familiar with vocational curriculum options, various teaching styles and strategies, and community-based training and employment opportunities; (e) act as a consultant and advisor to regular and vocational educators to help them identify and direct needed modifications to curriculum, instructional delivery, and equipment to accommodate mainstreamed students; and (f) know how to analyze and orchestrate school/community support systems to provide transition services for students once they leave the public schools.

According to the authors, the vocational specialist will spend a majority of time outside the confines of a vocational assessment laboratory. In addition, this person will have a pro-active, interventionist orientation rather than a reactive, medical-model orientation.

Finally, the role of the vocational assessment specialist will vary throughout a student's vocational education program. For example, at the beginning of the student's program, the assessor will concentrate on seeing that screening and placement purposes have been well met. There would be continual program planning and monitoring. Program review would occur at the end of the first year and, if the program is successful, not again until the student nears the end of the program and transitional planning becomes predominant.

## A Curriculum-Based Vocational Assessment Procedure (Porter & Stodden, 1986)

A second model for curriculum-based vocational assessment is that proposed by Porter and Ianacone (1986). The model is described as a "data collection, decision-making, and program-planning process for increasing the handicapped student's awareness and understanding of self in relation to work" (p. 123). The model was initially developed for the U. S. Department of Defense Dependents Schools (DODDS), Germany Region for the purpose of increasing appropriate participation of students in the Department's 49 middle, junior, and senior high schools.

The following considerations were crucial to model development:

1. Assessment data would reflect student performance levels upon completion of any career/vocational activity, course, or work experience.
2. Student performance would be directly related to instructional objectives for the curriculum context of each activity, course, or experience.
3. Assessment data would be descriptive of instructional outcomes, and could be used to supplement existing assessment and grading procedures.
4. Work-related behaviors and generalized skills would be assessed as they related to specific occupational skill areas.
5. Assessment data would be easily accessible to career/vocational instructors, work experience personnel, and/or job supervisors.
6. Collected data would fit the IEP evaluation and development procedures.
7. Assessment formats would be structured so as to be easily understood and interpreted by students, parents, and school personnel.

The model contains three levels of data collection that encompasses junior high school prevocational courses and activities, high school vocational courses, and cooperative work experience programs.

**Level I, initial assessment activities.** These activities begin in the junior high/middle school and assess student readiness and awareness skills through student participation in exploratory courses and activities.

**Level II assessment activities.** These begin when students start high school vocational coursework.

**Level III assessment activities.** These occur as students display work-related behaviors and skills in school/community cooperative work experience programs.

Assessment data is collected within three domains: work-related behaviors, generalized vocational outcomes, and specific skills outcomes. An example of a *work related behavior* might be student display of initiative or appropriate appearance. *Generalized vocational outcomes* might include the ability to understand written directions or demonstration of problem-solving techniques. Finally, *specific skill outcomes* might be the ability to use bonding processes or to operate a drill press. Instructors use a vocational assessment rating form to rate handicapped students' performance in each of these areas for each career/vocational course or activity in which they are enrolled. At the end of each quarter or semester, instructors send the rating forms to a case study committee chairperson. This individual logs in the completed form and shares the information with the case study committee. Assessment data from each instructor for each student is then considered in making programming and placement decisions for the next evaluation period. Vocational information may also be used in the development of IEP goals and objectives, and in the development of instructional modifications necessary to ensure student access and performance in the vocational curriculum.

According to the authors, this model is designed to provide ongoing assessment of student performance during and following instruction resulting in a sequenced performance record that reflects student's progress across several career/vocational courses and work experiences. Data then will be helpful for subsequent instructors in planning an individualized vocational curriculum. The ultimate application of assessment data would be to assist student transition into postsecondary vocational training opportunities or entry-level job placements.

The authors stress that the model provides an efficient means of transitioning handicapped youth through a sequenced career/vocational curriculum with community-employment outcomes. The model's curriculum-based vocational assessment procedures encourage a match of student interests and strengths with career/vocational instructional options. Also, according to the authors, the model planning and implementation process can be replicated within any secondary school career/vocational program sequence. Data continues to be generated from the DODDS-Germany Region program, and we would recommend the reader search the current literature for further reporting on the model's effectiveness.

## THEORY-BASED VOCATIONAL ASSESSMENT

As we stated in Chapter Three, we believe that a major problem with traditional career development approaches with handicapped populations is that they are not based on any philosophical or theoretical foundation. Thus, we would stress the importance of examining the specific reasons for implementing various career/vocational education programs. At present, implementation of such programs is based either (a) on traditional career/vocational approaches, regardless of whether such approaches are appropriate and/or beneficial for participants; or (b) on the basis of the desire on the part of vocational, special and regular educators to be provided with *cookbook* techniques that càn be incorporated into the existing curriculum.

Although both of these approaches can be useful with certain students and in specific circumstances, neither use highly-researched, theory-based assessment instruments as guides to design individualized career/vocational programs with promising prognoses for continued post-school job success and stability. One problem with career/vocational approaches that *are not* based on theoretical foundations is the lack of empirical evidence to support their effectiveness. Typically, evaluation criteria consist of observational data and surveys and questionnaires. Although such information is valuable, we believe that empirical studies are needed to determine such things as: (a) long-term program effects; (b) comparisons between handicapped and nonhandicapped populations; and (c) comparisons of program efficacy related to specific handicaps. We also believe that theory-based approaches to assessment provide more information about developmental and personality variables that allow for comparison between career development of handicapped and nonhandicapped populations.

Thus, for the remainder of this chapter, we will describe three theory-based approaches to career/vocational assessment that seem appropriate for use with mildly handicapped individuals.

## The Minnesota Theory of Work Adjustment (Dawis, Lofquist, & Weiss, 1968)

We have already described the basic tenets of this theory and its potential for use when considering career/vocational program development for mildly handicapped youth. Therefore, we will briefly review the theory, emphasizing relevant assessment instruments.

According to Brolin (1982), the theory "holds much promise for understanding the development of a work personality and attainment of satisfactory vocational adjustment by handicapped individuals" (p. 68). According to the theory, the development of a stable work personality is dependent upon the interaction between the individual and the environment. The work personality begins forming shortly after birth, and its development is dependent upon a combination of hereditary characteristics and the characteristics of reinforcers experienced in the environment. According to the theory, each individual is born with a unique set of response potentials (behavioral characteristics) that determine how that person will respond to reinforcers that are available in the environment. Reinforcers that are positively perceived and that occur repeatedly will contribute to a developing set of abilities that eventually become part of the work personality. The individual also interacts with environmental reinforcers (or lack of them) to develop a set of specific needs that also contribute to the work personality. If early experiences have been positively reinforced and encouraged, the individual should have developed a fairly stable set of needs and abilities by the age of 16 or 17. Work-related abilities include cognitive abilities, motor abilities, sensory abilities, interpersonal skills, physical abilities, and independent living skills. Work-related needs include such things as achievement, authority, autonomy, creativity, independence, responsibility, and the like.

According to the theory, appropriate career/vocational goals are achieved when an individual's abilities fit those required by the job, and when that person's individual needs are met within the work environment. Thus, a second theoretical concern is that of the characteristics of the work environment. Since each job or occupation has its own, unique set of *job requirements* and *job reinforcers*, then the work environment must be evaluated to determine its appropriateness as a job-site for a specific individual. According to Brolin (1982), "a well-conceived and well-conducted vocational program should reveal the individual's pattern of abilities and needs so that his interests and potential can be identified and so that training and an appropriate work environment can be planned" (p. 73).

Brolin (1982) describes the theory as (a) having direct applicability to both job placement and follow-up efforts, (b) essentially a placement theory since it is concerned with placing individuals on jobs that meet their basic abilities and needs, and, finally, (c) as being operational because of the measures designed to predict work adjustment. These instruments include:

1. *The General Aptitude Test Battery (GATB)* to measure individual vocational abilities.
2. *Occupational Aptitude Patterns (OAPs)* to measure ability requirements of jobs.
3. *The Minnesota Importance Questionnaire (MIQ)* to measure 20 vocationally-relevant needs. Since the MIQ requires at least a fifth-grade reading level, a form S version has been developed for use with individuals with lower reading abilities. However, Dawis (cited in

Brolin, 1982) cautions that the Form S is still experimental, and should be used for research purposes only.

4. *The Minnesota Job Description Questionnaire (MJDQ)* to measure reinforcers available in specific jobs and the levels at which they exist.

5. *The Minnesota Satisfactoriness Scales (MSS)* to measure how satisfactorily individuals perform on their jobs.

6. *The Minnesota Satisfaction Questionnaire (MSQ)* to measure satisfaction of individuals' needs through work.

To summarize, there have not been many studies to test the effectiveness of this theory, especially with regard to its potential for use with handicapped populations. However, we agree with Brolin (1982) and Osipow (1983), who state that the theory holds promise for use by career/vocational educators in planning appropriate programs for mildly handicapped youth. Thus, we advocate the need for future studies to determine the theory's applicability for handicapped populations.

## Career Development Assessment Model: A Four Phase Process (Biller, 1985; Super, 1983)

This model is developed in detail in Biller's (1985) text, *Understanding and Guiding the Career Development of Adolescents and Young Adults with Learning Disabilities,* and we recommend it as a viable theoretical approach to use in career/vocational program planning for learning disabled students. According to Biller, the assessment model is based on Super's (1983) revised developmental career assessment framework, and it corresponds to specific tasks of the adolescent career exploration stage. According to Biller, the assessment model provides the framework and procedures to assess life-stage determinants and components which in turn are turned into specific objectives in the related Exploration Career Life-Stage Curriculum outlined in Chapter Seven of Biller's book.

The Career Development Assessment Model (CDAM) consists of four phases: Phase I, Information and Assessment; Phase II, In-Depth View; Phase III, Assessment of All Data; and Phase IV, Counseling. We will briefly describe each of these phases and their relationship to career/vocational education programs, specifically as they relate to students with learning disabilities.

**Phase I, Information and Assessment.** Phase I is similar to most traditional career/vocational models in that the individual designated as the vocational assessment specialist (teacher/counselor) is responsible for conducting the assessment and gathering relevant data already on file. An initial intake interview takes place for the purpose of (a) establishing rapport with the student; (b) gathering data pertaining to medical, social, psychological, educational, and socioeconomic factors; and (c) determining student needs and career goals. Biller also stresses the importance of determining student reading levels to ascertain what modifications may be needed to be made in assessment measures. It is also crucial to collect data from home and community sources since many learning disabled students demonstrate traits and behaviors in these environments that may be different from those demonstrated in the school milieu. Finally, Biller states that the student should fully participate in all phases of the assessment.

**Phase II. In-Depth Assessment. Work Importance and Maturity.** The purpose of assessment in this phase is two-fold: (a) to determine the student's commitment to the importance of the diverse work roles of study, work and career, home and family, community service, and leisure activities. Super suggests that this assessment be done subjectively, primarily from interview data; and (b) to determine if the student is ready (career mature) to cope with career decision-making tasks required in Super's career exploration life-stage. The *Career Development Inventory* (CDI) (Super, et al., 1983) is used in Phase II as an overall measure of career maturity. The CDI is made up of 8 separate scales:

1. The first two scales, *Scale CP, career planning* and *Scale CE, career exploration* are attitudinal measures. Scale CP measures one's planning orientation to careers, and Scale CE assesses an individual's willingness to effectively use available resources to learn about educational and occupational opportunities. These first two scales focus on (a) awareness of the possibility of career choice or the need for it, and (b) the concern or motivation to respond to this awareness or need (Biller, 1985). These two objectives are the foundation for all further development activity. Also, the CE scales are useful in program planning since responses identify the career planning activities students are involved in, and they indicate career exploration resources being used by students.

2. The next three scales, *Scale DM, decision making, Scale WW, world-of-work,* and *Scale PO, knowledge of the preferred occupational group,* are cognitive measures. Scale DM measures the ability to apply knowledge and insight to career planning and decision making. Scale WW assesses student knowledge of career development tasks, of the occupational structure, of sample occupations ranging from semi-skilled to professional,

and of job-seeking and keeping skills. Finally, Scale PO helps students identify the occupational group that interests them the most, and it is structured to measure understanding of the classification of work that is of most interest to the student. According to Thompson et al. (cited in Biller, 1985), the PO scale is most useful with students who score average or better on the first four CDI scales. Thus it may not be applicable until late in the 10th grade or later. It is suggested that students above the sophomore level who score below average on the Scale PO receive assistance to help them learn more about career fields of interest.

3. The final three scales of the CDI, *Career Development — Attitudes* (CDA), *Career Development — Knowledge* (CDK), and *Career Orientation Total* (COT), represent combinations of the previous five CDI scales and provide additional information about career attitudes, cognitive awareness, and overall career maturity respectively.

CDI outcomes provide reference points for diagnosing, assessing, and enhancing desired attitudes and competencies related to effective career growth. This delineation of desired attitudes and competencies allows the specification of objectives for instructional and counseling projects designed to promote mature career development (Biller, 1985).

Biller cautions that the CDI may not be appropriate for some learning disabled students since it has a reading vocabulary of approximately a 10th-grade level, and since it was not normed on an LD population. However, Biller reports that the CDI may be appropriate for most learning disabled students when certain administration procedures are followed. The interested reader will find these listed in Biller's book.

*Abilities, Interests, and Potential Functioning.* Biller suggests that traditional career assessment activities are appropriate to make predictions about an individual's work potential if they are used appropriately and the data is considered in proper perspective. These include interest and aptitude testing, psychological testing, work samples, community or situational assessment, and on-the-job tryouts.

**Phase II: Assess Determinants of Career Maturity.** These determinants include locus of control, self-esteem, future perspective, cognitive complexity, and problem solving abilities. According to Biller (1985), not all learning disabled students will be affected by deficits in these determinants. However, if assessment results in Phase II indicate abnormally low maturity and/or motivation, then Phase II option testing is done to determine if these personality determinants are impeding the career development process. Biller (1985) discusses a variety of instruments for measurement of these determinants.

**Phase III and IV.** In these remaining two phases, career assessment data is reviewed, and career/vocational counseling occurs to determine what special accommodations will be needed to initiate instructional plans for teaching the Exploration Career Life-Stage Curriculum. For a detailed description of the curriculum, we would refer the reader to Chapter Seven of Biller's text.

In summary, the Career Development Assessment Model is based on Super's Developmental Self-Concept Theory of Vocational Behavior. Biller (1985) has done an excellent job of translating Super's theory into an assessment model that has application for mildly handicapped, and specifically learning disabled, students. The CDI, seems especially appropriate for providing a developmental approach to career/vocational planning for learning disabled students. We especially like the idea of assessing students throughout the adolescent stage of Career Exploration, with the idea that program development will be fluid and based on the students' individual needs and abilities.

## Holland's Theory of Vocational Personalities and Work Environments (Holland, 1985a)

As we stated in Chapter Three, Holland's theory assumes that career choices are an extension of an individual's personality, and that job satisfaction and stability is highest when an individual works in an environment with characteristics that are congruent with that individual's interests and personality. We agree, and propose that many mildly handicapped adults are not successful in their jobs because career/vocational programs frequently train them for stereotypic occupations that are frequently incongruent with their interests and personalities. While nonhandicapped persons are considered to have a variety of occupational interests, handicapped individuals are often occupationally stereotyped and trained for and placed into a more limited variety of occupational environments (Cobb & Larkin, 1985; Cummings & Maddux, in press). If mildly handicapped individuals have as much variety of occupational interests as nonhandicapped persons, then developers of career/vocational programs for this population should consider these interests in terms of training and counseling approaches. One way to determine personality and occupational interests is by administering occupational interest inventories.

In comparison to vocational assessment in general, little has been written concerning the value of assessing occupational interests of intellectually handicapped individuals. Several writers offer explanations for the lack of attention that is paid to interest assessment of mentally handicapped persons. Timmerman and Doctor (1974) suggest that occupational interest may be ignored in intellectually handicapped individuals because: (a) most of these individuals have not seriously been considered for employment; (b) the general attitude that intellectually handicapped persons do not have the ability or social maturity to make valid occupational choices; and (c) we lack appropriate instrumentation in terms of reading levels and career cluster choices.

Stodden, Ianacone, and Lazar (1979) state that such commonly-used interest inventories as the Strong-Campbell Vocational Interest Inventory and the Kuder occupational Interest Survey have proved to be unsatisfactory for use with mentally handicapped populations since high verbal ability and a wide range of experience are necessary to accurately respond to test items.

In spite of the weaknesses of some interest inventories, assessment of occupational interest should be a critical component of a career/vocational assessment program for handicapped individuals. However, Stodden et al. (1979) point out several cautions when using vocational interest assessments with mentally handicapped adolescents:

1. Many of the instruments and/or techniques used to assess interests have been criticized because (a) they frequently present limited forced choice career areas that may or may not be appropriate for mentally handicapped persons; (b) they often have strong occupational, sex, race, and regional biases that discriminate against the choices of many mentally handicapped adolescents; (c) they have inappropriate reading levels, instrument length, and lack necessary motivation and awareness activities as prerequisites to assessment; and (d) they are lacking in research as to stability of occupational interests of mentally handicapped subjects.

2. Without proper attitudes and philosophies of individuals responsible for administration of assessment activities, the use of information acquired from assessment may be meaningless or even harmful for the assessed individuals.

3. Validity of occupational interest inventories used with mentally handicapped individuals is determined by the context and purposes for the use of such instruments. The authors explain their position with the following statement:

> Occupational assessment must be conceptualized as a vehicle to produce demonstratively useful information for the client's exploration and growth, rather than a set of data from which to predict chances of occupational success. When occupational interest evaluation is viewed as part of a sequence of growth activities in career exploration, experimentation, and discovery, the concept of evaluation becomes a non-threatening series of activities with emphasis upon client change and growth. (p. 297)

Olshansky (1969) also emphasizes the importance of proper professional attitudes and philosophies in administration and interpretation of assessment information. He states these improper attitudes and philosophies often arise because of certain misconceptions including beliefs that: (a) we have knowledge pertaining to level of intelligence required for different types of jobs; (b) a slow learner is a poor learner; (c) intelligence is a constant and global quality; (d) mentally handicapped individuals can tolerate boring tasks; and (e) all mentally handicapped persons have the same interests and personality characteristics. Olshansky points out that since many of these misconceptions continue to exist among professionals, practitioners, and employees working with mentally handicapped person, accomplishing meaningful occupational interest assessment is frequently quite difficult.

From this discussion, it is apparent that occupational interest measures have both strengths and weaknesses when used with mentally handicapped populations. However, when included as part of a client-centered series of developmental growth and awareness activities, occupational interest evaluation becomes one of several variables necessary in appropriate career/vocational programming for mentally handicapped youth (Stodden et al., 1979). Only through such programming is the assurance of a high degree of work satisfaction and success possible. According to Stodden et al., education and rehabilitation personnel should become more involved with occupational interest evaluation as they work to meet the career/vocational needs of mentally handicapped individuals.

## The Holland Theory

One theory that has generated a great deal of discussion and research (Conte, 1983; Osipow, 1983) is Holland's (1985a) Theory of Vocational Personalities and Work Environments. Although Holland has not been primarily interested in handicapped individuals, his theory appears to provide a basis for formualting ways to look at handicapped individuals in a nonstereotypic manner (Cummings & Maddux, 1984; in press). We have already discussed the theory in detail in Chapter Three. Therefore, we would like to limit our present discussion to a description of Holland's instrument to measure occupational interests, the *Self-Directed Search,* and possibilities for its use with mildly handicapped populations. We also will present findings of recent research relevant for handicapped individuals and suggest implications of the theory's appropriateness for such individuals.

**The Self-Directed Search (SDS) (Holland, 1985b).** The *Self-Directed Search* is the instrument developed by Holland to assess occupational interests and personalities. It is self-administered, self-scored, and self-interpreted, and it is based on Holland's theory of vocational choice and occupational classification system. According to Holland (1985a), personalities and work environments can be classified into one of six categories—Realistic (R), Investigative (I), Artistic (A), Social (S), Enterprising (E), and Conventional (C). Job satisfaction and stability occur more often if personality type and work environment are congruent. For example, a Realistic type is happiest in a Realistic work environment while a Realistic type in a Social evironment is likely to be dissatisifed.

The SDS has five sections (228 items) used to assess a person's similarity to the six Holland types. To take the SDS, an individual fills out the assessment booklet and obtains a three-letter occupational summary code with the first letter of the code (the high-point code) representing that person's predominant Holland type.

Holland has also developed the Self-Directed Search Form Easy (SDS-E) for adults and adolescents who are poor readers. The format is similar to that of the SDS except that it has 25 fewer items, directions and statements requiring responses are more simply written, and two instead of three summary codes are obtained.

Over 400 studies have been conducted with the SDS (Osipow, 1983), and it is generally considered to be a reliable and valid instrument for determining vocational interests and predicting job success. The SDS affects the user in several positive ways (Holland, 1985b; Krivatsy & Magoon, 1976; McGowan, 1977; Redmond, 1973) that do not depend on a person's age, race, sex, or intelligence (Barker, 1978; Collins & Sedlacek, 1972; Croft, 1976; Holland, 1985a; Kimball, Sedlacek, & Brooks, 1973; Lewis & Sedlacek, 1972). No negative effects of the SDS have been documented (Holland, 1985b).

Holland (1985b) states that the classification system is useful as a tool and a framework for developing an occupational exploration plan with a student or a client. We agree, and believe that application of Holland's theory to mildly handicapped populations could be useful in terms of understanding their occupational characteristics and helping them attain job satisfaction and personal achievement.

To date, there has been little investigation of the theory related to handicapped populations. However, the authors have conducted several studies to determine the efficacy of use of the SDS and/or the SDS-E with learning disabled students. One of these studies (Cummings & Maddux, in press) compared Holland personality types among learning disabled and nonlearning disabled high school students. Results indicated that there was no difference between the two groups. In other words, the learning disabled students displayed as much variety of work personalities as did the nonhandicapped students. In light of these results, career/vocational education programs for learning disabled should focus on preparing them for occupational roles as diverse as those filled by nonlearning disabled individuals. We are also in the process of comparing learning disabled students' expressed vocational aspirations with their measured interests in an effort to determine whether or not the occupational aspirations of this population are realistic.

Also, since no studies have been done with Holland's newer form, the SDS-E, we conducted two studies to determine if the SDS-E could be considered an alternate form of the SDS (Maddux & Cummings, 1986), and if learning disabled students made fewer errors on the SDS-E than on the SDS (Cummings & Maddux, 1987). Results of both studies verified our hypotheses: the SDS-E was found to be an alternate form of the SDS, and learning disabled students made significantly fewer errors affecting Holland high-point codes on the SDS-E.

Although preliminary findings suggest promising potential for application of Holland's theory with mildly handicapped students, additional research is needed in several areas. Additional studies should compare the SDS with the SDS-E to determine if the SDS-E should be the instrument of choice for use with handicapped populations. Also, longitudinal studies should be made to determine predictive validity of the SDS and SDS-E when used with mildly handicapped individuals.

## SUMMARY

The success of career/vocational education programs for mildly handicapped students depends on the appropriateness of such programs for each student. One way to ensure that students are placed in programs suited to their individual needs is to include a well-designed career/vocational assessment component. Assessment should measure more than just work skills and aptitudes. According to Stodden and Ianacone (1981), the purposes for vocational assessment should be (a) to produce information that can be used to assist special education students and professionals who work with them in the career development process; (b) to provide information about the handicapped individual, the world of work, and specific work related skills; and (c) to determine how general and specific occupational information can be used to maximize the handicapped individual's options for successful employment.

In this chapter, we have discussed three approaches to career/vocational assessment: traditional approaches based on the vocational rehabilitation model of assessment; a curriculum-based approach; and a theory-based approach. While there are positive benefits to be gained from all three approaches, we believe that theory-based approaches are more suitable because they incorporate assessment instruments that have been validated through empirical studies and that have potential for providing more information about how developmental and personality variables affect career/vocational outcomes.

Chapter Five

# TRADITIONAL APPROACHES TO CAREER AND VOCATIONAL EDUCATION FOR THE HANDICAPPED

THE MOVEMENT toward career and vocational education for handicapped individuals is a relatively recent development within public education in this country. Vocational education is the older concept and is narrower in meaning than is career education. Vocational education refers to the teaching of skills needed by individuals in order to secure and keep paid employment. Career education, on the other hand, refers to teaching those skills and attitudes needed for adequate total life adjustment (Cegelka, 1985).

Brolin (1982) discusses the tendency to confuse the terms:

There continues to be confusion between the terms *career education* and *vocational education*. Many people in the field still refer to career education but essentially are talking about vocational education or preparation. (p. 27)

He goes on to define vocational education as:

. . . training the student for paid work, i.e., it emphasizes occupational preparation and is typically taught by vocational educators. It also focuses its efforts on secondary and postsecondary levels. (p. 27)

Career education, on the other hand, is defined as follows:

Career education is the process of systematically coordinating all school, family, and community components together to facilitate each individual's potential for economic, social, and personal fulfillment and participation in productive work activities that benefit the individual or others. (p. 43)

127

# THE HANDICAPPED IN CAREER AND VOCATIONAL EDUCATION

Traditionally, vocational education for the handicapped has been carried out through work-study programs started in the early part of the century. As Sitlington (1981) points out, however:

> Since the beginning these work experience programs have been geared almost exclusively to the mentally disabled adolescent. Little, if anything, has been done for other disability areas, particularly learning disabled and behavior disordered students. (p. 593)

Career education was officially introduced in 1971 by the U. S. Commissioner of Education, Sidney P. Marland, at a conference for high school principals. The concept grew out of increasing dissatisfaction with irrelevant curriculum and with the high rate of drop-outs in secondary schools (Brolin, 1983).

Actually, neither career nor vocational education programs have been made widely available to large numbers of handicapped students. Weisgerber, Dahl, and Appleby (1981) suggest that "the benefits of vocational education have been very limited for handicapped students" (p. 64).

These authors point out that in 1978, only 2.1 percent of students enrolled in vocational classes were handicapped, even though approximately 12 percent of students were classified as handicapped. They suggest that these figures are especially discouraging in light of the statement by the Bureau of Education for the Handicapped staff that 80 percent of handicapped individuals are unemployed after they leave school (U.S. Office of Education, 1975). Similarly, Brolin and D'Alonzo (1983) state that less than 2 percent of vocational enrollments are made up of handicapped students.

## BARRIERS TO PROGRAMS FOR THE HANDICAPPED

Given the poor life adjustment and vocational adjustment records of handicapped students after they leave school, it may appear puzzling that career and vocational education programs have not been widely used with these students. Weisgerber, et al. (1981) have presented some of the most frequently-encountered obstacles to excellent career and vocational education for the handicapped:

> Resistance to the handicapped stems from a variety of factors, but principally from

- a feeling of personal responsibility that most vocational educators have about the safety of their students when they are working with power equipment or are otherwise exposed to some type of hazard
- an unwillingness of vocational educators to compromise on standards of achievement or alter the curse completion requirements to reflect individual differences
- an assumption that it would be harder to place handicapped graduates in jobs, coupled with a recognition that program effectiveness in vocational education depends in large part on the placement rate of course graduates
- a lack of experience by vocational educators in dealing with the handicapped and little knowledge about their capabilities and potential
- a lack of aggressiveness by the handicapped in obtaining assignments to vocational classes (p. 65)

As mentioned in Chapter One, another contributing factor in the public school's failure to provide excellent career and vocational training for the handicapped has been the tendency to institute secondary special education programs modeled after elementary counterparts. These programs focus on academic skills such as reading and arithmetic and neglect career or vocational goals. Hohenshil (1984) has commented:

> In the past, the goals of most secondary special education programs were similar to those provided in the elementary schools. Many special educators seemed to believe that if their students didn't learn to read, write, and do arithmetic in the elementary grades, then they should get another 6 to 8 years of the same. (p. 51)

The academic orientation of secondary educators is undoubtedly a problem. We would hasten to add, however, that while vocational education is primarily a task for the secondary school, the same cannot be said for career education. Career education can and should be implemented throughout the public school curriculum, beginning during kindergarten and continuing throughout the grades.

Heller (1981) also discusses additional causes for the lack of good career and vocational education for handicapped students. He mentions the subject-matter orientation of many secondary school teachers and the emphasis on elementary practicum experiences for special education teachers-in-training.

Another contributing factor has been the lack of professionals specially trained to provide vocational and career education services to handicapped learners (Levinson, 1984). Educators trained in special education who traditionally have been responsible for educating handicapped students often lack knowledge and skills in vocational and career education (Cummings & Maddux, 1984; Levinson, 1984). Consequently, they have emphasized academic rather than career and vocational preparation of handicapped learners (Kokaska & Kolstoe, 1977). Vocational and career educators, on the other hand, while knowledgeable about career and vocational development and programming, often know little about educating handicapped students (Cummings & Maddux, 1984; Levinson, 1984).

Other problems include a lack of prerequisite courses needed by handicapped students to qualify for vocational and career education electives and lack of training on working with handicapped students by professionals who administer vocational assessment instruments and who use the results to help write IEP items.

Brolin (1983) includes a discussion of five possible reasons for the failure of career education to be implemented in American schools. He includes:

1. The fact that there are many other pressures being brought to bear on school districts in the 1980s including strong pressure to cut educational costs by reducing faculty and supplies that might have been used for career and vocational education.
2. The difficulty of persuading educators to change.
3. The fact that there is little time for planning and implementing changes and frequently no reward for doing so.
4. The fact that many educators do not understand the scope of career education and have not been convinced that a change to such an orientation is any better than what they are currently doing.
5. The fact that implementing career education requires educators to reveal what they are doing to other educators and to the public.

A final, major factor underlying all of these difficulties may be that vocational theory builders have developed their theoretical assumptions after formal and informal experiences with normal, nonpathological populations, and have been little concerned with handicapped groups (Conte, 1983). We believe that this final factor has been especially injurious. Vocational theory builders have almost completely ignored the handicapped. Therefore, no clearly-defined models have evolved for vocational or career education of the handicapped.

## THE NEED FOR A THEORETICAL FOUNDATION

We would have liked to call the present chapter *Models of Career and Vocational Education for the Handicapped.* However, the collection of activities, cautions, and techniques presently found in the literature are not clearly defined nor consistently theory-based. Therefore, we do not believe they should be termed *models*. It is the lack of a comprehensive and well-researched theory base that we believe is the current most critical deficiency in career and vocational education.

Indeed, we believe that the lack of coherent theoretical foundations underly many of our problems in education, and that the field has long been diverted from attention to this problem. We've been hearing and reading a great deal lately about the crisis in teacher preparation. As teacher educators, we are concerned that colleges of education seem to be convenient targets for an array of special interest groups who are upset about everything from the alleged decline in teacher competencies in basic skills to declining SAT scores and the teaching of evolution in public schools.

We believe these kinds of criticisms require thoughtful replies. But we don't consider them critical. There have always been controversial issues in education and there have always been vocal critics of teacher education. In the long run, this criticism is probably healthy, since it causes us to continually re-examine what we have been doing.

It seems to us that a *critical* problem in teacher education is our failure to convince our students (and sometimes each other) of the value of theory. In our experience, most teachers, even after the completion of a master's degree, see theory and practice as two entirely different things. Most regard theory as what is to be written down on tests for education classes, while practice is what is actually done in the classroom every day.

We have failed to demonstrate to students that theory *is* practical. Actually, we believe the two are inseparable, and that what is done (practice) depends almost totally on how we choose to look at the world (theory). Gage (1963) makes the point that it is impossible to function without theory:

> (Men) . . . differ not in whether they use theory, but in the degree to which they are aware of the theory they use. The choice before the man in the street and the research worker alike is not whether to theorize but whether to articulate his theory, to make it explicit, to get it out in the open where he can examine it. (p. 94)

We believe that it is important for educators to be more theoretical than most presently are.. By that, we mean that we all need to make more of an effort to bring out theories to the conscious level so that we can examine them. That's important, because when we do this, we may recognize an absurdity. What we are saying is that we need to have *con-*

*scious* theories rather than *subconscious* ones. And that may be the real difference between the educator who places a high value on theory and the one who insists that practice is the only important thing. In actuality, educators who believe they are atheoretical are only fooling themselves. There is actually a theory that underlies every action we take. We may, however, be unaware of the details of that theory. The educator who holds a conscious theory can be constantly thinking about it, evaluating it, and revising it by applying logic and new knowledge. The *practical* educator drifts blithely along, extolling the virtues of trying to ignore theory, while his every action is dictated by a theory (or, more likely, bits and pieces of many theories) whose very existence is unknown to him.

Most of our students continue to think in terms of this false dichotomy of theory vs. practice. They maintain they don't need theory because they *use what works*. There are many problems with this, not the least of which is how to know what is working. But even if we ignore the evaluation problem, if we attempt to operate without theory, how do we choose what *might* work in the beginning? And when it quits working, how will we know what to try next? Our alternatives will sound familiar because we have lived with them for years in education. Without conscious theory we may rely on experts to tell us what to do, we may use what's currently popular, we may resort to trial and error, or we may simply continue doing what we've always done, whether it *works* or not. Without conscious theory, we are forced to fall back to methods and materials, and educators become mere technicians.

We fear that this *atheoretical* orientation has characterized much of the program development work in vocational and career education, both for handicapped and for nonhandicapped populations. Because of this, we find the field to be fragmented and incoherent. Some techniques may *work*, but we have little to judge them by, and no guidelines to help us decide what to try next when existing techniques fail.

We believe the lack of theory is responsible for this sad state of affairs. We would hasten to add, however, that those who espouse the benefits of theory must take care not to become *true believers*. Weizenbaum (1976) cautions that we must keep in mind the fact that there is no such thing as a *true* or a *false* theory, only theories which are more or less useful for a given purpose. It seems to us that we, in the field of education, have often become absorbed in fruitless, divisive debates about the *truth* or *falsity* of various theories.

Weizenbaum (1976) likens a theory to a map of a partially explored territory:

And (again) there is no single correct map of a territory. An aerial photograph of an area serves a different heuristic function, say, for a land-use planner, than does a demographic map of the same area. One use of a theory then, is that it prepares the conceptual categories within which the theoretician and the practitioner will ask his questions and design his experiments. (p. 142)

If we accepted the above idea, would we really continue to put so much time and energy into *proving* that some particular theoretical approach isn't *valid?* Or would we realize that just as different travelers need different maps, and that just as different children need different approaches, so too may different practitioners do best with different theoretical stances?

Along these lines, Reese and Overton (1970) warn against arguments which they term *paradigm debates:*

Even within a single field of knowledge, theories can be classified into "families." A family is a set of theories that are based upon the same model, although not necessarily the same specific content area. Controversies about theories from different families involve paradigm debates, which are, as we have seen, futile. (p. 4)

One of the best examples of a paradigm debate in psychology and, more recently, in special education has been the fruitless argument between advocates of behavioral and cognitive theory. We have discussed this debate and its negative consequences to the field of learning disabilities in Chapter One of this book. As Weizenbaum suggests, the argument can never be resolved, since each model of man is based on a different world view.

We will endeavor not to become true believers in any particular theoretical approach. But we will attempt to rectify some of the problems described above that we believe stem from the atheoretical stance of many career and vocational educators.

When we present our model for career and vocational education, as we will do later in this book, we will attempt to ground it firmly in a theoretical framework that has withstood the scrutiny of research and the test of time. Since we did not feel that there were a number of legitimate models in career and vocational education, we chose to title this chapter *Traditional Approaches to Career and Vocational Education for the Handicapped.* For the remainder of this chapter, we will present and comment upon the approaches of some of the most articulate and influential experts in the field of career and vocational education for the handicapped.

# THE LIFE-CENTERED CAREER EDUCATION APPROACH

In our opinion, Donn Brolin's Life-Centered Career Education approach (Brolin, 1982; Brolin, 1983; Kokaska and Brolin, 1985) comes closest of all the approaches in career and vocational education to qualifying as a true model. The approach has also been called the Life-Centered Career Education (LCCE) Competency-Based Curriculum model (Brolin, 1982). The approach is implemented with a curriculum that is competency-based. Brolin states that it was developed over many years and with the help of many different educators (Kokaska & Brolin, 1985).

Brolin bases the curriculum on the belief that he has identified the skills (competencies) needed by handicapped people to adjust to community living after leaving the public school system. By studying these adult skills, he chooses important areas of emphasis for students still in school.

The curriculum is organized within three major dimensions:

1. The skills and competencies.
2. Location of resources used to teach the skills and competencies. Some of these can be found in school, some in the community, and some at home.
3. The stages or levels of career development.

The following sections will further present and discuss each of these dimensions.

## The Skills and Competencies Dimension

There are 22 major competencies, or skills in the LCCE curriculum. They are further broken down into more than 102 subcompetencies. In order to understand this organization, an example might be helpful. Competency number five is *Buying and preparing food*. This major competency is further broken down into six subcompetencies:

5.1 Demonstrate appropriate eating skills
5.2 Plan balanced meals
5.3 Purchase food
5.4 Prepare meals
5.5 Clean food preparation areas
5.6 Store food

Competency number 21 is *Obtaining a specific occupational skill.* For this competency, the subcompetencies cannot be the same for everyone and will depend on the occupation chosen.

All of the competencies and subcompetencies can be further classified as falling into one of three major curriculum areas:

1. Daily Living Skills
2. Personal-Social Skills
3. Occupational Skills

The example above competency number five dealing with buying and preparing food fits into the Daily Living Skills category, while number 21 on obtaining an occupational skill falls under the Occupational Skills category.

It would be excessively lengthy to list all of the competencies and subcompetencies here. A complete listing can be found elsewhere (Brolin, 1983; Kokaska & Brolin, 1985). The following are the 22 major competencies:

1. Managing family finances
2. Selecting, managing, and maintaining a home
3. Caring for personal needs
4. Raising children — family living
5. Buying and preparing food
6. Buying and caring for clothing
7. Engaging in civic activities
8. Utilizing recreation and leisure
9. Getting around the community (mobility)
10. Achieving self-awareness
11. Acquiring self-confidence
12. Achieving socially responsible behavior
13. Maintaining good interpersonal skills
14. Achieving independence
15. Achieving problem-solving skills
16. Communicating adequately with others
17. Knowing and exploring occupational possibilities
18. Selecting and planning occupational choices
19. Exhibiting appropriate work habits and behaviors
20. Exhibiting sufficient physical-manual skills
21. Obtaining a specific occupational skill
22. Seeking, securing, and maintaining employment

(Adapted from Kokaska and Brolin, 1985, pp. 46-47.)

Numbers one through nine fall in the broad curriculum area of Daily Living Skills, numbers 10 through 16 fall in the Personal-Social Skills area, and numbers 17 through 22 fall in the Occupational Skills category.

## The Location of Resources Dimension

Resources are located at school, in the family, or in the community. The role of the special educator in the LCCE approach tends to be toward becoming a consultant to other people who deal with the child. In addition, the special educator acts to coordinate services and service agencies concerned with the child and those concerned with the efforts of the family. According to Brolin (1983), some direct instruction will also be necessary in the form of tutoring or if necessary instruction is otherwise not available at home, in the community, or from regular educators.

Thus, it is apparent that Brolin's approach is a mainstreaming approach that emphasizes the importance of the special educator as consultant. We see this as a major potential problem for those attempting to implement LCCE. Although the consultant model for special education has been shown to be workable, it presents many problems in implementation. Research has shown that the success of the consultant role is highly dependent on interpersonal skills of the consultant, and that the consultant must be a master teacher with excellent communication skills.

Brolin stresses the importance of the regular classroom teacher in helping to cultivate a success environment for handicapped students and in fostering social acceptance by nonhandicapped peers. Brolin emphasizes the importance of home economics and industrial arts teachers as well, and includes a table showing the various regular educators who can be instrumental in teaching each of the twenty-two skills and competencies at the junior high school and at the senior high school level (Kokaska and Brolin, 1985, p. 51). For example, the chart shows that skill number nine, *Getting around the community* can be facilitated at the junior high level by the home economics teacher and at the senior high level by the driver's education teacher.

Brolin (1978) also emphasizes the importance of family involvement as the second component in this dimension:

> Parents can assist their children by structuring responsibilities, developing career awareness, teaching specific skills, and providing a secure psychological

environment where self confidence and independence can be developed adequately. Family members should also be encouraged to participate in class activities. (p. 15)

Brolin emphasizes the potential power of parents who band together in advocacy groups. He points out that many parents have developed sophisticated advocacy skills by serving on political action committees or other community advocacy committees, and that these skills can be put to excellent use on parent advocacy committees aimed at securing good career and vocational education for handicapped students.

Also related to the family role is the influence of the family upon their handicapped child's awareness of vocational roles as well as upon the child's attitude toward the feasibility of working toward securing various jobs or careers. Brolin warns against the danger that parents may erroneously assume that certain careers are unattainable given their child's handicap. Such parents may then fail to make the child aware of that career, or may fail to present that particular career as a viable choice.

We agree with Brolin about the dangers of such family attitudes and actions. In fact, we believe this problem is a specific case of a more general serious problem that is currently impeding progress in career and vocational education of the handicapped. The problem is that many people, including special educators and vocational educators, hold a stereotypic view of what jobs handicapped people are capable of successfully performing. Such a stereotypic view becomes a self-fulfilling prophecy when it is used as the underlying rationale for educational programs. Since certain careers are viewed as unattainable, educational programs do not attempt to train handicapped students for these careers, resulting in *underrepresentation* of handicapped workers in these jobs. Since other careers are viewed as attainable and desirable, these careers are overstressed in training programs even though some handicapped individuals may lack the specific aptitudes and interests needed to successfully perform in such careers. The result is *overrepresentation* of handicapped individuals in these careers, thus strengthening existing stereotypes.

We have conducted research into the vocational interests and personalities of mildly handicapped individuals (Cummings & Maddux, in press), and we have shown that they are every bit as varied in this regard as are nonhandicapped individuals of the same age, sex, and socioeconomic status. At the same time, there is research evidence that mildly handicapped individuals are most frequently trained for and placed in jobs calling for only one kind of vocational interest and personality. We believe that this narrow focus is due to a stereotypic view of the characteristics and abilities of mildly handicapped individuals. This may help account for part of the reason that many mildly handicapped individuals are less well adjusted vocationally than are nonhandicapped peers. We will discuss this phenomenon and the research related to it later in this chapter.

Brolin also emphasizes the importance of maintaining excellent communications with parents and with parent training. He also believes that parents can be effective in working with their children and helping them achieve the 22 career development competencies and the related subcompetencies. He includes a list of 12 suggestions for families to help them in working with their handicapped children. The following is a condensation of that list:

1. Provide physical activities each day that call for both fine motor and gross motor skills.
2. Provide a home workshop to help children learn the names and uses for common tools.
3. Assign jobs to children and require their completion within a given time frame.
4. Take children to visit job sites and discuss them.
5. Discuss the work of family members in front of the child.
6. Carry out family activities such as trips that will help the child develop recreational and social skills.
7. Require the child to make some decisions on his own and then to live with the consequences.
8. Allow the child to take part in family decisions.
9. Stay in close contact with school personnel.
10. Help the school plan and implement community activities such as field trips.
11. Encourage part-time jobs in deverse settings.
12. Participate on school advisory committees.
    (Adapted from Kokaska, & Brolin, 1985, p. 200-201)

The third component of the Location of Resources Dimension involves the community. This component is further divided into resources found in community agencies and organizations and those found in business and industry.

Brolin mentions agencies such as state vocational rehabilitation agencies, social service agencies, employment services, mental health agencies and others as examples of sources of professionals who can be of help in career and vocational education. He also suggests the use of organizations such as the YMCA, YWCA, Red Cross, Jaycees, Rotary, Lions, and others. Kokaska and Brolin (1985, pp. 356-360) present a five-page table of professional organizations important to career development of handicapped individuals. This comprehensive table lists the organization name and address, publications available (if any), and a short description of activities.

The LCCE approach makes extensive use of resources found in business and industry. The following list of suggestions for building a collaborative effort with business and industry is from Kokaska and Brolin (1985, p. 215):

Identifying trends in the economy
Furthering contacts with business and industry
Becoming advocates for handicapped workers
Serving as a classroom resource
Providing program consultation
Providing work experience
Participating in conferences and workshops
Providing instructional and resource materials

These authors provide a discussion of each of the above suggestions in their recent book entitled *Career Education for Handicapped Individuals* (Kokaska, & Brolin, 1985, pp 215-224). They also provide an excellent list of common objections of employers who are approached to employ or train handicapped workers. Also included are ways to allay the fears of employers who voice these objections.

## The Stages or Levels of Career Development Dimension

The LCCE includes four levels of career development:

1. awareness
2. exploration
3. preparation
4. placement, follow-up, and continuing education

All four stages are ongoing throughout the individual's life, though activities begin at different stages. Career awareness begins at birth and should be a primary concern of the elementary school curriculum. Career exploration begins during the elementary school years and receives increasing emphasis as the child grows older. Kokaska and Brolin (1985) describe this level:

Career exploration is the link between career awareness and career preparation. During this stage, young students begin to think seriously about their particular set of aptitudes, interests, and needs and how these can be directed toward meaningful and successful adult roles. Sequential exploration activities and experiences should be planned so that by the time students are ready for high school, a more highly individualized educational plan can be designed, and a more relevant career preparation program can be offered. (p. 56)

The career preparation stage is also ongoing throughout the individual's life, but is especially emphasized during the high school years when students should be able to choose from many vocational courses and community jobs.

The career placement, follow-up, and continuing education stage occurs during secondary and post-secondary years. Work-study programs play an important role. Nonpaying adult work roles are also stressed, as well as work for pay.

Brolin (1978) has published a manual for the LCCE approach. This manual begins with a very brief discussion of the rationale behind the approach. It then presents 84 pages of detailed competency units designed to teach the 102 subcompetencies. Each unit specifies the domain, the competency, and the subcompetency to be taught. The units are presented in chart form displaying objectives, activities/strategies, and adult/peer roles.

For example, under the domain of Daily Living Skills, one unit teaches competency number one, Managing Family Finances, and Subcompetency number two, Make Wise Expenditures. One of the four objectives listed is for the child to learn to categorize purchasable items in regard to quality and quantity. One of the four activities or strategies to teach this subcompetency calls for the students to go on a mock shopping trip in which they differentiate items in regard to quantity and quality. One of the two adult/peer roles listed specifies that representatives of Consumer Protection should discuss levels of quality.

Although the competency units are extensive and detailed, they are not to be regarded as a *canned approach*. Brolin (1978) advises that many decisions must be made by teachers who decide to use the LCCE approach. Common faculty concerns relate to scope and sequence, grade level specification, modification of activities, use of alternate activities, etc. Such concerns are not addressed in the units because Brolin believes that "Curriculum development must take place in the local school system" (p. 18).

Also included in the manual is a suggested form for Individualized Education Programs, a Competency Rating Scale and Manual, and a chapter on sources of instructional materials and other resources. For school districts interested in implementing LCCE, there is another publication entitled *Trainer's Guide to Life Centered Career Education* (Brolin, McKay, & West, 1978) which helps school districts train personnel.

Kokaska and Brolin (1985) sum up the LCCE approach by listing unique contributions of the approach:

1. It provides an interface between education and work.
2. It is a K-12 effort involving as many school personnel as possible.
3. It is an infusion approach.
4. It does not replace traditional education.
5. It conceptualizes career development as occurring in stages.
6. It requires a strong experiential component.
7. It is based on developing life skills, affective skills, and general employability skills.
8. It requires the school to work closely with the family and with community resources. (Adapted from Kokaska, & Brolin, 1985, pp. 58-60)

## Evaluation of the LCCE

Brolin's contribution can hardly be overstressed. He has almost single-handedly sensitized a generation of special education teachers and administrators to the importance of career and vocational education for the handicapped. He has produced a highly structured, detailed, and well-thought-out set of competencies from which a coherent curriculum can be produced. His printed material is logical and complete, and he has even produced some excellent material to help school districts train their own personnel. Donn Brolin must be regarded as a highly influential and expert pioneer in the field of career and vocational education for the handicapped.

The LCCE approach does have some weaknesses however. As we stated earlier, we do not find that the approach is heavily theory-based. Although LCCE seems highly consistent with practical experiences of Brolin and others, we have already discussed our belief that while practical considerations are crucial, they cannot substitute for a strong theoretical foundation.

Another problem is related to the selection of the competencies and subcompetencies. Brolin states that the curriculum was devised based on research conducted in the seventies, and lists only four such studies. Thus, the curriculum appears to have been generated based on a relatively small number of research studies. Partially allaying this criticism is the fact that one of the primary studies cited was part of a grant-funded project involving 12 school districts across the nation and over 300 school personnel (Brolin, Elliott, & Corcoran, 1984).

The third problem we see with LCCE is the heavy reliance on infusion. Infusion models in special education have not been highly successful in the past. This has probably occurred because they rely on the expertise and good will of regular educators, some of whom have not received adequate training in the education of the handicapped, or who have negative attitudes about serving such students. Good preservice and inservice teacher training can help reduce such problems, but we remain unconvinced that infusion approaches will be highly successful across large numbers of school districts and school teachers.

We hasten to point out, however, that all educational approaches have certain weaknesses, and our criticisms of LCCE should not be misinterpreted. We believe that the LCCE approach represents the most substantial contribution to date to the career and vocational education of handicapped individuals.

## THE VOCATIONAL REHABILITATION AGENCY APPROACH

Vocational Rehabilitation Agencies are projects of the state and federal government and exist to aid handicapped and injured individuals enter or reenter the world of work. Thus, we are discussing a collection of governmental services rather than an *approach* in the traditional sense of the term. The two primary objectives of such agencies are to help disabled persons become gainfully employed, and to help them develop independent living skills if at all possible (Weisgerber, Dahl, & Applyby; 1981). These agencies provide services such as comprehensive evaluation, counseling and guidance, training, transportation, and follow-up services.

Specifically, they work with people disabled by mental retardation, mental illness, alcoholism, drug addiction, amputations and other orthopedic impairments, epilepsy, cancer, stroke, tuberculosis, congenital deformities, neurological disabilities, and learning disabilities (Brolin, 1982). The inclusion of learning disabled persons is a relatively new development. Historically, learning disabled individuals have been excluded from rehabilitation services because eligibilty criteria did not recognize learning disability as a mental or physical disorder (Gerber, 1981). The Rehabilitation Services Administration has now mandated that learning disabled individuals are eligible for services. LD adults are thus eligible to receive employment assistance in the least restrictive environment and may take full advantage of the delivery of services needed for successful adjustment (Gerber, 1981; Gray, 1981).

Although learning disabled individuals are eligible for rehabilitation services, and rehabiliation literature is beginning to address their needs, many problems presently exist in serving this group. Rehabilitation handbooks and guides are often inaccurate in advising rehabilitation counselors of their responsibilities to learning disabled clients. Assessment and evaluation procedures often are too simplistic to realistically measure the specific needs of this group. Rehabilitation counselors whose training has traditionally emphasized the needs of physically handicapped individuals with more definitive disabilities often experience considerable uncertainty, recognizing that they do not adequately understand the unique problems associated with learning disability.

Although guides and handboooks can provide some background information about the learning disabled population, they often do not describe the multiplicity of problems these individuals experience. Through intensive inservice workshops the rehabilitation counselor can acquire basic information and skills needed to work with these clients. Although the uninformed rehabilitation counselor can provide some emotional support, without appropriate training the counselor is often not aware of critical problems of learning disabled clients such as social misperception, spatial disorientation, and inadequate motor skills. Such counselors do not take these problems into account when planning a vocational program for their clients. It is likely that until vocational counselors acquire sufficient information and skills pertaining to learning disabilities, these clients will be as inappropriately served by rehabilitation agencies as they have been by the public schools.

Vocational rehabilitation agencies have done slightly better in helping clients who are mentally retarded and emotionally disturbed. However, most employees of such agencies are not oriented toward clients with milder problems and do better with more severely affected individuals.

Brolin (1982) summarizes four problems of vocational rehabilitation agencies. These problems were revealed in a five-state federal audit conducted in 1978:

1. One-half of the clients did not have an individualized, written rehabilitation plan (IWRP).

2. Over half were not aware of their right to appeal ineligibility determination.
3. About three-fourths were placed in an occupation that was contrary to their agreed-upon job goal.
4. Only 8 percent were referred to another agency after being declared ineligible for VR services. (p.11)

In summary, vocational rehabilitation programs have been of great service to many older, physically handicapped individuals. They have not historically been of great service to mildly affected school-age learning disabled, mentally retarded, or emotionally disturbed students. One other problem is that their services are generally not made available until the client is about 16 years of age. Until vocational rehabilitation employees become more school-wise and school-oriented, they are not likely to become highly beneficial to school-age handicapped children.

# GARY M. CLARK'S SCHOOL-BASED CAREER EDUCATION APPROACH

Clark has formulated an approach he calls "A School-Based Career Education Model for the Handicapped" (Clark, 1979). (We have already discussed the fact that we do not consider any of the career education plans we have seen to be true models, since they are not sufficiently theory-based.) Clark chose a school-based approach from the following four ways of facilitating career education goals. These four ways were identified by the U.S. Office of Education:

1. The employer-based approach
2. The home/community-based approach
3. The residential-based approach
4. The school-based approach

Before describing Clark's school-based approach, we will briefly present the rationale behind each of the four approaches listed above.

The *employer-based approach* involves business and industry as well as schools and targets the thirteen- to twenty-year-old age group. Participation is voluntary and is intended as an alternative to the traditional classroom program. The individual needs of students are determined and actual work situations found to meet those needs.

The *home/community-based approach* is intended for those students who have completed their public school education. The target group is the eighteen to twenty-five-year-old group who spend most of their time at home such as pregnant women, mothers of preschool children, unemployed persons, or handicapped persons with disabling conditions. Television, radio, or other media is used to motivate home study, or neighborhood centers are established to provide career guidance referral, and other services.

The *residential-based approach* is often used in rural settings. The target group is isolated, disadvantaged families who move to a setting offering diverse services such as day care, kindergarten, counseling, etc.

Clark attributes the *school-based career education approach* to Sidney P. Marland, who emphasized occupational guidance and skill acquisition programs. Clark endorses this approach, but criticizes it for being too work-oriented and thus neglectful of other life career roles (Clark, 1979, p. 18):

> The school-based model attempts to create a comprehensive awareness of job options while increasing a student's ability to enter employment in a selected occupational area or go on for further education. But the model also seeks to develop a concept of self in relation to work, personal characteristics (like initiative, resourcefulness, and pride in work), and a realistic understanding of the relationships between the world of work and education. . . . There is no doubt that . . . . supporters of the model view career education as a unique program whose ultimate outcome is a satisfied and satisfying worker in our society. (Clark, 1979, p. 18)

Clark has stated that he perfers a school based model that "maintains a focus on work careers, but gives equal importance to other competencies critical to life careers and involves roles in addition to worker roles" (p. 20). Accordingly, Clark's curriculum has four major elements:

1. values, attitudes, and habits
2. human relationships
3. occupational information
4. acquisition of job and daily living skills.

Clark's model is based on the premise that career education must emphasize the competencies of the whole person, rather than simply competencies directly related to the performance of a specific job. We will present a brief synopsis of Clark's vision for how these four curriculum areas should be implemented.

## Values, Attitudes, and Habits

Clark believes that values are essential in career education, and the values component of the career education curriculum should be the primary component in elementary school. In defense of this position, he points to research indicating that values, attitudes, and habits are more important to the vocational and personal success of handicapped individuals than are specific job skills.

Clark does not advocate the teaching of specific values. Instead, he recommends that children be taught to choose their own values and to defend them effectively. In addition, he believes that children should be taught to recognize why they think and act as they do, how their actions are related to their beliefs, and what the possible consequences of their actions will be.

Clark sums up the importance of this aspect of his curriculum:

> Career education programming for handicapped elementary school children should focus on developmental levels and the critical values, attitudes, and habits children form during the elementary years. These critical values, attitudes, and habits center upon children's self-concepts, their perception of their own value as persons, their assessment of the school experience, their valuation of effort or working, their relative desire for a "normal" life, and their hopes for the future. (Clark, 1979, p. 31)

## Human Relationships

Clark stresses the importance of teaching about human relationships in the curriculum because of the special problems of handicapped persons related to social relationships and peer interaction. He recommends that the elementary years should emphasize teaching handicapped students to understand and communicate with others as well as helping them work through feelings of anger and hostility related to their disability. Teaching self-control is also highly valued.

## Occupational Information

Clark advocates teaching about all aspects of the world of work that are important for people to know about. Specifically, he includes "occupational roles, occupational vocabulary, occupational alternatives, and basic information related to some realities of the world of work" (Clark, 1979, p. 70).

Of particular interest are Clark's eight realities related to the world of work. These are:

1. Society is work-oriented.
2. Work occurs in a particular locale — usually outside the home.
3. Paid work tends to be impersonal.

4. Work has its reward systems.
5. Work is bound by time and the wasting of work time is always frowned upon.
6. Most work is done in the company of others and it is important for the worker to interact well with people at work.
7. There is dependence and interdependence among workers and work groups.
8. Not everyone is able to work or to work in the job of their choice.

## Acquisition of Job and Daily Living Skills

Clark suggests that job and daily living skills are inseparable. He believes that these skills can be categorized as *cognitive skills, affective skills,* and *psychomotor skills*. The affective skills have already been discussed above under the areas of *values, attitudes, and habits,* or *human relationships*. Cognitive and psychomotor skills thus make up the emphasis in the curriculum area titled *acquisition of job and daily living skills*.

The cognitive skills include:

1. Reading
2. Knowledge of safety
3. Memory
4. Vocabulary
5. Spelling
6. Basic math facts
7. Problem-solving
8. Semi-independent travel and mobility
9. Semi-independent self care
10. Semi-independent use of money
11. Decision making
12. Independent travel
13. Independent self-care
    (Adapted from Clark, 1979, p. 121)

The psychomotor skills include:

1. Eye-hand coordination
2. Finger dexterity
3. Manual dexterity
4. Strength
5. Stamina

(Adapted from Clark, 1979, p. 121)

Clark includes a chapter on each of the four curriculum areas discussed above. At the end of each of these chapters he includes a detailed list of goals for acquisition of the skills for that area. This list is broken down into goals for the primary level (K-3) and for the intermediate level (grades 4-6). Also included are selected activities, followed by selected materials for achieving the goal/objective statements. Each of these sections are also broken down into primary and intermediate levels. The final chapter in the book is on implementing career education programs for the handicapped.

## Evaluation of Clark's Approach

Gary Clark has made an important contribution to the literature in career education for the handicapped. His ideas could definitely be used as the basis for a comprehensive curriculum developed by a school district. We believe that the strength of his program is its breadth. The four curriculum areas are comprehensive and avoid the trap of conceptualizing *career* as if it is synonomous with *job*. The weaknesses of his approach are its lack of a theoretical and research base and the fact that it focusses only on the elementary-aged student.

# SITLINGTON'S CAREER EDUCATION APPROACH FOR THE HANDICAPPED

Sitlington (1979, 1981) has outlined an approach that is organized around vocational education based on an excellent assessment program. She makes the case that assessment has become more important because of recent requirements for increased involvement of regular educators in programs for the handicapped, and for more systematic planning for vocational programming for the handicapped. Although she recommends a comprehensive career education program, her interests are largely in the vocational education component within career education.

She advocates an approach in which classroom activities are coordinated with on-the-job experiences. She suggests that program staff members must determine what kinds of assessment information is required in their particular programs. This information may fall into the following categories:

1. medical
2. educational
3. personal/social

4. interests
5. work habits and attitudes
6. gross and fine motor skills
7. preferred learning modes and type of effective reinforcers

Thus, Sitlington's recommendations are intended to help educators design and implement a systematic, assessment-oriented, experience-based program. Brolin (1979) has referred to similar programs as falling into a category called *Experience-Based Career Education* (EBCE). Sitlington makes use of the five primary components of the work experience sequence identified by Thompson and Wimmer (1976). These include:

1. prevocational experience
2. job analysis
3. in-school work experiences
4. community placement
5. after graduation placement and followup

Sitlington recommends actual skill training at the secondary and postsecondary levels by public schools, community colleges, or technical institutes in the following semiskilled and skilled occupations:

1. business and office education
2. distributive education including retailing, wholesaling, storing, financing, and restaurant and hotel work
3. health occupations
4. home economics
5. trade and industrial education
6. vocational agriculture
   (Adapted from Sitlington, 1981, p. 595)

Skills falling under the above categories are taught either through school-employer cooperative arrangements, or school laboratory settings.

Obviously, most of Sitlington's recommendations are for vocational education activities from junior high level through the postsecondary level. She does, however, go on to recommend that Clark's career education approach be implemented at the elementary school level. We have already described that approach earlier in this chapter.

## SUMMARY

Vocational education refers to skills needed for paid employment, while career education is broader concept and refers to skills needed for adequate total life adjustment. The movement for career and vocational education for handicapped individuals is relatively recent. Many barriers to excellent programs for the handicapped remain in place, although some progress has been made.

We believe that a major problem in designing and implementing excellent career and vocational programs for handicapped individuals is the lack of a coherent theory on which to base such programs. Although we have found many excellent suggestions relating to programming for the handicapped, we do not believe that any of these suggestions or approaches can qualify as true *models,* since they all lack theoretical grounding.

The approach that comes closest to a model is Brolin's Life-Centered Career Education Approach. We have reviewed this approach as well as the vocational rehabilitation agency approach, Clark's School-Based Career Education Approach, and Sitlington's approach.

The next chapter will present and discuss some of the critical issues in vocational and career education for the mildly handicapped.

Chapter Six

# ISSUES IN CAREER AND VOCATIONAL EDUCATION FOR THE MILDLY HANDICAPPED

A S WE HAVE stated earlier in the book, the movement to provide career and vocational education programs for the handicapped is a relatively new one. Because of its newness, there are a number of unresolved issues related to it. In this chapter, we will discuss some of these issues and make some recommendations for how we would resolve the problems presented by them.

## HOW SHOULD PROGRAMS FOR MILDLY HANDICAPPED BE DIFFERENT?

Career and vocational education programs for the mildly handicapped should be different from programs for the moderately/severely handicapped in several ways. The mildly handicapped generally have a more positive prognosis with regard to potential for success in semi-skilled and skilled jobs, ability to live independently, etc. In other words, their potential for normalization is greater than that for the moderately/severely handicapped. Therefore, the thrust of training programs should be to help prepare students for eventual independent functioning with limited or with no further support.

The fact that mildly handicapped individuals are capable of learning how to succeed in occupations that are at a high level of complexity has obvious implications for skill training, job placement, etc. There are a number of issues related to career/vocational programs for mildly handicapped students. One of the most acute problems is related to the unfortunate stereotyping of handicapped individuals by educators, employers, and the public at large.

# THE PROBLEM OF STEREOTYPING

As we have discussed elsewhere in this book, there is an abundance of evidence that mildly handicapped individuals are not being well-prepared for life after school. We believe that a major reason for this may be that public schools are not providing these students with appropriate career and vocational education programs (Cummings & Maddux, 194; Sitlington, 1981).

Too often, mildly handicapped students do not receive appropriate vocational education courses. This happens because they drop out of school, because they are forbidden to enroll in vocational courses due to the fear that they will injure themselves or others, because they are enrolled in regular vocational education courses where they fail due to their instructors' unwillingness or inability to modify requirements, or because they are enrolled in special vocational courses organized around a narrow, stereotypic view of the kinds of professions suitable for the mildly handicapped.

A common view of the occupational capabilities of mildly handicapped individuals is that they can be successful only in low-level, menial jobs requiring little more than motor skills and strength. Thus, when special vocational programs are in existence for this population, they often prepare them for jobs such as assembly-line work, mechanic's helper, manual laborer, etc. These jobs may be quite appropriate for some mildly handicapped students, but would be tailor-made for failure for others, depending on their abilities, disabilities, personalities, interests, etc.

Plue (1984) conducted a study illustrating the narrow range of jobs available to the handicapped. He analyzed all jobs held by 3,177 mildly handicapped individuals over a six-year period and reported that the jobs generally required unskilled or semi-skilled work involving sorting, motor speed, manipulation of parts, separating, matching, assembly, and tool use.

This study and others bring up a important cause-or-effect question: *Do mildly handicapped individuals end up in jobs of this type because their personalities and interests lead them to seek out such work environments, or because vocational programs, counselors, educators in general, and other helping professionals hold a stereotypic view of suitable jobs for the handicapped, and thus make decisions about career/vocational education and job placements that result in the continuation of the stereotype?*

We believe the latter to be the case, and we have conducted research that leads us to this conclusion (Cummings & Maddux, in press). To understand this research, we must first review some generally accepted concepts in career/vocational education.

To begin with, we know that the success of career/vocational education programs depends on ensuring that the program is appropriate for each student. To achieve this fit between the needs and abilities of the student and the program itself, a well-designed assessment component is essential. This assessment component must be comprehensive and must include more than measurement for mere skills and aptitudes. Student personalities and interests should also be considered before students are placed in a program. These facts are well-accepted in career/vocational education, but well-designed assessment components are seldom incorporated in programs for the handicapped (Sitlington, 1979).

Even when assessment is included in career/vocational education programs, there is evidence that measurement of career interests, values, and work personality is frequently ignored (Stodden and Ianacone, 1981). (The reader is referred to Chapter Four for a full discussion of career and vocational assessment.) The reason that assessment programs should include measurement of vocational interest and personality is that research has shown that job satisfaction, stability, and achievement are highly dependent on a match between vocational interest and personality and the type of job an individual chooses (DeVoge, 1975; Gottfredson, 1977; Mont & Muchinsky, 1978; Wiggins, 1976).

The research we conducted made use of John Holland's theory of vocational personality and work environments (Holland, 1985). We have presented a thorough explanation of Holland's theory in Chapter Three of this book. Therefore, we will present only a brief review in this chapter. Holland suggests that an individual's career choice reflects that person's personality and behavioral styles. Both vocational interests (personalities) and work environments can be classified into one of six categories: (a) Realistic, (b) Investigative, (c) Artistic, (d) Social, (e) Enterprising, and (f) Conventional.

People classified as Realistic tend to be asocial, conforming, inflexible, and uninsightful. They prefer physical, highly concrete activities and avoid abstract problem situations. Realistic job environments involve activities such as using machines and tools.

Individuals classified as Investigative tend to be analytical, intellectual, complex, and precise. They prefer activities which involve abstract problem-solving, organizing, and understanding. Investigative job environments require abstract problem-solving skills and scientific curiosity.

Artistic personalities are complicated, disorderly, emotional, expressive, and imaginative. Artistic environments reward people for display of artistic abilities.

Social types are cooperative, friendly, helpful, warm and understanding. Social occupations include teaching, counseling, and social work.

Enterprising personalities are adventurous, ambitious, energetic, self-confident, and extroverted. Examples of Enterprising environments include sales, corporations, and political occupations.

Conventional types are careful, conforming, conscientious, orderly, and methodical. Accounting and clerical work are examples of Conventional environments.

Holland has developed and refined three instruments for measuring vocational personality as expressed by the six types described above. These include the Vocational Preference Inventory (VPI) (Holland, 1977), the Self-Directed Search (SDS) (Holland, 1979), and the Self-Directed Search form E (SES-E) (Holland, 1979).

Over 400 research studies have been conducted to validate the theory or to refine the instruments (Osipow, 1983). As a result of factor-analytic research, Holland discovered that a hexagon can be used to express the relationships among the six personality types (Holland, 1979). A capital letter standing for each of the six types is placed at each of the corners of the hexagon. Beginning at the upper left corner of the hexagon and proceeding in a clockwise direction, the order of the letters is RIASEC. The factor analytic studies performed using Holland's assessment instruments revealed that physical proximity of letters on the hexagon represents similarity and difference of any two categories. The closer any two letters are to each other, the more similar are the personality types and work environments for which they stand, and vise versa. Letters directly across the hexagon are physically farthest away from each other and therefore stand for the most dissimilar personality types.

This relationship is depicted graphically in Chapter Three. To locate the most dissimilar personality type in the absence of a drawn hexagon, simply find the letter of interest in the sequence RIASEC. Then skip the next two letters. The next letter in the sequence would fall directly across the hexagon and would be the most dissimilar personality type from the original letter. For example, to find the personality type most dissimilar from the Artistic type, skipping over the next two letters (the S and the E) results in the C being chosen. Indeed, the Conventional personality type or job environment is most dissimilar from the Artistic type and job environment. Similarly, to find the personality type most dissimilar from the Enterprising type, skipping two letters brings one back to the beginning of the sequence to the I (Investigative type).

The matter of similarity or difference is crucial because of the importance of congruency between personality type and job type. Individuals are happiest, most successful, and most vocationally stable when their personality type matches their job environment, and vice versa. An investigative personality would thus be likely to be most satisfied, successful, and stable when placed in an Investigative work environment, and least so when placed in an Enterprising evironment.

This brings us back to the study we referred to above in which jobs of mildly handicapped individuals were studied (Plue, 1984). We reanalyzed Plue's data by looking up in the Dictionary of Holland Occupational Codes (Gottfredson, Holland, & Ogawa, 1982) all the jobs held by the mildly handicaped individuals included in the study. This reference book lists the Holland category for thousands of jobs. With very few exceptions, the jobs held by Plue's mildly handicapped individuals fell into the Realistic category.

The finding that almost all handicapped individuals in Plue's sample were working in Realistic environments led to our research. We wondered if mildly handicapped individuals might be doing poorly vocationally partly because many were being placed in job environments incongruent with their occupational interests and personalities. We know that nonhandicapped people have diverse occupational personalities falling all around the Holland hexagon. If the same is true of mildly handicapped people, then many must be working in incongruent environments since nearly all jobs held by Plue's handicapped workers were classified as Realistic.

We then set out to design an experiment to investigate whether mildly handicapped high school students are as diverse in their occupational personalities as are nonhandicapped peers. We decided to begin our investigation with learning disabled students, and we secured permission to examine the permanent records of all learning disabled high school students in a large school district in Texas. There were 190 students so designated. We submitted the permanent records to a panel of three experts in learning disabilities. Each member of this panel independently evaluated each record to determine whether the student labelled learning disabled by the school district actually met the Federal criteria for learning disabilities. Panel criteria for inclusion in the study was set at agreement by at least two of the three experts that the Federal requirements were met. One hundred three students of the original 190 met this criteria for inclusion. Seven students dropped out of the study, leaving a final sample of 96 learning disabled students.

These 96 learning disabled students were then matched with 96 non-handicapped high school students on the basis of sex, ethnicity, and socioeconomic status. All students were then administered the Self-Directed Search under highly standardized conditions and in the presence of a proctor. All tests proctocols were corrected for errors in self-administration and scoring, and the predominant (high point) Holland code was determined for each student. The number of students falling into each of the six Holland categories (Realistic, Investigative, Artistic, Social, Enterprising, and Conventional) were determined for both learning disabled and nonlearning disabled students.

The numbers of learning disabled students classified into each of the six categories (RIASEC) were 33, 5, 8, 38, 6, 6 respectively. For the nonlearning disabled students, the numbers were 25, 8, 8, 37, 14, 4 respectively.

A 2 by 6 chi-square test of homogeneity was then calculated. This is a statistical test to determine if two distributions are alike or different. In this case, the chi-square test was used to determine if there was a different distribution of high-point codes in the two groups (learning disabled vs. nonlearning disabled). The chi-square value was 5.41 (df = 5, p = 0.37).

This nonsignificant chi-square value indicates no difference in the distribution of students into the six categories when learning disabled and nonlearning disabled students are compared. In other words, *vocational interest and personality among the learning disabled sample is no less diverse than vocational interest and personality among the nonlearning disabled sample.*

These findings have profound implications for career/vocational education of the mildly handicapped. If mildly handicapped persons are just as diverse as nonhandicapped individuals in their vocational interests and personalities, yet are working in job environments almost exclusively Realistic in nature, then many of them must be working in job environments incongruent with their personalities. Since incongruence between occupational personality and work environments is known to be associated with job dissatisfaction, failure, and instability, incongruence may help explain the poor career and vocational adjustment of the mildly handicapped.

Another important finding of the study was that more learning disabled students were categorized as S (Social) than R (Realistic). This is serious because if Social types are placed in Realistic job environments, a high degree of dissatisfaction, failure, and instability would be expected, since the S is located directly across the hexagon from the R. Holland has found that Social types have an aversion to activities, competencies, and interests preferred by Realistic types and vice versa (Holland, 1985).

In a different study which we have not yet completed, we studied approximately 50 individuals who had been labeled learning disabled during school and who are now 25 to 30 years of age. We interviewed these persons and determined what jobs they had been placed in by vocational counselors and other educational professionals. Without exception, these jobs fell into Holland's Realistic category.

We are currently in the process of replicating these studies with mildly mentally retarded and mildly emotionally disturbed individuals. From the preliminary evidence as well as from our own previous experiences, we believe we will find the same results with these samples as we did with the learning disabled individuals. That is, we expect to find that the vocational personalities and interests of the mildly retarded and mildly emotionally disturbed are just as varied as those of the nonhandicapped population.

After completing the first of the studies described above, we concluded:

> To prevent inappropriate job placement, assessment of interests and personalities should be part of career/vocational training programs for learning disabled individuals. Once student interests are determined, then career/vocational programs should prepare students for occupations suited to those interests. For example, learning disabled students with high social interests could be trained to work in social settings such as schools, churches, etc. Students with artistic characteristics and interests could be trained to work in artistic environments such as art galleries, theaters, etc. When occupational interests and personalities of learning disabled individuals are considered in job training and placement, they may be more likely to experience job satisfaction and success. (Cummings and Maddux, In Press)

We think these studies illustrate the absurdity of the stereotype that handicapped individuals should be trained only for Realistic job environments. Mildly handicapped individuals are just as varied in their vocational personalities and interests as are nonhandicapped individuals, and job training should be selected only after comprehensive assessment produces a profile of strengths and weaknesses as well as vocational interests.

## THE PROBLEM OF POOR SOCIAL SKILLS

Zigmond and Brownlee (1980) define social skills as the abilities necessary for effective interpersonal functioning. It has long been acknowledged that a lack of appropriate social skills is a major career and vocational problem for handicapped individuals (Irvine, Goodman, and Mann, 1978). A host of research studies have shown that social skills are crucial to the successful continued employment of the handicapped (Lignugaris/Kraft, Rule, Salzberg, & Stowitschek, 1986).

For example, Foss and Bostwick (1981) surveyed rehabilitation service providers to determine problems encountered with handicapped adults. These providers reported that social and interpersonal skills were the greatest problems of developmentally disabled adults.

Goldstein, Sprafkin, Gershaw, and Klein (1980) carried out a similar study in which they surveyed employers. The employers stated that problems related to vocational adjustment of the handicapped were associated more closely to social behavior than to job performance.

Sheldon, Sherman, Schumaker, and Hazel (1984) studied crucial vocational skills of handicapped workers. They found that skills involved with following directions, accepting criticism, and negotiating conflict situations were just as critical as job performance.

Much of what is known about social skills have been derived from anecdotal accounts of social service providers who work with the handicapped, or from studies of skills needed in sheltered workshop settings. Little research has been carried out to determine social skills needed in more typical work settings. One exception is the work of Lignugaris/Kraft et al. (1986). These researchers studied selected aspects of social behavior of successful handicapped and nonhandicapped employees at work and described the social interactions among these workers.

It was found that the successful employees were active interactants who conversed more with co-workers than with supervisors. In two-thirds of the observations conversation was exclusively work related. Requesting help, criticizing others' work, or joking about a work-related topic occurred in 40 percent of the observations. Nonwork-related conversations occurred in only 6 percent of the observations. The only difference between handicapped and nonhandicapped workers was that the nonhandicapped joked and laughed with coworkers more often. Since successful workers were so social, the researchers recommended that "If individuals were taught some minimal job-related conversational repertoires, they might be better prepared to socially adapt and retain employment" (p. 27).

Gardner, Beatty, and Gardner (1984) list common vocational problem areas for mildly handicapped adults. These problem areas include inability to get along with co-workers or bosses, inability to accept responsibility for their own life and career, a tendency to blame others for their own failures, lack of an understanding of self related to work, and inappropriate work attitudes.

Alley and Deshler (1979) have stated that the degree to which learning disabled individuals can interact successfully on a social basis is a critical determinant of their success and adjustment. Schumaker, Pederson, Hazel and Meyen (1983) maintain that social competence might well outbalance academic deficits and allow mildly handicapped adults to compete successfully in the job market and to life independently.

Chelser (1982) studied 560 learning disabled adults, ages 18 to 36. These individuals rated social relationships and skills as the area in which they felt they had the greatest need for assistance. (Career counseling was rated second.)

White (1985) surveyed the literature and reported that research has established that mildly handicapped individuals have a number of social-skills related problems. These problems include an inability to make friends, dissatisfaction with contacts with parents and relatives, a restricted range of social contacts, and a variety of emotional and psychological problems.

There is evidence that social skills are extremely important to successful vocational adjustment of the nonhandicapped as well. Wilms (1984) surveyed a large number of major employers and reported that personnel officers for these firms maintain that they prefer good work habits and positive attitudes over specific job skills. These employers stated that they would prefer to teach specific job skills on the job, and rely on public schools to instill work habits and positive attitudes toward work.

Adelman and Taylor (1986b) have referred to the current interest in social skills training:

> As research and feedback from teachers, students, and parents indicate the need to continue to evolve ideas for correcting learning and related behavior problems, newer directions are being pursued. For example, there is renewed interest in programs that deal directly with social and emotional functioning. In particular, social skills training is being widely discussed (Bryan & Bryan, 1984). (p. 22)

Unfortunately, the interest in social skills has cooled considerably in the last year or so. Special education in general seems plagued with fleeting fads of this sort. Social skills were *hot* for about two years, but have been replaced with the current concern for transitional programs.

Most disciplines go through periods of fashionable concern for certain topics, and there is nothing inherently damaging about this. However, in special education, topics seem to remain in vogue for such a short time, and are so completely abandoned, that there is frequently little progress made before the currently popular topic is replaced by something new.

We do not know what the solution is for this problem. We would recommend, however, that journals exercise restraint in devoting theme issues to newly-popular topics. Additionally, editors should take deliberate steps to find and publish articles which reflect ongoing inquiry into crucial topics, regardless of whether or not these topics are currently *in*.

The Federal Government should exercise the same restraint in their funding priorities. Funds should be made available for in-depth research over a period of five to ten years. By totally revising funding priorities too frequently, the Government encourages transitory interest in *hot topics,* and the abandonment of promising lines of research that are not as likely to be funded.

Even though social skills training is not the topic currently in vogue, as illustrated above there is substantial agreement that it is crucial to the life adjustment of the handicapped. With such abundant testimonials to the importance of social skills training for mildly handicapped individuals, it is puzzling that this is such a neglected area in career/vocational education. Although most published material concerning career/vocational education of the handicapped recommends that social skill training be made an important component of such programs, few schools include such training.

In light of the evidence presented above, we suggest that the social skills training components of published career and vocational education programs not be ignored or underemphasized. In addition, we suggest that both regular and special education teachers take steps to initiate specific social skills training of handicapped students during elementary school. In fact, social skills training should be initiated as soon as school begins and should continue throughout the lives of handicapped individuals. Strain and Odom (1986) do a good job of summarizing why social skills training is important:

> Initially, social skill deficits are observed in all categories of exceptional children. Second, social skill deficits which appear in the early years tend to become more debilitating without active intervention. Third, an absence of social skills inhibits the development of intellectual, language, and related skills. Finally, defi-

ciencies in social skills during childhood stand as the single best behavioral predictor of significant adjustment problems in adulthood. (p. 543)

Adelman and Taylor (1986b) present an excellent discussion of the problems involved in social skills training:

> How promising are programs for training social skills? Recent reviewers have been cautiously optimistic about the potential value of several proposed approaches. At the same time, however, concerns have been expressed that such skill training seems limited to what is specifically learned and to the situations in which the skills are learned. Moreover, the behaviors learned seem to be maintained only for a short period after the training. These concerns have been raised in connection with (1) training specific behaviors, such as teaching a person what to think and say in a given situation, and (2) strategies that emphasize development of specific cognitive or affective skills, such as teaching a person how to generate a wider range of options for solving interpersonal problems. (p. 258)

One problem that is particularly difficult involves the transfer of training from one domain to another. Psychologists and educators have been plagued by this problem for years. The general consensus now is that transfer does not occur automatically and must be carefully planned for and nurtured. Adelman and Taylor (1986b) suggest that failure to achieve transfer has resulted from a lack of emphasis on motivation:

> As with other skills training approaches, the limitations of current approaches seem to result from a failure to understand the implications of recent theory and research on human motivation. It is evident that many social skills training programs lack a systematic emphasis on enhancing participants' motivation to avoid and overcome interpersonal problems and to learn and continue to apply interpersonal skills to solve such problems. (p. 258)

Adelman and Taylor (1986b) include an excellent chapter on motivation which should be read by anyone planning to implement social skills training. In addition, they present some helpful specific recommendations for social skills trainers, including suggestions to help maximize transfer.

They suggest that several assumptions should underlie programs for social skills training of the handicapped. These include the assumption that not all social problems result from a person's lack of social skills, and that social skill assessment should be conducted only after steps are taken to reduce environmental conditions contributing to the problem and to maximize the student's motivation for learning to cope successfully.

Suggestions are included for topics pertaining to direct discussion, sentence completion, Q-sort activities, role playing, and audiovisual presentations. The use of videotapes is said to be particularly advantageous. Activities are organized around a four-part sequence:

1. Interpersonal problem situations are analyzed.
2. Options for handling the problem are generated and analyzed.

3. An option is chosen and evaluated.
4. If the option is unsuccessful, another option is chosen.

For educators looking for specific suggestions for implementing social skills training for the mildly handicapped, we recommend two other books to parents and teachers. The titles are *Teaching Social Skills to Children,* (Cartledge & Milburn, 1986), and *Social Development of Learning Disabled Persons,* (Kronick, 1981). Our earlier book might also be useful for such educators, since we included techniques for social skills training (Cummings and Maddux, 1985b). These suggested techniques are intended for use by both teachers and parents.

## THE PROBLEM OF TRANSITION

Transition will be dealt with more completely in Chapter Eight of this book. At this point, suffice it to say that the lack of good transitional programs to bridge the gap between public school and full-time employment and independent living is responsible for much of the poor after-school adjustment of the handicapped.

Wehman, Kregel, and Barcus (1985) have developed a good definition of vocational transition:

> Vocational transition is a carefully planned process, which may be initiated either by school personnel or adult service providers, to establish and implement a plan for either employment or additional vocational training of a handicapped student who will graduate or leave school in three to five years; such a process must involve special educators, vocational educators, parents and/or the student, an adult service system representative, and possibly an employer. (p. 26)

No matter how good the career and vocational education program in the public school, the success of the entire effort hinges on careful planning before the student leaves school and appropriate follow-up services provided after public schooling is completed.

## THE PROBLEM OF UNREALISTIC
## PARENTAL EXPECTATIONS

One of the most tragic problems relating to career and vocational education for mildly handicapped students is the problem of unrealistic parental expectations. Such expectations cause untold heartache and frustrations for countless handicapped persons and their parents.

Although a few parents of mildly handicapped children develop expectations that are too limited and constricted, the opposite is more often the case. We have known dozens of parents of learning disabled children, for example, who have stubbornly insisted that their severely learning disabled child can and will succeed academically, first in high school and later in college. A few severely learning disabled students can meet such lofty expectations, though many who do pay a fearful cost in terms of anxiety, fear, and social isolation.

There are probably several reasons why parents form such unrealistic expectations. One reason is that denial is part of the natural reaction to the shock of having a handicapped child. Good counseling and understanding professionals can do much to guide the parent through the denial stage and help him or her accept the handicapped child.

Such good counseling by knowledgeable professionals is relatively rare, however. Unfortuantely, we believe that misguided professional advice and counsel is frequently responsible for causing or maintaining unrealistic parental expectations. We referred to this problem in the preface of our book on parenting the learning disabled (Cummings & Maddux, 1985b):

> One of the authors is the parent of a learning disabled nineteen-year-old and an active participant in parent organizations at the state and local level. The other author taught learning disabled children in public school for five years.
>
> The outcome of our experiences has been ongoing frustration at the number of professionals who seem unable to work effectively with parents of learning disabled children. Although professionals may be knowledgeable about effective counseling techniques, these professionals often provide parents with inaccurate and misleading information. The often tragic outcome is that parents develop unrealistic expectations for their learning disabled children.
>
> As a result of these misconceptions and false expectations, and as the literature is recently beginning to show, many learning disabled children are leaving school unprepared for college, for work, for adult relationships, and for independent living. (p. vii)

One of the problems associated with unrealistically high expectations is that parents may be led to overemphasize academics and in so doing, restrict opportunity for the important normal socializing experiences of childhood and adolescence. These experiences are particularly important for the mildly handicapped, since such children frequently have particular difficulty with interpersonal and social skills. Denial of opportunity for normal social interactions exacerbates this difficulty.

Parents who form unrealistically high expectations for their handicapped children often submerge them in academics.

> The assumption seems to be that if Johnny can just put in enough extra hours studying, he will be fine by the time he graduates. As a result of such thinking, parents may insist that their children be placed in mainstreamed academic subjects. They may spend hundreds of dollars on special tutors and special schools. They often meet their already exhausted children at the door with demands that they do their homework. No thought may be given to any other educational alternative to the academic program. In fact, many parents of learning-disabled children may become offended if the possibility of vocational training is even suggested to them. (Cummings and Maddux, 1984, pp. 83-84)

School psychologists, counselors, and teachers should be careful not to overemphasize the *mild* nature of the problem when meeting with parents of mildly handicapped children. They should remember that a learning disabled child is *mildly* handicapped compared to a profoundly retarded child, but compared to nonhandicapped children, most learning disabled children have severe problems.

We have worked with parents of learning disabled individuals who have been led to believe that all learning disabled children have above-average or even gifted abilities in certain areas. We referred to this problem in an earlier journal article:

> Parents frequently do not understand why their learning-disabled children are having so many difficulties. After all, the special education teacher pointed out that some renowned individuals such as Nelson Rockefeller, Albert Einstein, and Thomas Edison were learning disabled. The implication is that parents of children with learning disabilities should not worry. They may be the parents of a future Einstein! In fact, some overzealous parents may even consider the learning disability to be a precursor to greatness. (Cummings and Maddux, 1984, p. 81)

We do not suggest that educators should not mention to parents that some notable, high-achieving individuals were learning disabled. But they should emphasize that these individuals were not *typical* learning disabled people, but were highly intelligent, gifted, atypical individuals who were *also* learning disabled. Unlike such extraordinary individuals, most learning disabled people have average intelligence. Counselors and others working with parents should point out that if the likes of Einstein and Edison had problems in school, many learning disabled children with *average* intelligence may find academic success highly elusive if not unattainable.

Over the last few years, we have worked with many learning disabled college students. A few did well so long as good support services such as tutoring and counseling were available. Most, however, struggled painfully and hopelessly in a losing battle to keep up with their studies and obtain a degree.

A colleague, Larry Faas of Arizona State Universiy, is completing a research study of characteristics of successful learning disabled college students. He informs us that his preliminary findings indicate that the vast majority of such students are forced to study continuously and have no social life whatsoever. One could question whether or not a college degree will be worth such a heavy price.

We would not presume to answer that question for handicapped individuals. However, we do suggest that parents frequently put undue pressure on their mildly handicapped children, and this may result in those children pursuing a college degree not for its own sake, but in order to please parents. This can have several undesirable consequences.

First, mildly handicapped children may suffer emotional problems as a result of pressure to succeed in academic environments. We are acquainted with a 25-year-old severely learning disabled young woman who is a sad case in point. She works as a teacher's aide in a program for severely handicapped children, and she enjoys this work immensely. However her parents are determined that she graduate from college.

The young lady is highly verbal, but her social skills are exceedingly poor. She cannot take adequate notes in lecture courses, she does not read well, and she lacks the interpersonal skills to communicate her problems to her teachers or to ask them to modify assignments. She has been attending college sporadically for five years, attending briefly, failing, and dropping out for awhile. She is acutely unhappy and considers herself a failure even though she is a valued employee at her job as an aide. She feels she has disappointed her parents and considers herself lazy even though she studies unsuccessfully for many hours every day. We have watched helplessly as her emotional condition has deteriorated and she is currently under treatment for anorexia nervosa.

Second, the majority of mildly handicapped children who are pushed to follow college preparatory, academic programs do not succeed in obtaining a college degree. Most drop out of college after a semester or two and return home with no marketable skill and with the psychological scars caused by yet another failure.

Third, parental pressure for academic success and the attendant private tutoring, summer school, and homework leaves no time for adequate career/vocational training and no time for after-school or summer employment. The result is that once academics are finally abandoned, the individual has nothing to fall back on to aid post-school adjustment to the world of work and independent living.

And lastly, so long as parents continue to insist on academic programs exclusively for their mildly handicapped children, schools are likely to continue offering such inappropriate programs and neglecting the instituting of appropriate career and vocational education.

The problem of unrealistic parental expectations has several implications for professionals. First, it should be explained to parents that even though the handicap is referred to as mild, there is no guarantee that problems will be minor. Parents should be made aware that both academic and social problems are common, and that undue emphasis on academics can exaggerate the social skills problems.

Second, parents should be made aware that a college degree is no guarantee of vocational success or high earning power, and that many attractive jobs do not require a college degree. Wilms (1984), for example, reports that only 9 percent of entry-level jobs in this country require a postsecondary degree and that employers often prefer good work habits and attitudes to college degrees or specific skills training.

Third, parents should be encouraged to make the home a haven and a refuge for the pressures of academics. Rather than insisting on inordinate levels of homework, private tutoring, and summer school, parents should encourage enjoyable family activities such as hobbies, camping, and other recreational pursuits.

Fourth, parents should be guided to make abundant social experiences available for their children. Closely supervised activities providing for interaction with both peers and adults are beneficial. After such experiences, parents should discuss the experiences and alternative solutions to behavioral problems that arose.

Fifth, parents should be encouraged to help provide work experiences for their children at an early age. In our experience, mildly handicapped students who are successful vocationally have nearly always been involved in paid part-time employment situations for many years before full-time employment was attempted.

Sixth, parents can be led to demand appropriate career/vocational programs from their public schools. These programs should begin in elementary school and continue throughout the school years.

Seventh, parents can emphasize the importance of punctuality and dependability. They should also attempt to model these qualities in their own lives. These skills are extremely important to employers and are often considered more important than specific job skills. We have all heard the common employer lament that *you just can't get good help these days.* Punctuality, dependability, and a desire to do one's best are the characteristics employers find difficult to locate.

## SOME MISCELLANEOUS PROBLEMS

There are many other problems and issues in career and vocational education for the mildly handicapped. Greenan (1982) has identified four problems: (a) attitudes, (b) personnel preparation, (c) funding, and (d) interagency cooperation and agreements.

### Attitude

The attitude problem referred to by Greenan (1982) is that educators frequently do not think of vocational education as a valuable addition to the curriculum for mildly handicapped students. In addition, Greenan suggests that special educators should integrate work world activities into the curriculum, especially in subject areas such as math and social studies. To successfully accomplish this integration, special educators must be willing to enter into dialogue with vocational teachers, work-study coordinators, and community people and resources. Inservice education programs should also be conducted in order for educators to learn more about vocational services which are available to their students.

### Personnel Preparation

Personnel preparation problems involve making teachers-in-training aware of career and vocational education goals, objectives and services. Greenan suggests such training should also involve vocational educators-in-training. The thrust of the training for regular and special educators should be an emphasis on integrating career and vocational concepts into the regular curriculum's academic activities.

### Funding

Funding problems referred to by Greenan are related to ensuring that Federal funding be made availabe for career and vocational education. The funding intended for needs assessment, in-service training, program maintenance, and program evaluation will continue to be forthcoming only if the various states include career and vocational goals and services in their state PL94-142 plans. Local educators must continue to support such plans and make every effort to receive all funding available for career and vocational education.

## Interagency Cooperation and Agreements

Greenan also identifies interagency cooperation and agreements as a major problem. He makes the point that vocational educators are frequently left out of IEP meetings. This results in handicapped students being excluded from vocational courses. In addition, special educators should be certain that vocational educators receive all assessment information about handicapped students in their classes. This will aid the vocational teacher in adapting or modifying materials and expectations for such students.

Conversely, the vocational teacher should provide special educators with all vocational assessment data on handicapped students. Special educators should also be asked to help plan new vocational assessment programs for handicapped students or help modify existing programs.

Greenan also emphasizes that vocational teachers should always be consulted about the feasibility of placing handicapped students in their programs. Special educators can then help vocational teachers modify their programs. Appropriate modifications may include:

> . . . taped versions of written material, language at appropriate reading levels, simplified versions of regular material, oral texts and/or reports, visual materials and use of peer tutors. (Greenan, 1982, p. 235)

Also included in the category of interagency cooperation and agreements is Greenan's recommendation that special educators help vocational teachers evaluate handicapped students' progress and assess the effectiveness of their programs. When problems arise, the vocational teacher should immediately consult with the special educators for help in devising solutions to the difficulty. Greenan also suggests that regular and vocational educators should consider establishing formal policies and agreements that might even be put in writing.

## Misinformation About the Handicapped

White (1985) identifies the general public's lack of accurate information about the handicapped as a major problem. He maintains that employers often demonstrate prejudices against handicapped applicants and employees.

A good example of the misinformation commonly held about the handicapped is that many people suggest that mild handicapped young people should consider a career in the military. Yet Harnden, Meyen, Alley, and Deshler (1980) administered the *Armed Services Vocational Aptitude Battery* to a large number of learning disabled high school students and found that only 29 percent scored high enough to quality for the Army, while only 4 percent scored high enough to qualify for the Air Force. To counter misinformation and prejudice, a public information campaign should be mounted to inform the general public about the characteristics of handicapped individuals.

## Lack of Training in Adult Education

Another problem identified by White (1985) is that before good programs for adults can be put into place, training in adult education must be made available to professionals. At present, very few adult educators know anything about special education, and very few special educators are expert in working with adults. University teacher-training programs could respond to this need, as could state and local education agency in-service programs.

## An Empirical Approach to Problems

Greenan and Phelps (1982) took an empirical approach to problems in vocational education. These researchers surveyed all state directors of vocational education and special education, and consultants responsible for vocational special needs education in the Unived States and surrounding territories. The purpose of the survey was to identify the major policy-related problem areas that confront state education agencies in providing vocational education to handicapped learners.

Eight problem areas were identified and are listed as follows from most often to least often mentioned:

1. Interagency cooperation and agreements
2. Funding and fiscal policy
3. Service delivery and program alternatives
4. Personnel preparation
5. State legislation, plans, and policies
6. Attitudes
7. Program evaluation and improvement
   (Adapted from Greenan and Phelps, 1982, p. 409)

Further, these researchers found that over 50 percent of the problems listed fell into the two areas of interagency cooperation and agreements and funding and fiscal policy. They attribute the heavy emphasis on the first of these two problems to recent changes in Federal law resulting in "expanded efforts to work cooperatively in providing a continuum of vocational education opportunities and services for the handicapped population" (p. 410).

The funding and fiscal policy problems identified seem to be caused by inadequate funding and complex and inadequate funding formulae at the Federal, state, and local levels. They identified other problems:

> Other problems and concerns less frequently mentioned by the state education agency personnel included: (a) lack of appropriate preservice and inservice training for vocational and special education personnel; (b) lack of specific statewide policies and guidelines pertaining to vocational education for the handicapped; (c) the restrictiveness and vagueness of federal regulations; (d) negative educator and employer attitudes; and (e) lack of job placement follow-up and programmatic evaluation. (p. 410)

## Lack of Follow-Up Services

The current emphasis on normalization of experiences for the handicapped has resulted in increased program efforts to prepare handicapped individuals for competitive employment. Dineen (1981) found that 64 percent of the 60 developmental centers and sheltered workshops in Washington include competitive job placement as a goal and a service. However, Ford, Dineen, and Hall (1984) have identified the lack of follow-up services as a major barrier to effective vocational programs for the retarded:

> While vocational training and job placement are clearly important facets of preparing an individual for living an independent, satisfying life, experience indicates that competitive placement is only the beginning of the services needed. Mentally retarded clients who have been trained to competitive levels in vocational skills remain handicapped by the lack of adequate systems for maintaining them on the job and assuring that the quality of their lives is in fact enhanced by competitive employment. (p. 291)

These authors identify three problem areas. First, sheltered workshops are environments where a great deal of feedback and reinforcement is typically provided. This is usually not possible in competitive employment environments. Therefore, performance standards are difficult to maintain. After keeping records for six years, the researchers report that lack of maintenance of job skills was a factor in 47% of job losses.

Second, social skills deficits and life skills deficits become more important and debilitating in competitive employment than in sheltered workshop settings and may result in loss of job. Social skills problems were a factor in 42% of job losses studied. These problems were further broken down into poor social interactions with employers and/or coworkers, emotional outbursts, and inappropriate language. The life skills deficits noted included problems of managing grooming, money, transportation, child care, health care, and housing. Other problems included quitting a job even though the client had no other job to go to, poor attendance, theft, and hygiene.

Third, agencies working with the retarded frequently do not continue services for long after placement, even though job threatening problems will continue to occur long after such placement. The researchers report that of 53 clients who were placed and worked at the same job at least one year, only eight needed no intervention services after the first six months, and only two of ten clients who found their own jobs were able to remain employed at that job for at least six months.

The authors concluded with four recommendations:

1. The training program must provide on-the-job training for clients involving close monitoring of performance levels.
2. There should be long-term follow-up to ensure maintenance.
3. Support services such as recreational programs should be provided at hours when handicapped clients are not working.
4. Financial support needs to be made available for long-term follow-up services and agencies need to be reinforced for maintenance as well as for initial placement.

## SUMMARY

This chapter has reviewed a number of critical issues and problems in career and vocational education. We began our discussion by presenting evidence for rejecting the stereotype that handicapped individuals should be placed exclusively in *Realistic* job environments requiring fine and gross motor ability and tool manipulation. Since handicapped people have the same diversity of vocational interests and personalities as nonhandicapped peers, such narrow placements may account for part of the reason that handicapped workers do not generally make good vocational adjustments.

We then discussed the importance of social skill training for mildly handicapped students. Since most job dismissals are the result of poor social skills rather than an inability to perform the work, more attention needs to be given to these skills in programs for the mildly handicapped.

Transitional programs will be dealt with more completely in another chapter. A brief definition of transition was given and the importance of programs to bridge the gap between school and independent living was discussed.

Other problems presented were problems of attitude of regular educators toward vocational education, the need for better personnel preparation, funding problems, problems of interagency cooperation and agreement, the problem of misinformation about characteristics and needs of the mildly handicapped, the need for training in adult education, and the problem of lack of long-term follow-up services after job placement.

## Chapter Seven

# RECOMMENDATIONS FOR CHANGES IN THE PUBLIC SCHOOLS

IN THE PAST, mildly handicapped students have had few career/vocational options available in the public schools. Typically, these students have been channeled into academic programs emphasizing reading, writing, and mathematics. Even though these students continued to demonstrate difficulties in these academic areas when they reached junior and senior high school, their educational programs continued to emphasize remediation in academic subjects. One reason for this continued emphasis on academics was the hope by educators and parents that with experience and maturation, the student would eventually "catch-on," successfully complete school, and become a well-functioning, independent adult. Unfortunately, it has recently become apparent that many students, identified as mildly retarded, behavior disordered, and learning disabled have not responded to academic remedial efforts (Kendall, 1981). Many of these students are graduating from high school unprepared for college, vocational-technical school, or for transition into the adult life of work (Crimando & Nichols, 1982; Cummings & Maddux, 1984, in press; Faford & Haubrich, 1981; White, et al., 1983).

A recent survey of learning disabled adults conducted by Hoffman, et al. (1986) found that "learning disabled adults have major academic, social, personal, and vocational needs that must be addressed if they are to attain adult competence" (p. 50). The authors also reported the following: (a) learning disabled adults surveyed had received little or no career/vocational education; (b) career/vocational education is a critical need area for learning disabled students; (c) provision of these services should minimize the need for post-school vocational rehabilitation services; (d) employment and job training are the most critical needs of learning disabled adults at the present time; and (e) these needs can be met only by secondary, transitional, and postsecondary vocational programs.

We believe that the poor post-secondary adjustment of mildly handicapped individuals results from several problems related to effective development and delivery of career/vocational education programs for mildly handicapped students. First of all, although vocational education programs have been in place in the secondary schools for years, they have traditionally been designed either for nonhandicapped students or for moderately-to-severely mentally retarded students (Kendall, 1981; Sitlington, 1981). Few, if any, programs have been developed for learning disabled, behavior disordered, or mildly retarded students. We consider the needs and abilities of this group of students to be different from those with more severe handicaps, and we think that career/vocational education programs for mildly handicapped students should consider and address these differences.

Another problem with traditional public school career/vocational education programs is that they are usually initiated at the secondary level, and most frequently at the high school level. We disagree with this approach, and agree with those who assert that career/vocational education should begin at the elementary school level (Brolin, 1982; Brolin, Elliott, & Corcoran, 1984; Clark, 1979; Kokaska, 1983; Kokaska & Brolin, 1985; Sitlington, 1981). These programs should include career awareness activities to develop values, attitudes and habits, human relationships, and daily living skills; social skills development; and functional academics. These elementary-school activities would develop some prevocational skills and lay the groundwork for secondary-school career/vocational education programs. These would include continued development of prevocational skills in addition to actual job-skills training at the middle- or junior-high school, and actual on-the-job training for high-school students. As a result of such intensive, long-term education and training, mildly handicapped students should graduate from high school more fully prepared to compete in the adult work environment.

A final public-school programming consideration is the need to combine the expertise of both special and vocational educators. Both special education and vocational education have much to offer mildly handicapped students. However, each of these disciplines have certain disadvantages when taken separately. Separate special education work experience programs tend to remove handicapped students from the mainstream of education, and they prepare students for menial, low-level jobs fitting a stereotypic view of interests and abilities. In addition, they are typically designed with more severely handicapped students in mind. Finally, while special education teachers have training and expertise in dealing with academic needs of handicapped children, they often have not been trained in career/vocational education.

Conversely, public school vocational education programs usually do not begin until the 10th or 11th grade which is often too late for most handicapped students, even those with mild handicaps. These programs frequently consist of specific skill training, assuming that participants have already developed necessary prevocational and employability skills. In addition, the vocational education curriculum, without modification, may be too difficult for handicapped learners (Sitlington, 1981). While vocational teachers can teach electronics, carpentry, or mechanics, they usually have no background in special education, and they may be uncertain about how to modify instructional materials to accommodate handicapped students.

The solution of these problems is to coordinate efforts of regular vocational and special educators. One benefit of such coordination would be the sharing of information. For example, vocational education teachers could develop minimal competency criteria for handicapped students to master before they could participate in vocational education courses. These criteria could then be shared with special education teachers who, in turn, would use them to teach handicapped students essential skills necessary for successful participation in regular vocational education programs. Thanks to the Carl Perkins Vocational Act of 1984, such cooperation is mandated and funds are available to encourage cooperation between public school vocational and special education teachers.

A third problem related to effective career/vocational programming for mildly-handicapped students has to do with parent education. Since we have dealt with this problem at length in another chapter, we will provide only a brief overview at this point. Because most learning disabled, mildly behavior disordered, and mildly retarded individuals appear more normal than handicapped, parents of these students may believe they will eventually outgrow their difficulties. One consequence of such thinking is that these parents often expect their children will attend college after high school graduation. Thus, it is usually a difficult task to convince these parents of the need for career/vocational educational programming as early as the elementary years. Usually, only after the child continues to experience academic difficulties at the secondary level do the parents admit the need for vocational training. As we have already said, initiation of career/vocational education at the secondary level is often inadequate for many handicapped youngsters. Thus, unrealistic parental expectations may result in some mildly handicapped youth missing out on years of valuable training and preparation for work.

Consequently, meaningful, early involvement of parents in educational planning is essential to helping parents form realistic expectations and long-term goals for their handicapped child. It should be the responsibility of educators and other special-education professionals to convince parents of the value of long-term career/vocational planning for their children. For example, parents should be made aware of the outdated concept of *college for everyone.* According to one report (Wilms, 1984), a postsecondary credential is the minimum requirement for only 9 percent of entry-level jobs. We believe that many individuals can be adequately prepared to function in society with technological or other non-college training. Thus, one responsibility of professionals should be to give parents examples of interesting, fulfilling jobs that are available to individuals who do not hold college degrees, but who have received appropriate career/vocational training.

Lately, special education professionals have begun to look more closely at the career/vocational needs of mildly handicapped students. Hopefully, the current attention being paid to these needs will not be diverted by another, newer special education fad, but instead will continue to focus on developing viable, career/vocational education programs to prepare these youngsters for competitive employment and fulfilling lives as adults.

We are encouraged by the recent movement to provide quality career/vocational education programs for mildly handicapped individuals. However, we believe that any changes will be short-lived without some rather dramatic changes in existing public school programs. For the remainder of this chapter, we will present seven specific special education reforms related to the career/vocational preparation of mildly handicapped students. We will also discuss specific issues related to the development of elementary, middle/junior high, and high school career/vocational programs. Finally, we will describe some practical ideas for implementing these programs at each educational level.

# REFORM OF SPECIAL EDUCATION RELATED TO CAREER/VOCATIONAL PREPARATION OF MILDLY HANDICAPPED INDIVIDUALS

If public schools are going to adequately prepare mildly handicapped students for work and adult living, we believe several reforms will need to occur:

1. Career/vocational education should begin early and continue throughout the public school years. It frequently takes many repetitions for mentally handicapped youngsters to learn a new concept. In spite of this fact, we frequently expect that a short dose of vocational education during the last two years of high school will be enough to instill good work habits and work skills in mildly handicapped students. This will not work! We believe that career/vocational training should begin in kindergarten and continue until graduation.

Elementary teachers in resource rooms and in self-contained special education classrooms should emphasize career awareness activities, appropriate work behaviors, and social skills training. These activities should be incorporated into the elementary special education curriculum, and children should engage in these activities daily. Academics should also be taught with the career/vocational needs of the *handicapped adult* in mind. By the time they finish sixth grade, mildly handicapped youngsters should have an understanding of work values, attitudes and habits, human relationships, and daily living skills.

By the time they enter seventh grade, these youngsters should have a solid understanding of the myriad of occupational opportunities available to them. They should understand the requirements of hundreds of jobs. They should have internalized the value of appropriate work habits such as dependability, punctuality, and relating appropriately to employers and fellow employees. They should also have a basic knowledge of how to manage their paycheck; appropriate hygiene; and how to keep house, wash clothes, cook and so on.

The junior high/middle school curriculum should include job-skills training, both in simulated work environments in the school, and in actual community employment locations. Older junior high/middle school students could even serve as apprentices in various businesses, and these should not be limited to food service occupations, janitorial work, and assembly line work. Mildly handicapped students, especially those with behavior disorders and learning disabilities are likely to become bored with low-level, menial jobs that fit the stereotypic view of what handi-capped persons can do. (This may even be true to more severely handi-capped persons.)

By the time students enter high school, they should be prepared to begin actual on-the-job training. Throughout their school years, stu-dents should be taught functional academics—reading, writing, math—as they apply to everyday realities; they should be taught social skills; and they should be taught independent living skills.

As a result of such longitudinal planning and intensive prevocational and vocational training, mildly handicapped students would graduate from high school better prepared to live and work in an adult world. As we have already stated, *transition from school to work* is the trendy new phrase in special education. It is our contention that with more effective public school education and training, mildly handicapped students would not need transitional programs to succeed in the adult world.

2. Cease using the elementary model of special education in the sec-ondary schools. We believe that for many mildly handicapped young-sters, continuing with tutoring and remediation in junior/high/middle school, and especially in senior high school is frequently a wasted effort. For all but the most mildly affected, it makes more sense to give students a practical education with an emphasis on equipping them to deal with the realities of the adult world.

Another problem with the elementary model at the secondary level (and this is the fault of many teacher-training programs and state de-partments of education) is that many special education preservice teach-ers enroll in either a generic or a dual elementary/special education program, yet state departments of education issue them a K-12 special education teaching certificate. There is no problem with this arrange-ment if these teachers are assigned to an elementary classroom.

However, if teachers receiving such a certificate are assigned to a sec-ondary school classroom they are likely to be lost. In the first place, they must deal with adolescent handicapped students—students who are much different from those they learned about in their child development courses. Secondly, if they are assigned as resource room teachers, they may have to tutor students in a variety of subject areas including chemistry, algebra, and English literature. This is a bit too much to ask a new college graduate who was trained to teach elemetary-school chil-dren elementary-school subjects.

Obviously, it is time that colleges and state departments of education recognize the need for at least two special education models, an elementary model and a secondary model. (It is possible that four models would be even better: an early childhood model, an elementary model, a junior high/middle school model, and a high school model). In conclusion, one major advantage of the secondary model versus the elementary model is that university secondary/special education curricula could include a strong career/vocational education component. Thus, preservice teachers would be better prepared to teach handicapped adolescents and provide quality career/vocational training for their students.

3. Combine the expertise of special and vocational educators. As we have already said, both special and vocational education have much to offer mildly handicapped students. Although vocational/special education programs are available in public schools these are usually (a) designed for more severely handicapped students; (b) self-contained; and (c) based on the traditional model of preparing participants for stereotypic, low-level jobs. Regular vocational programs, on the other hand, often (a) are too difficult for handicapped participants, (b) consist of specific skill training exclusively, (c) do not begin until high school, and (d) are taught by instructors who have no special education training.

Thanks to the Carl Perkins Act, efforts are underway to coordinate the expertise of special and vocational educators. We believe that this movement is long overdue and holds much promise for providing excellent career/vocational education for mildly handicapped learners.

4. Teach social skills and independent living skills from elementary school through high school. Results of numerous studies provide evidence that handicapped students do not pick up these skills incidentally. Thus, they must be methodically taught over a long period of time. Perhaps if such skills were taught from elementary school on, most handicapped students would acquire them by the time they graduated from high school.

5. Mildly handicapped students should be trained for nonstereotypic occupations. The authors have conducted research comparing the occupational interests of learning disabled and nonlearning disabled high school students (Cummings & Maddux, In press). The results of our study provided evidence that no significance differences existed in the diversity of occupational interests of both groups of students. The learning disabled students had personalities and interests that were as varied as those of the nonhandicapped students.

We believe it is a mistake to think that handicapped individuals are only capable of performing tasks such as those required by assembly-line work, food service occupations, or domestic services. Our research (Cummings & Maddux, In press) revealed that more LD students than nonhandicapped students had occupational interests in the Social category, and as many LD as nonLD students had occupational interests in the Artistic category. Yet, many career/vocational education programs for these students train them for occupations where they will have little contact with people, and assembly-line and janitorial work is far from artistic! Thus, we believe that it is imperative that occupational interests and personalities of handicapped students be considered in vocational education programs. Then, once those interests are determined, students should be trained for a broad variety of occupations suited to their personalities and interests. Although a learning disabled person with high Artistic interests may not be a great painter or sculptor, that individual might enjoy working in a museum or in a florist's shop.

Also, we often hold the stereotypic notion that students with learning disabilities are "good with their hands" and encourage them to enroll in programs to train them to become auto mechanics, carpenters, and the like. However, since one of the characteristics of many learning disabled persons is a lack of motor coordination, it may be unrealistic to think that most of them will be excellent workers in occupations requiring skills in manual dexterity.

6. Parents need to be educated to plan realistically for their mildly handicapped children. None of the first five reforms will be effective unless professionals, including special education teachers, who work with mildly handicapped students are willing to encourage parents to plan realistically for their children's futures. Parents who insist, against all evidence, that their child attend college, and who stress academics to the exclusion of any other options, may be opening the door to a future of failure and life-long dependency for their children.

7. Develop theory-based, empirically-validated career/vocational education programs. At present, there is a lack of empirical research to investigate the efficacy of existing career/vocational education programs, and to provide impetus for looking at the career development of handicapped individuals. Traditionally, development of special education vocational models has evolved more from practical experience than from any solid research base. The consequence has been an attempt to fit all handicapped children into a model based on a narrow, stereotypic view of the occupational abilities and interests of handicapped populations—a model that is most appropriate for more severely mentally and physically handicapped students.

We believe that the solution to this problem is to consider existing career/vocational theories that have been developed for nonhandicapped populations, and use these theories as foundations on which to design and implement research paradigms for handicapped populations. The result should be appropriate career/vocational education programs that consider the unique needs and abilities of every handicapped group.

We believe that these reforms are vital if public schools are going to provide excellent career/vocational education programs that are suited to the unique needs of handicapped participants. We disagree with the traditional method of providing vocational/special education programs in segregated settings to severely handicapped students while at the same time offering only academic options to mildly handicapped students. We believe that all handicapped students can benefit from career/vocational programs. We also believe that these programs should be integrated with regular vocational education as much as possible, yet be designed to address the unique needs of handicapped participants, regardless of the severity of the handicap. Finally, if such programs are to be successful, they should be developed on the basis of empirical research findings, and they should prepare participants for a variety of occupations.

## CAREER/VOCATIONAL DEVELOPMENT PROGRAMS: K-12

According to Brolin and West (1985), it has become apparent that career development begins early and continues throughout life. Unlike vocational education which focusses on specific skill training, career education involves knowledge of all productive adult roles including that of family member and citizen. Consequently, many special and vocational educators have begun to recognize the importance of introducing career education concepts into the K-12 curriculum long before students begin vocational training in specific skills. Career development concepts that should be included throughout the curriculum include (a) early development of work personality traits such as occupational interests; motivation; good work habits, ethics, and values; and punctuality; (b) increased self-awareness; (c) development of a good self-concept; (d) awareness of a wide array of employment opportunities; (e) exposure to the regular vocational education curriculum; and (d) exposure to a variety of hands-on experiential work activities. When handicapped students are exposed to continuous career/vocational educational opportunities throughout their public school careers, they should be well-prepared to enter the adult world.

For the remainder of this chapter, we will provide a look at proposed curriculum development for elementary and for secondary programs. We will also present some practical strategies for use in elementary and secondary career/vocational courses.

## Career/Vocational Programs in the Elementary Years

Career education skills are developmental in nature and begin during the early years of a child's life. According to Gillett (1983), the elementary years are vital to the development of career concepts for mildly handicapped children. She believes that attitudes are formed during these years that will affect the child's vocational adjustment later in life. Consequently, a child's education and training for adult living should begin early and continue throughout the school years. If career/vocational education is postponed until adolescence, it will be difficult, if not impossible, to negate years of inappropriate behavior patterns. Kokaska, Lazar, and Schmidt (1970) also believe that a special education program should include a continuum of vocational experiences which lead the student through progressive levels of work experience to the final status of an independent worker. They believe that such preparation is more difficult if the student's first exposure to vocational education is in high school.

Brolin, Elliott, and Corcoran (1984) describe elementary students as being in the developmental stage of career awareness. They state that it is important for students to begin to develop an understanding of the roles people assume in the occupational world, and in the larger society. Such training will create a basic self-awareness, enhance the growth of a positive self-image, and develop a respect for others. Development of these traits will prepare the child to engage in career fantasy and role-playing, and to begin to make tentative career choices (Brolin, et al., 1984). Children observe the activities adults undertake, sometimes inquiring why adults engage in such activities. Later, they will fantasize about being in similar work situations and act out their fantasies mimicking the behavior of adults through role-play. Brolin and his colleagues believe that adults may discourage or deter young handicapped children from acting out their fantasies because of the belief that the child lacks the potential to pursue the fantasized goal. Such behavior results in children becoming discouraged and certain options are thereby squelched at an early age. Instead of discouraging children, adults should ecourage them to act out their perceptions of themselves in occupational and social roles since engaging in these activities allows a work personality to begin to take root in children.

It is also necessary that children understand and respect the worth of personal traits and attributes. According to Gillet (1983), character training at the elementary level is not only important to social development, but is important for the development of future job skills. Employers want employees who are dependable, and who exhibit initiative, realiability, perseverence, and cheerfulness. Since more employees lose their jobs because of poor character traits rather than lack of skill, it is important to begin training early to develop positive personality attributes in mildly handicapped children.

According to Gillett (1983), one goal of career education for the mildly handicapped child at the elementary level should be the development of social skills necessary in job, family, and personal adjustment. Many mildly handicapped students have difficulty with social perception which includes the ability to intepret social cues and respond appropriately. Consequently, they need to be taught to interpret the behavior of others and to understand the meaning of facial expressions, gestures, and voice inflections. If the reader is interested in curriculum designed to teach social skills, we recommend Doreen Kronick's book, *Social Development of Learning Disabled Persons.*

Career/vocational growth is also dependent on the development of basic academic skills that are developed during the elementary years. These include (a) knowledge of the calendar; (b) time concepts; (c) money, shape, and color recognition; (d) mastery of a basic written and spoken vocabulary; and (e) skill in communication. According to Gillett, these are skills that are essential to success in the world of work and should be incorporated into the regular elementary curriculum. Thus, she believes that career education should not replace the academic program or call for a separate curriculum.

Instead of replacing the regular academic curriculum, a well-conceived, carefully-developed career/vocational program in the elementary grades may motivate the student's interest in school and academic learning (Gillett, 1983). When curriculum activities are related to careers and the world of work, students may better perceive the relevance of school activities to their own futures.

How career education activities are included in the elementary curriculum depends on the developmental stage of the student, the kind of program placement, prerequisite skill development, IEP goals and objectives, and the teacher's philosophy (Gillett, 1983). Following are examples of activities designed both for the regular classroom and for the resource room.

**Regular Classroom Activities.** The special education teacher may work with regular classroom teachers on a consultant basis, making suggestions for the provision of career education instruction within the regular classroom setting. Gillett provides a list of activities that are appropriate for use in the regular classroom:

1. Use a variety of multisensory activities.
2. Use transparencies and other visual aides to accompany verbal explanations.
3. Show a sequence of job-related activities using pictures rather than printed materials.
4. Provide opportunities for students to apply the newly-learned skills in a variety of situations different from that in which the original learning occurred.
5. Provide self-tests and checklists so that students can monitor their own progress.
6. Clarify new material by the use of diagrams.

Donohoe (1976) presents ideas for learning centers in the regular classroom to teach independent living skills. Activities at the learning centers teach such things as dealing with an emergency, supermarket shopping, using the yellow pages, and following a recipe. Figure 2 is an example of an activity for teaching how to order from a menu.

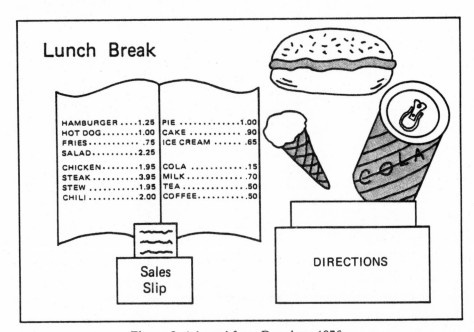

**Figure 2.** Adapted from Donohoe, 1976.

This center could be used in an elementary math class to help teach computation skills, or in a language arts class to help teach reading and following directions. The child goes to the center and gets instructions from a question sheet or from an audiotape. For this activity, the child might be told that he is traveling and has stopped at a restaurant. He has a total of three dollars and must choose items from the menu which do not exceed this amount. A sales slip could be provided and the child would write down each item, the price of each item, and the total cost of the meal. A calculator could be included for the child to check his work. He might also be asked to tell how much change he would receive if his order is less than the allotted amount.

Wilson and Barnes (1974) suggest activities for developing survival learning materials for classroom use. These materials are organized under the headings of following directions, locating references, interpreting forms, and obtaining personal information. The authors intend their suggestions to be used as "starter ideas" for reading teachers to use in developing their own packet of materials. They suggest that teachers first gather a variety of materials from sources such as magazines, newspapers, old textbooks, and the like. The materials are then packaged in *pocket folders,* with the reading materials in one pocket and the questions in the other (see Figure 3).

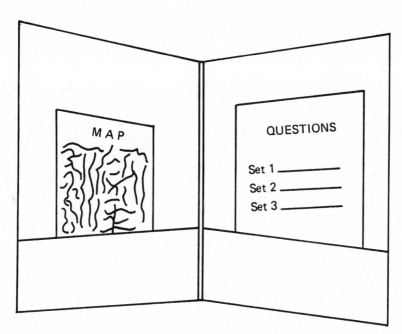

**Figure 3.** Adapted from Wilson and Barnes, 1974.

For self-correction purposes, answers can be placed on the back of the sheet which contains the questions. Three sets of questions are included. They are designed to require the student to locate directly stated facts, interpret what has been read, and to make some application of what has been read.

An example of this activity is a packet dealing with map reading skills. The packet includes a local area map and questions which ask what town is shown, the quickest route from one site to another, and the distance from one site to another.

Brolin (1978) has constructed an extremely useful manual for life centered career education. This 199-page manual provides practical suggestions for teaching daily living skills, personal-social skills, and occupational guidance and preparation.

One example from the manual is that of activities for teaching money identification and change-making skills in a math classroom. Suggestions include:

a. practicing with authentic money
b. constructing money puzzles
c. quizzing with money flashcards
d. constructing money posters with magazine pictures
e. playing structured money games such as monopoly
f. constructing bulletin boards
g. operating a store to practice making change

Halverson (1974) presents a rationale and activities for career development in the elementary school. Included are the following suggestions: for language arts class, children could write essays about their career interests. In arithmetic class, they might work on job-related story problems. In social studies class, they could study occupations in other cultures or in other times.

Gillett (1983) and Turner (1982) suggest the following newspaper activities which could be used in a language arts or social studies class to promote career awareness:

a. Circle all jobs on a given page
b. Label pictures by job category
c. Cut out ads and name all associated jobs
d. Cut out an article and list associated jobs
e. Categorize jobs in want-ads as *jobs I like, jobs I want to learn more about,* and *jobs I don't like*
f. Categorize jobs in want-ads as *indoor/outdoor jobs, jobs requiring experience,* or *seasonal jobs*

g. Students write the ideal job description for an ad they would like to answer.

h. Students look at the sports page to see what kind of jobs (other than athletics) are available at sporting events.

i. Students keep a file of stories about on-the-job accidents and develop a list of job hazards

Finally, Kokaska, Lazar, and Schmidt (1970) provide suggested vocational objectives and corresponding classroom activities appropriate for the regular elementary classroom. The authors deal with two general objectives: the dignity of work and a positive self-concept. They believe that teaching students about the dignity of work is one of the most neglected goals of both regular and special education curriculums. Teachers' and parents' attitudes about specific jobs may interfere with a child's natural curiosity about certain jobs. Thus, children should be taught about the positive attributes of all fields of work, since it is not certain at the elementary level what future occupations children will be best suited for.

Kokaska et al. emphasize the importance of providing children with information that enhances pride, recognition, and reward. They stress that both the teacher and the student should be aware that there are forms of recognition and reward other than a salary. One such positive reward is the feeling that there is a place of importance for an individual within a complex society.

The development of a positive self-concept is also important. The authors suggest that teachers should not only emphasize the *independence* of each worker, but should also endeavor to teach the concept of the *interdependence* of workers. When students recognize that others are as dependent on them as they are on others, the outcome should be an enhanced sense of self-esteem and pride in work.

Kokaska et al. (1970) recommend that teachers ascertain the feeling of students towards various occupations by developing curriculum units that teach children about various occupations. Teachers could then arrange class discussions or have students classify jobs into those they like and those they dislike. At the end of the instructional unit, the teacher could identify and evaluate students' positive and negative responses to determine attitudes that need to be modified to develop more positive student attitudes.

The authors also suggest allotting classroom tasks to enhance self-concepts of handicapped students. Students should be encouraged to undertake tasks which they can achieve successfully. Such tasks might include filing papers, delivering messages, or doing housekeeping chores. A detailed job description can be prepared for each task that includes information about why, how, and when the task must be accomplished. During the initial stages of the task, the teacher should review all of the steps involved in accomplishing the task and walk the student through the entire job. After the student has demonstrated that the task can be successfully performed under the teacher's supervision, the child should be allowed to work independently. Finally, the child might describe the duties of the job to the next student who is assigned the task. As the student achieves self-confidence in task performance and demonstrates improvement, he or she should experience increased self-confidence. Teachers should make students understand that beginning failures in task performance do not affect the teacher's judgment of them, since it takes time and effort to learn to perform a job well. However, the authors caution that teachers should be careful to design classroom tasks so that possibilities of failure are kept to a minimum.

**Resource Classroom Career/Vocational Activities.** Gillett (1983) presents several career/vocational activities that are appropriate for the resource room. She suggests that resource room teachers work individually with students to begin nurturing thoughts about work perferences and future vocational training. She also encourages resource room teachers to relate academics and specific subject areas to the world of work and future careers. Class activities that involve teamwork listening, or following directions are excellent precursors to occupational training. Also, the use of simple written directions, pictorial step-by-step presentations or taped verbal directions provide variety.

Gillett describes procedures for resource room teachers to use to give a career orientation to process training activities. For example, job-related environmental sounds can be used to develop auditory discrimination. Auditory memory can be enhanced through the use of work-related terms, names of careers, and so on. Visual tracking activities might include tracing a bus route from a starting point to a given destination. Finally, grouping specific jobs into job families can be useful classification activity.

Gillett describes other general academic activities that can be given a career education focus including the following:

1. Complete word hunts using career names, tools, etc.
2. Use sequencing cards that show step-by-step procedures necessary to perform a job or carry out a daily living task.

3. Identify vocabulary words in relation to job *products* and job *services*.
4. Compile an *All About Me* notebook that incorporates concepts and skills such as time relationships, prepositional word identification, organizational skills, and sequencing.

Gillett describes numerous other career-related activities for the resource room and for the self-contained classroom. We would refer the interested reader to her excellent article, *It's Elementary! Career Education Activities for Mildly Handicapped Students* (Gillett, 1983).

We have presented a sampling of career-related activities that are appropriate for use in the elementary school classroom. We believe that early training is imperative if mildly handicapped students are to achieve success in the adult world. Since issues related to future adjustment to work and adult living are important and are relevant for all children, handicapped or not, we think that including such activities within the regular elementary curriculum will make academics more relevant for all children who participate in these activities.

## Junior High/Middle School Career/Vocational Programs

According to Brolin, Elliott and Corcoran (1984), the onset of genuine career exploration usually occurs at the junior-high school level. During this period, young people begin to let go of their images and fantasies of adult roles, and begin to take a realistic look at their abilities and interests. These abilities and interests begin to be manifest in hobbies, extra-curricular activities, and part-time jobs. These experiences, in turn, have the effect of fine-tuning individual interests and abilities. Unfortunately, the career development of mildly handicapped junior-high school students may lag behind that of their peers resulting in an obstruction of their career choice process (Bingham, 1978; Brolin, Elliott, & Corcoran, 1984; Mori, 1982).

This transitional career development stage of exploration involves effective use of perceptual, cognitive, and affective abilities. Because they frequently have deficits in these areas, mildly handicapped students may be susceptible to misinterpretation of information relevant to making tentative career choices. The result may be the development of unrealistic tentative choices. Another consequence may be a restricted range of options for exploration. Finally, because of a history of frustration resulting from school failure, many mildly handicapped youngsters may exhibit impulsive, impatient, and uncooperative behavior during the middle years (Bingham, 1981; Brolin, et al., 1984).

Unless substantial career-related experiences have been provided in the elementary grades, teachers at the junior-high/middle-school level will have to create learning situations conducive to developing career awareness in mildly handicapped students. Teachers of junior-high/ middle-school mildly handicapped students should work to develop youngsters' self-confidence, and abilities and assets should be highlighted and emphasized to facilitate healthy career exploration (Brolin, et al., 1984). At this time, a thorough career/vocational assessment is necessary to uncover abilities, interests, and attitudes. Career/ vocational education programming should be designed so that these interests and assets can be developed. Evaluation is also necessary to make junior-high/middle-school students aware of the wide array of occupational and personal options available to them. Finally, hands-on work-related experiences in the community can make students further aware of available employment options.

Just as a well-designed career/vocational program during the elementary school years prepares mildly handicapped students for the career exploration stage during the middle school years, a similar program is necessary before students can be successful in the career preparation stage that usually occurs at the high school level.

## High School Career/Vocational Programs

According to Brolin et al. (1984), many mildly handicapped students find the high school curriculum complex, and their academic skill development often plateaus at this time. However, if satisfactory career awareness and career exploration has been accomplished, the mildly handicapped high school student is ready to begin career preparation for eventual competitive employment. During this time, students become more knowledgeable about their individual interests and abilities. Coursework should include more than just work-related activities. Components of the high-school curriculum should also include information pertaining to adult life-roles of family member, community involvement, avocational activities, and personal-social responsibilities.

Those students desiring to obtain employment after high school graduation should be offered coursework that provides specific-skill training and plenty of hands-on work experience activities. To achieve this goal, special and vocational educators must work together to see that regular vocational education programs are available to mildly handicapped students. Vocational educators should communicate what competencies students need to successfully complete their courses, and special educators should provide information pertaining to ways in which vocational education courses can be modified to meet the needs of handicapped students.

Finally, for those mildly handicapped students who have the ability and desire to pursue post-secondary educations, the high school curriculum should include instruction in coping and study skills.

There are many books and articles that describe secondary career/vocational education curriculums (Kokaska & Brolin, 1985; Collier & Bruno, 1984; Cummings & Maddux, 1985; Edge & Burton, 1986; Kronick, 1978; Stephens & Confar, 1984; Vautour, Stocks, & Kolek, 1983). However, in light of the recent emphasis on the integration of handicapped students into the regular vocational education program, we will present a secondary curriculum approach that teaches those skills needed for locating, securing, and maintaining employment (Brody-Hasazi, Salembier, & Finck, 1983). Generic skills essential to living and working independently such as functional reading and computational skills, personal management, and social skills are included as curriculum components. The program requires that special and vocational educators work together to ensure that students benefit from a program that is consistent with individual skills, interests, and future work environments.

The following objectives provide a framework for planning and evaluating the curriculum from a student-centered and from a programmatic perspective:

## 1. Student-Centered Objectives

A. Assessment procedures should be developed to identify abilities and interests that are related to current and future training and employment opportunities in the community. Personal perference inventories, parent interviews, and direct observation are often the best ways to collect relevant information. In areas of demonstrated interest, students could be taught to reach criterion performance levels on simulated or actual job tasks in either school or community training sites. Work-related skills can be assessed by collecting daily measures on attendance, productivity, and time required to reach criterion performance.

B. Provide necessary support services to ensure access to mainstream vocational classes. Special educators should be responsible for making information available to vocational educators about strategies that have proven to be effective in mainstreaming handicapped students into regular academic programs. These strategies include cooperative learning, peer tutoring, and learning strategies. If cooperative efforts are going to be successful, school administration should provide needed support services such as resources to provide for curriculum development and adaptation, and time for special and vocational teachers to plan together.

C. Provide several work experiences, six to eight weeks each, in identified areas of interests and abilities for high school students. Many handicapped students do not have adequate career exploration experiences. Thus, from the time they enter high school, they should be provided with plenty of work experiences based on identified interests. Such experiences allow for assessment of student performance in a variety of work environments as well as providing the student with information about adequate training opportunities. Options might include in-school work experience, community work experience, and finally, on-the-job experiences where student aptitudes and interests are matched with income-producing jobs.

D. Assist the student in locating and securing employment prior to graduation. The authors recommend *The Job Counselor's Manual* (Azrin & Besalel, 1981) as a systematic approach for teaching job search skills such as identifying and contacting potential employers and resume preparation. The program can be adapted for use by students with severe reading and written expression deficits. The program is unique in that students are trained to engage in job-seeking activities themselves rather than depending on a work-experience coordinator or job developer to find the jobs for them. Brody-Hasazi et al. (1983) believe that this approach may be more effective for mildly handicapped students. They also believe that the skills they acquire in the process will be generalizable to future job-seeking efforts.

E. Provide supervision and follow-up services to students in full-time or part-time employment until graduation (or the student's twenty-second birthday). These services may be necessary for students working both part-time and full-time. The length of time needed for continuing follow-up services depends on adjustment and performance of the student. The specific nature of the follow-up services for each student should be determined with both the employer and with the student. For some students, it may be necessary to work closely with the student and with the employer to ensure that the originally agreed upon job expectations are being met by both parties.

Rusch and Mithaug (1980) identify the functions of follow-up as (a) identifying problems, (b) providing on-the-job intervention, (c) seeking validation, (d) intervention, (e) fading follow-up checks, and (f) evaluating adjustment. Rusch and Mithaug also developed a work performance evaluation form to measure three broad areas they consider critical to job retention: social skills, vocational skills, and special considerations.

G. Work with agencies such as vocational rehabilitation, community colleges, state employment services and the like to develop individual transition plans for students who need continued service after high school graduation. The transitional plan should be developed jointly by vocational and special educators, parents, the student, and appropriate adult service workers. The plan should be written at least eighteen months before graduation, and it should be updated every six months. Components of the plan should include future residential and employment options, services needed to successsfully achieve these options, names of agency representatives who will be working with students to achieve outcomes, and a description of and timelines of completion of the activities. In addition, a teacher should be assigned as the school-based case manager to serve as an advocate for the student with adult service providers.

## 2. Program-Centered Objectives

A. Provide flexible teacher schedules to meet training and monitoring needs of students placed in community settings. If student-centered objectives are going to be successfully developed and implemented, then teachers should have time for program development and to supervise community training activities. Some teachers may have to work afternoons and early evenings, or early mornings and afternoons if a student has a job placement that does not correspond with regular school hours. Also, teachers will need time to develop programs, and plan monitoring and training strategies appropriate for the various work environments in which students are placed.

B. Design and implement a follow-up evaluation process. Following graduation, students should be contacted to determine employment status, use of social services, relationship of school vocational preparation to actual employment experiences, and other relevant information. A teacher designed as case manager should be responsible for contacting students and/or parents six months, one year, and eighteen months after the student graduates.

C. Develop a system for identifying all handicapped students who need vocational components included in their IEPs prior to those students entering secondary school. Such a system could serve as an initial screening and planning vehicle to identify specific resources needed by each mildly handicapped student requiring a vocational program in the high school.

According to Brody-Hasazi et al. (1983), to be successful, this program will require administrative support, inservice training for special and vocational education teachers, intensive parental involvement, community cooperation, and interagency collaboration. They state that "our challenge as educators is to shape the existing service delivery systems so that vocational education and training can be delivered in a way which meets the needs of mildly handicapped students in the 1980s" (p. 209).

## SUMMARY

In this chapter, we have provided several recommendations for changes in public school career/vocational education programs including (a) developing programs from the elementary grades through high school and beyond; (b) the need for teacher-training institutions and state departments of education to provide certification in secondary as well as in elementary special education; (c) the need to combine the expertise of special and vocational educators; (d) teaching social and independent living skills from elementary through high school; (e) the need to train mildly handicapped students for nonstereotypic occupations; (f) educating parents to plan realistically for their mildly handicapped children; and (g) developing theory-based, empirically-validated career/vocational education programs. Of these seven recommendations, we consider the need to develop theory-based, empirically-based K-12 career/vocational education programs of greatest importance. We believe that once this is accomplished, we can intervene early with appropriate programming. As a result, mildly handicapped youngsters should begin to make valid career choices by the time they enter junior high school, and be ready for actual work experiences in occupations suited to their interests and abilities by the time they enter high school. By the time they leave high school, these students will be so well-prepared for work that the need for transitional services will be minimal.

Chapter Eight

# TRANSITION AND POSTSECONDARY
# RECOMMENDATIONS

THROUGHOUT this book, we have emphasized the fact that many mildly handicapped individuals are not making satisfactory post-school adjustments. Although estimates vary greatly, it appears that between 50 and 75 percent of all disabled people are unemployed (Wehman, Kregel, & Barcus, 1985). Hasazi, Gordon, and Roe (1985) reported on postschool employment status of 462 handicapped individuals and found 55 percent had jobs. No severely or profoundly handicapped persons were included in the study. In addition, even for those who were employed, the nature of their work was cause for concern. Bellamy (1985) commented on their jobs:

> A significant part of this employed group were in seasonal, part-time, or intermittent jobs with many working below the minimum wage. The employment picture that emerges depicts a high level of joblessness; those who do find work often participate in the secondary or marginal work force where wages, job security, advancement, opportunities, and benefits are traditionally low. (p. 475)

In a similar vein, White (1985) studied 50 learning disabled and 50 nonlearning disabled young adults and found equal proportions were employed. However, he also reported:

> LD young adults were employed in jobs with significantly lower social status than the NLD young adults. LD young adults expressed significantly greater dissatisfaction with their employment situation than their NLD counterparts. LD young adults expressed significantly lower aspirations for future education or training than NLD young adults. (p. 232)

We feel strongly that much of the cause for these adjustment problems can be traced to the lack of good vocational transition programs.

Wehman, Kregel, and Barcus (1985) have defined *vocational transition:*

Vocational transition is a carefully planned process, which may be intitiated
either by school personnel or adult service providers, to establish and implement a plan for either employment or additional vocational training of a
handicapped student who will graduate or leave school in three to five years;
such a process must involve special educators, vocational educators, parents
and/or the student, an adult service system representative, and possibly an
employer. (p. 26)

We like this definition, but we would like to make one qualifying statement: *No transitional program, regardless of its comprehensive nature or high
quality, will be successful with large numbers of handicapped students unless career
and vocational education has been provided during the elementary years, preferably
beginning at kindergarten and continuing throughout the elementary grades.* Although the current interest in transitional issues is healthy, there is one
potential problem. We must not become so focussed on developing services in secondary schools that we lose sight of the importance of ensuring high-quality career and vocational educational services throughout the grades.

## THE CURRENT INTEREST IN TRANSITIONAL PROGRAMS

Transition became a popular topic soon after the publication of a
number of reports on the status of education in America. As a response
to the depressing statistics relating to postschool adjustment of the handicapped, a number of Federal laws and policies came into being. These
initiatives addressed transition from school to independent living.

Especially influential was the publication of *Unfinished Agenda*
(National Commission on Secondary Vocational Education, 1984). This
report was a reply to one of the more influential (and critical) reports on
American education, and outline several areas in need of development
including:

1. Personal skills and attitudes.
2. Communication and computational skills.
3. Employability skills.
4. Broad and specific occupational skills.
5. Foundation for career plannig and lifelong learning. (West, 1985)

Also in 1984, Madeline Will, Assistant Secretary of the Offices of
Special Education and Rehabilitative Services (OSERS), made a

number of statements responding to the need for establishing a national priority on improving transition from school to working life for individuals with disabilities (Will, 1984a, 1984b, 1984c, 1984d).

In these documents, Will states that the time has come to launch "the second stage of a revolution — an enormous effort to create or totally reorganize a system of services for disabled people in our nation" (Will, 1984a, p. 11). She goes on to say:

> The major challenge we face is not primarily one of limited resources. It is rather a question of will and character, both of which I think Americans have in ample supply. The major challenge to special education in the next decade is to *will* the means to accomplish our ends. One of these involves looking beyond traditional services boundaries to collaboration among human service delivery systems. (p. 12)

In discussion interagency cooperation, she goes on to say:

> Experience has taught me that the service delivery systems at the state and local level cannot be integrated without further effort to coordinate entitlement and discretionary programs for the disabled through the federal government. The Office of Special Education and Rehabilitative Services, or OSERS, was created as a single agency to bring special education and adult rehabilitation programs together in one department. Although these programs are now housed in one department, much more work needs to be done to achieve full functional integration of these two components of OSERS. We need partnership, not only between the Office of Special Education and the Rehabilitation Services Administration, but with government at every level, with the private sector, and as well with the community of disabled citizens. (p. 12)

Will goes on to make the point that Part C of the reauthorization of The Education of the Handicapped Act established a new priority:

> To strengthen and coordinate education, training, and support services for handicapped youth in order to foster their effective transition from school to the adult world of work and independent living. (Will, 1984a, p. 12)

Will then identifies specific problems she sees in meeting the goals she has identified:

> Let me identify and discuss four barriers I see to the achievement of our ultimate goals. These barriers, which disabled Americans know well are not primarily physical, are intellectual, moral, organizational, statutory, and regulatory. They involve problems of inadequate and inaccurate communications. I challenge special educators (and commit OSERS) to breaking down these four artificial barriers in the next decade.
>     1. The barrier between special and regular education.
>     2. The barrier to full integration of handicapped individuals in a heterogenous society.

3. The barrier between the nursery and the school.
4. The barrier between the school and the work place.
   (Will, 1984a p. 12)

She then addresses each of these barriers and makes specific suggestions for how to overcome them. With regard to the barrier most relevant to transition (barrier four), she makes the point that a prime goal of education is to make the student qualified for employment. However, she asserts that "joblessness, rather than employment, is the norm among persons who have disabilities." (Will, 1984a, p. 15) To remove this barrier, we must also remove related barriers to independent living, transportation, and worthy use of leisure time.

She then makes a series of specific recommendations related to transition. First, Will suggests that we must improve the curriculum of the secondary school and make it more relevant to the realities of the work place. Therefore, there must be an appropriate balance between academics, vocational education, and independent learning skills. She asks a number of questions related to curriculum development in the secondary school:

> Should there be a concentrated effort to increase the speed at which tasks are performed by handicapped students? How much teaching time should be devoted to improving social behavior or time management? What can be done to ensure that handicapped youngsters are not forced into vocational education when alternatives are preferable and desirable, or forced to make career choices long before their nonhandicapped peers are required to do so? Lastly, what implcation does the development of new and, perhaps different, secondary and transitional models have for our personnel preparation policies? (Will, 1984a, p. 15)

Will's second suggestion is that we must improve post-secondary services. With regard to these improvements, she says:

> The array of post-secondary services available in any community should be broad enough to enable each student with a disability to enter employment, either immediately after leaving school, or after a period of further education or adult services. Like other citizens, people with disabilities should have access to appropriate educational opportunities that are relevant to individual interests and to the job market. Community colleges, vocational-technical schools, and other institutions of higher education can respond by reducing barriers to participation, developing relevant programs, and providing needed accomodation. (Will, 1984a, pp. 15-16)

In addition, she suggests that incentives must be developed for employers. These incentives would encourage employers to support the excess costs involved in hiring handicapped workers.

# THE OSERS TRANSITION PLAN

Eventually, Will presented more specific plans for the Federal initiative towards transition (Will, 1984b, 1984c, 1984d). Although specific elements of this plan have been called a "model" (Halpern, 1985), we do not agree with such a designation. As we discussed in Chapter Six, a true model must be based upon a theoretical framework. We do not find an underlying theory in the OSERS plan, and we do not, therefore, refer to it a a "model." As we review the OSERS material in this chapter, we shall refer to it as the OSERS *plan*.

Will (1984d) defines transition:

> The transition from school to working life is an outcome-oriented process encompassing a broad array of services and experiences that lead to employment. Transition is a period that includes high school, the point of graduation, additional post-secondary education or adult services, and the initial years in employment. Transition is a bridge between the security and structure offered by the school and the opportunities and risks of adult life. Any bridge requires both a solid span and a secure foundation at either end. The transition from school to work and adult life requires sound preparation in the secondary school, adequate support at the point of school leaving, and secure opportunities and services, if needed, in adult situations. (p. 3)

Will then specifies three assumptions that underlie the OSERS transition approach. The first of these is that the array of post school services is extremely complex. The simplicity and relative consistency of services provided by public school is replaced by complex, confusing, and widely diverse services and service-providers in the community. She asserts that this complex system is necessary to meet diverse needs of handicapped individuals, but that appropriate and diverse combinations of services and opportunities must be developed to effect successful transition of handicapped people.

The second assumption is that all handicapped individuals should receive transition consideration. Will estimates that this includes at least 250,000 to 300,000 students.

The third assumption is that sustained employment is an important outcome of education and transition for all citizens. Therefore, the OSERS goal is that all handicapped students who leave the school system will obtain employent either immediately, or after appropriate post-school training. Although paid employment is important, there should also be emphasis on social, personal, leisure, and other adult roles. Thus, another way to assess the success of transitional programs is to evalute the degree to which handicapped individuals are integrated into the total community. Paid employment is seen as promoting community integration since the workplace itself should be integrated, and since salaries earned provide buying power to purchase integration.

Will (1984b, 1984c, 1984d) presents a five-part conceptual framework for transition represented through a simple graphic (see Figure 4).

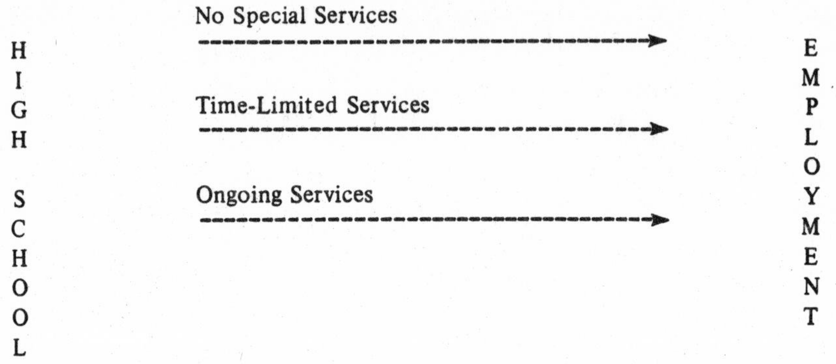

```
H          No Special Services                              E
I          ------------------------------------------>      M
G                                                           P
H          Time-Limited Services                            L
                                                            O
           ------------------------------------->           Y
S          Ongoing Services                                 Y
C          ------------------------------------->           M
H                                                           E
O                                                           N
O                                                           T
L
```

**Figure 4**

Will refers to the high school as the *Foundation* of the transitional program. The high school provides "the foundation in skills, attitudes, personal relationships, and often, employer contacts that determines much of the success of later transition" (Will, 1984d, p. 4). She emphasizes the importance of special education acting in concert with vocational education and other school-based services to ensure that students leave school with entry level job skills appropriate for their particular community. The degree of integration of handicapped with nonhandicapped students and the importance of good counseling services are also emphasized.

The upper-most arrow, labeled *No Special Services,* refers to those students who move from high school to employment. These individuals require only those post-school services that are available to all citizens, whether handicapped or nonhandicapped, although some special accommodations may need to be made to meet their needs. These services would include postsecondary education provided by agencies such as community colleges, vocational and technical schools, and four-year institutions of higher education.

The middle arrow, labeled *Time-Limited Services,* include those temporary sevices that lead to employment. These are specialized, short-term services such as those supplied by vocational rehabilitation, post-secondary vocational education and other job training programs. Qualification for these services usually involve documenting the presence of a handicapping condition. These services are usually extended only to those clients thought capable of *making it on their own* after the short-term services is completed.

The bottom arrow, labeled *Ongoing Services* refers to a relatively new concept often called *supported employment*. Will asserts that the revolutionary aspects of this concept is that in the past, ongoing services were generally not aimed at employment and were actually an alternative to work. She further describes this new concept:

> The alternative proposed here is employment with whatever ongoing support is necessary to maintain that employment. For example, an individual using this bridge from school to working life might leave school and obtain employment as part of a small team of disabled individuals in an electronics manufacturing plant where the state agency responsible for ongoing services pays the company for a work supervisor. (Will, 1984d, p. 5)

In describing supported employment environments, Will suggests that industry could accommodate small teams of handicapped workers receiving publicly supported supervision. Another alternative might be a variety of jobs in a community, each of which hire only one handicapped worker. In such an arrangement, a publicly supported supervisor would rotate from site to site. Mobile crews working in community settings and former day programs operating successful businesses and employing handicapped workers are other alternatives.

Will discusses changes that must take place in employment, the target of all the efforts in the program. She makes the point that nothing will work without a variety of employment opportunities for handicapped workers. She asserts that such opportunities must be stimulated by family and neighborhood networks. In addition, problems related to minimum wage, incentives to employers, equal opportunity, and structural unemployment must be solved.

Will then outlines OSERS action in each of the five components of the transition program. Research, development, demonstration, and replication are planned to improve the secondary school foundation. She outlines some specific areas:

> Particular interests include: renewed efforts to develop cooperative programs with vocational education and vocational rehabilitation to serve all students with disabilities; improvement of community-based job training and placement within the school's vocational preparation program; and de-

velopment of service models for all students that allow regular and frequent contact with nondisabled peers. (Will, 1984d, p. 5)

She also discusses the OSERS role in post secondary education. She asserts that OSERS will attempt to stimulate research and program development in community colleges and vocational technical schools.

The OSERS role in time-limited services is to stimulate cooperation between special education, vocational education, and vocational rehabilitation. In addition, OSERS will strive to promote appropriate changes in on-site job training and placement programs.

To improve ongoing services, OSERS will provide initiatives to encourage states to change from day activity programs to work alternatives. OSERS will provide competitive grants to state agencies to pay for inservice training, program development and demonstration, and other start-up activities.

To improve employment opportunities, OSERS will promote interagency agreements. In addition, incentives will be provided to employers to make employment opportunities available to handicapped workers who need special equipment, building modifications, longer training periods, etc.

In addition, OSERS will attempt to promote research into transition to determine the numbers of handicapped individuals who find employment by each of the three bridges (no special services, time-limited services, and ongoing services). Other OSERS efforts will concentrate on "disseminating effective practices, providing assistance to states, and building the capacity of the professional community to deliver improved services." (Will, 1984d, p. 6)

## HALPERN'S TRANSITION PLAN

The OSERS plan, as illustrated by the graphic, emphasizes that employment is the primary goal of transition. This fact has generated some criticism. Halpern (1985) has evaluated the OSERS program and finds fault with the single-minded emphasis on paid employment. Although Halpern admits that the OSERS documents pay lip service to other dimensions of adult adjustment, he feels they are underemphasized and valued only for their contribution to employment potential:

What the authors of this policy seem to be suggesting is that the nonvocational dimensions of adult adjustment are significant and important only in so far as they contribute to the ultimate goal of employment. Such a position can be challenged both philosophically and empirically. (Halpern, 1985, p. 480)

Halpern goes on to suggest that the OSERS program should be modified so that *Community Adjustment,* rather than *Employment* is the ultimate goal of transition. Community adjustment is conceived as being buttressed by three pillars. These three pillars are actually the components of community adjustment and consist of *quality of the residential environment, adequacy of the person's social and interpersonal network,* and *employment.* Halpern goes to special pains to point out that in this approach, employment is no more important than the other two aspects of community adjustment, and suggests that if any of the three pillars are inadequate, "then the entire structure is in danger of collapse, and a person's ability to live in the community is threatened." (Halpern, 1985, p. 481)

Halpern accepts the OSERS description of problems and issues inherent in employment. He goes on to describe the second category of community adjustment: the quality of the residential environment:

> The second pillar of residential environment is equally complex. In addition to the satisfactoriness of a person's actual home, one must also consider the quality and safety of the neighborhood in which the home is located as well as the availability of both community services and recreation opportunities within reasonable proximity to the home. (Halpern, 1985, p. 481)

Halpern goes on to say that the third pillar, social and interpersonal networks, may be the most important of all. He describes it as follows:

> It includes major dimensions of human relationships such as daily communications, self-esteem, family support, emotional maturity, friendship, and intimate relationships. (Halpern, 1985, p. 481)

We agree that social and interpersonal networks enjoyed by the handicapped person are extremely important. A recent study by Schalock, Wolzen, Ross, Elliott, Werbel, and Peterson (1986) has provided data in support of this assertion. These researchers studied 108 learning disabled and retarded students who had graduated from a rural high school employing a community-based job exploration and training model. Nineteen predictor variables were studied to determine relationships to 11 employment-related outcome variables. One of three predictor variables found to be consistently related to the nine major outcome variables was level of family involvement. (The other two were number of semester hours in vocational programs and type of handicap.)

Halpern asserts that the OSERS model implies that success in employment will lead to success in the other two *pillars* or categories of community adjustment. He provides data from his own research showing that such is not necessarily the case. Halpern spent three years studying mentally retarded people living semi-independently in four Western states. He gathered data on employment status, satisfaction with work, neighborhood quality, neighborhood safety, family support, and social support.

He then constructed an intercorrelation matrix using these variables. Only one of the fourteen correlations were significant (family support with social support, r = .20, p < .05). All other correlations were nonsignificant and ranged from .00 to only .09. Halpern concluded that these variables were generally not related to one another:

> In other words, success in one area was often unrelated to success in either of the others. This means that successful programmatic efforts aimed at a single dimension of community adjustment are not necessarily going to produce improvements along the other dimensions. If our three-dimensional model is correct, this also means that success along only one or even two dimensions is not likely to be sufficient to support the desired goal of community adjustment. Programs will need to be directed *specifically* toward *each* dimension, with client needs determining the selection of specific services. (Halpern, 1985, p. 482)

The apparent discrepancy between the Halpern (1985) and the Schalock et al. (1986) findings are probably due to the fact that the former study examined individual correlation coefficients, while the latter employed multiple regression analysis. Thus, family support *by itself* may not be powerful enough to significantly influence variables such as current employment, living and financial status, but is extremely important when combined with other important variables such as student's handicap, days absent during school, gender, semester hours in vocational programs, and school enrollment.

Halpern (1985) goes on to present some additional findings from his study of secondary special education programs (Halpern & Benz, 1984; Benz & Halpern, 1986). This study was a survey of special education teachers, special education administrators, and parents of handicapped high school students in Oregon. The survey addressed a number of issues, several of which are relevant to the issue of transition programs.

Of particular interest was the finding that less than 50 percent of parents of handicapped secondary students reported that their children actually received instruction in vocational preparation, functional academics, home living skills, and community living skills. In addition, half of the teachers surveyed identified vocational education and community living instruction as areas in need of improvement. Indeed, vocational education was identified by teachers as the area of the curriculum *most* in need of improvement. Halpern (1985) summarizes his findings concerning vocational education:

> Several signs became evident quickly that all was not well in the vocational education of students with disabilities. In most specific areas of vocational education, such as service occupations or machine trades, half or more of the special education teachers indicated that instruction was not available to their students. Nearly one-quarter of the teachers stated that they had *no* involvement in the vocational education of their students. One-third of the teachers reported that vocational evaluation services were not available to *any* of their students. Not surprisingly, vocational education was identified by both teachers and parents as the curriculum area most in need of improvement. (p. 484)

In our experience, one of the most important and influential variables in providing good transition programs is the degree to which interagency collaboration and coordination is achieved. Halpern found support fo this assertion when he asked teachers to identify the weakest areas of their programs. Almost half of the respondents identified clear assignment of the responsibility for coordination of vocational and special education.

The need for improvement in this area is demonstrated by responses to another question on the survey relating to cooperation and coordination. When administrators were asked who had the responsibility for such coordination, 60 percent indicated that it was the responsibility of the special education teacher. Only about 30% of special education teachers, however, indicated that they were responsible for coordination, and fully 20% said no one had this responsibility. Clearly, cooperation and coordination of special education and vocational education is an important area in need of development.

In evaluating the OSERS program and Halpern's criticism of it, we are forced to agree that the OSERS approach seems too narrowly focussed on employment and neglectful of personal-social skills needed for independent living. We would never undervalue the importance of employment. However, we have known handicapped individuals who were able to sustain gainful employment, but were unhappy and maladapted individuals because they were unable to establish the social and interpersonal networks needed for self-fulfillment. We have also known successfully employed handicapped individuals who were relatively well-adjusted in terms of personal-social contacts, but who were unable to live independently because they lacked certain self-help skills such as cooking, housecleaning, etc.

Indeed, an ACLD survey of adult learning disabled individuals found that 52 percent were employed. However, 71 percent were being supported by their parents. We are just completing a study of learning disabled adults, and we have found significantly more of these individuals are living at home than are nonlearning disabled individuals matched by age, sex, and socio-economic status. Furthermore, most of these young adults would prefer to maintain their own living quarters if they were able.

We therefore support a more comprehensive approach to transition that strives to develop diverse competencies in handicapped persons. The goals of such a transition program include gainful employment and all other competencies and skills needed to promote attainment of an independent and productive life style leading to excellent mental and physical health.

## THE CARL D. PERKINS VOCATIONAL EDUCATION ACT

Another important Federal initiative with implications for transitional concerns is PL98-523, the Carl D. Perkins Vocational Education Act, which was signed into law on October 19, 1984 and became active as of July, 1985. The law is intended to make vocational education programs accessible to the handicapped and sets aside 10 percent of the federal money allocated under the act to be used to provide services to the handicapped. In addition, the law requires that the states match this 10% and use the money only for the excess costs involved in providing vocational education to handicapped individuals.

The law is fairly complex and has been more fully addressed in a previous chapter of this book. One requirement of the law that is relevant to the present discussion has been summarized by Vinup (1986):

> Guidance, counseling, and career development activities along with services designed to facilitate the transition from school to employment shall be provided by professionally trained counselors in the field. Grants to states under the act shall be used for programs to improve, expand, and extend career guidance and counseling programs and for activities to ensure that these programs are accessible to the handicapped. (p. 18)

The act also requires joint planning and coordination with a number of previously established federally funded programs. The law also requires that vocational goals and objectives be included in the special education student's IEP, that handicapped students be given vocational education in the least restrictive environment practicable, and that careful records be kept of data such as the number of handicapped students served by specific vocational education programs.

## WEHMAN'S APPROACH TO VOCATIONAL TRANSITION

Wehman, Kregel, and Barcus (1985) have presented another approach to vocational transition. These authors also call their approach a *model,* although like other approaches, it too lacks a coherent theoretical foundation.

We quoted these authors' definition of transition at the beginning of this chapter. It is reproduced at this point for convenience:

> Vocational transition is a carefully planned process, which may be initiated either by school personnel or adult service providers, to establish and implement a plan for either employment or additional vocational training of a handicapped student who will graduate or leave school in three to five years; such a process must involve special educators, vocational educators, parents and/or the student, an adult service system representative, and possibly an employer. (Wehman, Kregrel, & Barcus, 1985, p. 26)

We said earlier that we find this definition acceptable, although we emphasized that in our opinion, no transitional program will be effective unless career and vocational education is begun early in elementary school.

Wehman et al. (1985) go on to enumerate the assumptions implicit in the definition:

> The key aspects of this definition are that (a) members of multiple disciplines and service delivery systems must participate, (b) parental involvement is essential, (c) vocational transition planning must occur well before 21 years of age, (d) the process must be planned and systematic, and (e) the vocational service provided must be of a quality nature. (p. 26)

Wehman includes three steps or stages in his transition plan: (a) school instruction, (b) planning for transition, and (c) job placement.

The authors express a concern that is similar to our concern that the emphasis on transition in secondary schools may cause the field to lose sight of the importance of ensuring high-quality career and vocational education services throughout the school grades:

With the increased federal emphasis on transition, it is essential that service providers and agencies do not focus exclusively on the transition process while ignoring the quality of the foundation services offered by public schools and the range of vocational alternatives offered by community agencies. Previous efforts at interagency agreements which purported to ameliorate transition problems actually resulted, in all too many cases, in movement of a student from one inadequate school program to another inadequate adult program. (Wehman, Kregel, & Barcus, 1985, p. 27)

We agree fully. Transition is not a program that can be developed and refined in isolation. Secondary programs are based on elementary programs and post-secondary programs rely on elementary and secondary programs to build prerequisite skills.

The problem of overemphasis on transition is related to a problem we discussed in an earlier chapter. At that time, we referred to the transitory nature of popular issues in special education and the fact that some researchers move so rapidly from topic to topic that little progress is made in one area before it is abandoned and replaced with another. In the past, federal officials have been too quick to respond to the vagaries of fashion and to move grant monies from one *in* problem to another. This has resulted in sporadic, on-again, off-again research and a discipline where a little is known about many topics, but where very few topics have been explored in depth.

These problems have been further aggravated by declining enrollments and attendant financial crises on many university campuses. This has led to the establishment of a cadre of new academic entrepreneurs in many institutions. Many such professionals, often supported wholly or in part by Federal *soft money*, spend most of their energy attempting to anticipate the next *hot topic* in order to be the first applicants for associated funding. These individuals are little more than academic hustlers who care little or none at all about the topics they are funded to research or the programs they are funded to demonstrate. They and their institutions judge success not on the quality of their discoveries, but on the dollar amounts of grants obtained. Money is no longer a means to make possible the investigation of important topics. It is important only for its own sake. The means to an end has itself become the end.

One of the authors was once a professor at a university where the dean of the college called a meeting to discuss "the possibility of obtaining a large research grant in special education." When the dean was asked what he desired to research, he replied that he really wasn't concerned about the topic, only about the amount of money that could be obtained.

Such attitudes are not likely to contribute to a sophisticated, longitudinal research base that can be used to generate new theories or refine existing ones.

The topic of transition is the current *hot topic* in special education and related fields. That will not be destructive in and of itself, if the Federal Government and individual researchers resist the urge to abandon this topic in a year or two when another issue comes into vogue.

Wehman, Kregel, and Barcus (1985) move from their warning concerning the danger of focussing too narrowly on transition, to an explanation of their transition proposal. They provide a graphic representation of their program. However, we find the drawing to be confusing, and we prefer to convert it to outline form as follows:

I. Stage I. Secondary School Instruction
   A. Functional Curriculum
   B. Integration with Nonhandicapped Peers
   C. Community-Based Instructional Model of School Services

II. Stage II. Planning for Transition
   A. Individualized Transition Plan
     1. Specifies Transition Responsibilities
     2. Characterized by Early Planning
     3. Created with Appropriate Input
       a. Parent
       b. Student
     4. Interagency Cooperation Required
       a. School
       b. Rehabilitation
       c. Adult Day Program
       d. Voc-Technical Center

III. Stage III. Meaningful Employment
   A. Competitive Employment
   B. Work Crews/Enclaves
   C. Specialized Sheltered Work Arrangements
   D. Follow-up 1-2 Years Later

In discussion of Stage One, Wehman et al. (1985) suggest that the three components of functional curriculum, integrated schools, and community-based service delivery have been derived from research on effective secondary school programs. The functional curriculum is designed to prepare students for jobs actually existing in the community and calls for continuous assessment of community opportunities. The functional curriculum begins early in elementary school and continues throughout the grades.

Integrated schools are necessary and appropriate because most handicapped students will be working in community positions alongside non-handicapped peers. Also included in this concept is the importance of early and frequent exposure to natural work settings. This is not only beneficial to the student, but works to sensitize future employers to the feasibility of hiring handicapped workers.

Community-based instruction is important because handicapped workers require many opportunities to practice job skills in real work environments. Failure to provide real work environments is a common cause of job failure.

Stage Two is the planning component of the transition program. As can be seen from the outline above, this stage produces a formal individualized transition plan produced with input from the parents and the student. The plan calls for interagency cooperation. It is a written plan and specifies services both before and after graduation. The plan should include long term goals and short term objectives. Wehman, Kregel, and Barcus (1985) describe the individualized transition plan:

> Students must also be prepared to effectively use community services, manage their money, travel to and from work independently, and interact socially with other individuals. Plans must address all these skill areas to meet the comprehensive needs of handicapped students. Plans should also be individualized. . . . In addition, transition plans should identify who is responsible for initiating and following through on each specified activity. (p. 30)

The individual transition plan should be longitudinal and should first be developed four years prior to graduation and modified once each year. The transition plan should be considered part of the student's regular IEP and after leaving school could become part of his or her Individual Written Rehabilitation Plan.

A systematic parent education program is also advocated as a means of improving the potential of appropriate parental input. This program should include parental meetings designed to orient parents to community agencies and their diverse responsibilities, and prepare parents to work with these agencies. Parental visitations to service agencies are also recommended.

Wehman et al. (1985) also emphasize the importance of interagency collaboration and agreements but suggest that such agreements have not historically been beneficial. Various problems such as *turf protection* and attitudinal problems are identified. Solutions to these problems are suggested and include information exchanges, staff development restructuring of services to avoid duplication, and joint planning.

We agree that the lack of effective interagency collaboration and agreements are a major barrier to effective transition programs. We have been involved in a number of committees and meetings aimed at securing such cooperation and have seldom seen them succeed. A parent who served on such a committee once summed up the problem well when she signed "These meetings always seem to end up with each representative explaining why they are not responsible for the needed services."

Wehman et al. (1985) then discuss a variety of employment options. These include competitive employment, competitive employment with support, enclaves in industry, and specialized industrial training.

> With regard to supported employment, they explain: A supported work approach to competitive employment emphasizes structured assistance in job placement and job site training. A job coordinator is extensively available for individualized one-to-one training and follow-up. A strong focus of this model is helping individuals *maintain* their jobs. (p. 32)

Sheltered enclaves consist of small groups of handicapped workers who work in business and industry under daily supervision by some agency specialist. This arrangement often makes it possible for some handicapped workers who have previously been able to work only in segregated sheltered workshops to succeed in an integrated, natural work setting.

The final recommendation is that school districts institute a follow-up procedure that checks on every graduate of their program at least every two to three years. The results of the follow-up should be presented to the school board and to the state agency.

# A COMPARISON OF THE HALPERN, WEHMAN, AND OSERS PLANS

Both the Halpern and Wehman plans are broader than the OSERS plan in that both attach more importance to personal-social skills, self-help skills, and other competencies other than those directly applicable to employment. The OSERS plan implies that attaining successful employment will lead automatically to attainment of other competencies, while the Halpern and Wehman plans assume that other such competencies must be taught directly.

Perhaps the more narrow OSERS focus is understandable in light of the current Federal climate encouraging economy and cut-backs in social programs. If cost-saving is viewed as the main goal of a transitional program, then employment emerges as the natural aim of such programs.

We approve of the OSERS emphasis on transition, but we prefer the Halpern and Wehman approaches. We believe the strength of the Halpern plan is the equal emphasis on employment, social and interpersonal networks, and the residential environment with success in all three leading to community adjustment. The strengths of the Wehman plan are the written individualized transition plan, the creative variety of employment options, and the emphasis on the importance of follow-up activities. All three plans acknowledge the importance of interagency cooperation and agreements, though none of the three provide effective solutions to this very difficult problems.

The weakness of all three approaches is the absence of a theoretical base. Furthermore, there is little research cited as evidence for the specifics of any of the plans. Clinical experience seems to have been the main guide for the authors of all three approaches.

We believe that clinical experience is a necessary but not sufficient guide for those who would build educational programs. Clinical experience should be engaged in with theory and research helping to determine action. The action is then further modified as research tests the efficacy of various theoretically-derived alternatives. Actually, the whole process feeds on itself with each of the three components of theory, research, and clinical experience acting to refine and improve each other.

The problem with programs based only on clinical experience is that progress is painfully slow since trial and error is the main problem solving strategy. Choosing which alternative plan of action to use is another problem whenever difficulties arise which have not been previously experienced.

Greenan, Miller, and White (1985) have conducted a study that has relevance for the present discussion. These researchers conducted a survey to identify problems that need to be addressed through research and development. These problems are related to career development programs for exceptional individuals. They concluded:

> The data clearly demonstrates that the sampled members of the Division on Career Development believe that there is a continuing need to investigate issues relating to inter-and intraagency cooperation and a need to establish data-based instructional procedures that can be used within the learning environment. The data further indicate that the respondents did not signifi-

cantly differentiate the areas that required research focus. The respondents apparently believe that all areas noted on the questionnaire require further research and analysis and that it is premature to prioritize those areas at this time. . . . These results suggest that the field of career education has not yet established a clearly delineated research agenda. This phenomena is a two-edge sword that on one hand enables creative investigators to explore yet uncharted areas, but on the other hand suggests it is a field that has failed to establish primacy in any of its articulated interest areas related to inter- and intraagency efforts and programming. Increasingly, in an age of accountability, the field of career education must be able to demonstrate that it knows its own agenda, is following that agenda, and the outcomes are yielding efficacious results. (p. 41)

We have addressed the need for research and theory in another section of this book. Suffice it to say at this point that all three approaches suffer from a lack of theory and for that reason we do not consider any of them to be true *models*. They are however, important and useful beginnings that can serve as guideposts for the development of true transition models.

## THE SECONDARY TRANSITION INTERVENTION EFFECTIVENESS INSTITUTE

The University of Illinois at Urbana-Champaign has long been a major center for activities relating to vocational education of the handicapped and transitional issues. The College of Education maintains an Office of Career Development for Special Populations and has engaged in a number of Federally funded projects relating to issues in the field, including publishing a series of book-length documents in a series entitled Personnel Development Series. This series is a publication of the Leadership Training Institute/Vocational and Special Education with the Office referred to above.

In addition, OSERS funded the Department as a *National Network for Professional Development in Vocational Special Education*. This project ended recently but resulted in a series of accomplishments including:

1. Publishing 12 issues of *Interchange,* a professional journal relating to career education of the handicapped.
2. Conducting five national conferences regarding the role of special education, vocational education, and vocational rehabilitation in enhancing the transition from school to the workplace for youth with handicaps.

3. Sponsoring 6 regional networks.
4. Producing four conference proceedings documents.
5. Conducting a national networking needs study in vocational special education.
6. Sponsoring 20 miniconferences, which were directed by individuals around the country, on the topic of transition from school to work for handicapped youth.
7. Producing a national network resource directory and a monography on personnel preparation issues in the area of transition from school to work.

Some publications of the National Network are still available and can be obtained by writing to Janis Chadsey-Rusch, University of Illinois at Urbana-Champaign, 110 Education Building, 1310 South Sixth Street, Champaign, IL 61820.

The College of Education at Illinois was recently awarded a contract from OSERS to establish a Secondary Transition Intervention Effectiveness Institute. The purpose of the Institute, funded through 1990, is to assist in evaluating and extending the impact of the 1983 Amendments to the Education of the Handicapped Act. These amendments are intended to address the major educational and employment transition difficulties encountered by youth with handicaps. *Interchange* will be published by the Institute to disseminate evaluation and research findings from all federally funded transition projects. For further information about the Transition Institute, contact Frank R. Rusch, Director, Transition Institute at Illinois, University of Illinois at Urbana-Champaign, 110 Education Building, 1310 South Sixth Street, Champaign, IL 61820, or call (217) 333-2325.

One of the valuable documents available from the Institute, is a compilation of information on all of the funded transition project from 1985-1986. This document is entitled *Handbook for Project Directors* and contains information regarding the contact person for each project; the duration of the project; and the purpose, technical methods, and anticipated outcomes for each project. For a copy, contact Cindy Dobbs at the address listed above.

## THE PROBLEM OF INDEPENDENT LIVING

One of the reasons we like the Halpern (1985) approach is that it emphasizes the importance of the residential environment. We believe this is one of the most neglected of problems in the transition movement. The OSERS approach assumes that independent living will be a beneficial side effect of employment. That is not consistent with our experience with mildly handicapped individuals. Many of these young people can sustain competitive employment, yet remain unable to live independently and frequently live at home with parents.

Unfortunately, most of the emphasis on self-help or independent living skills is directed toward moderately or severely handicapped individuals. Even with these individuals, the thrust of residential programs seems to be to provide *permanent* community-based, yet supervised living arrangements, frequently with paid house parents.

For mildly handicapped individuals, and for some more severely handicapped persons, a similar, but *temporary* arrangement is needed. These halfway houses would emphasize and provide supervised practice in cooking skills, hygiene, housecleaning, financial management, and other skills needed for independent living.

When the handicapped person is deemed ready, assistance would be provided in finding suitable living quarters. Follow-up services would maintain the person's capacity for independent living.

We have found almost no interest in such arrangements for the mildly handicapped. Yet our own research as well as other studies have shown that mildly handicapped individuals frequently have major problems in attempting to establish their own living quarters away from their families. In addition, the inability to live independently is a source of concern for both handicapped individuals and their families.

## SUMMARY

Vocational transition is a new term and refers to services offered to smooth the movement from public school to adult adjustment. The current interest in transitional programs grew out of responses to several reports on the status education in America. Madeline Will, Assistant Secretary for the Office of Special Education and Rehabilitative Services (OSERS) has identified transition as a major problem and an area of emphasis for efforts emanating from her office.

OSERS has produced a plan for transitional services. This plan emphasizes competitive employment as the primary goal of transition. We find this goal to be to narrow and instead prefer plans set forth by Halpern (1985) and by Wehman, Kregel, and Barcus (1985). Both of these approaches are broader and give equal emphasis to employment and self-help/independent living skills.

The Carl D. Perkins Vocational Education Act is another recent Federal initiative with implications for transitional programs. The act requires that states set aside 10 percent of Federal money allocated under the act to be used to help provide services for the handicapped. In addition, states must match this 10 percent and use the money only for the excess costs involved in providing vocational education to handicapped individuals. Transition services are specifically identified as important services provided under the Act.

Transition is the newest issue in vogue in special education and related disciplines. This fact, together with available funding should not cause an overemphasis on secondary programs and reforms to the exclusion of concern about career/vocational education in elementary schools.

The University of Illinois has received several large Federal grants or contracts and has recently become a center for activity related to transitional issues for handicapped students. The most recently funded program established The Secondary Transition Intervention Effectiveness Institute with the College of Education. Several publications are available from the Project and more will be forthcoming.

Finally, a neglected area of transition is preparation for independent living for mildly handicapped students. Many such students can sustain competitive employment, but are unable to live independently. Such individuals need temporary, halfway houses where independent living skills such as cooking, money management, and housekeeping are taught. Once these skills are learned, such individuals need assistance in establishing independent living quarters and follow-up to ensure maintenance of the needed skills.

Chapter Nine

# A PROPOSED CAREER/VOCATIONAL
# CURRICULUM

THROUGHOUT this book, we have emphasized our belief that career/vocational education suffers from a lack of theoretical foundation. This is somewhat surprising, since there is no lack of theories available to those planning career/vocational programs. Chapter Three in this book reviewed a variety of interesing theories. We are not sure why there has been so little use made of these theories, but we suspect that one reason is that curriculum builders have been pressured to *do something* quickly, and have not taken the time needed to translate theory into action.

The purpose of this chapter is to present a plan for building a school-based curriculum based on a solid theoretical foundation. (The reader is referred to Chapters Three and Five for a more complete discussion of the relevance of theory to practice.) We will present a general conceptual plan on which such a curriculum could be built. We will not, however, attempt to detail actual activities, since such curriculum specifics would comprise a book-length document in itself and because local school districts need to tailor their curricula to their own specific needs and assets.

We will begin by presenting a conceptualization of the model curriculum which we will then fit into the framework of Holland's Theory of Vocational Personalities and Work Environments (Holland, 1985a). This curriculum outline consists of a combination of two previously-presented career/vocational approaches.

## THE MODEL CURRICULUM

In Chapter Five we reviewed some traditional plans for career/vocational education for the handicapped, and in Chapter Eight we

217

reviewed a number of transitional plans. We have selected a combination of two of these plans on which to build our model. The two plans are Brolin's Life Centered Career Education Plan (Brolin, 1983), and Halpern's transitional plan (Halpern, 1985).

We like Halpern's plan because of the inclusion of three components of *Community Adjustment* which Halpern makes the goal of transitional programs. The following outline shows the three components of *Community Adjustment:*

A. Quality of the Residential Environment
B. Adequacy of the Person's Social and Interpersonal Network
C. Employment

Although Halpern's plan is for *transition,* we find these components useful in thinking about the full range of career/vocational education throughout the school grades. Actually, it is reasonable that the ultimate goals of transition are also the ultimate goals of earlier educational programs since both K-12 education and transitional programs aim at successful adjustment of the individual into all aspects of community life.

Thus we would suggest that Halpern's goal of *Community Adjustment* is the ultimate goal of career/vocational education. Further, we suggest that his three components of *quality of the residential environment, adequacy of the person's social and interpersonal network,* and *employment,* are the enabling objectives leading to that goal.

For purposes of identifying the actual *activities* leading to accomplishment of the three enabling objectives and subsequent attainment of the ultimate goal, we like Brolin's work (Brolin, 1983). Chapter Five presents a comprehensive review of Brolin's plan. Briefly, Brolin has constructed a curriculum by identifying three primary categories of activities: *daily living skills, personal-social skills,* and *occupational guidance and preparation.* These categories of activities can be equated to Halpern's enabling objectives as follows:

1. Brolin's activities for teaching *daily living skills* would lead to the achievement of Halpern's enabling objective related to *quality of the residential environment.*
2. Brolin's activities for teaching *personal-social skills* would lead to the achievement of Halpern's enabling objective related to *adequacy of the person's social and interpersonal network.*
3. Brolin's activities for teaching *occupational guidance and preparation* would lead to the achievement of Halpern's enabling objective or *employment.*

Brolin's categories of activities can be viewed as curriculum areas which are broken down into 22 competencies. The 22 competencies are further broken down into 102 subcompetencies. These competencies and subcompetencies are potentially useful as a starting point for districts beginning the development of a career/vocational education scope and sequence. For curriculum developers in such districts, we recommend Brolin's excellent books, especially *Life Centered Career Education: A Competency Based Approach* (Brolin, 1983).

In summary, here is an outline of the curriculum:

### Ultimate Goal—COMMUNITY ADJUSTMENT

I. *QUAILITY OF THE RESIDENTIAL ENVIRONMENT* (Halpern, 1985)

(Enabling Objective #1)

A. *Daily Living Skills Activities*
  1. managing family finances
  2. selecting, managing, and maintaining a home
  3. caring for personal needs
  4. raising children and family living
  5. buying and preparing food
  6. buying and caring for clothing
  7. engaging in civic activities
  8. utilizing recreation and leisure time
  9. getting around the community
     (Categories of Activities from Brolin, 1983. See Brolin for a further breakdown of the above into 42 subcompetencies and for suggestions for specific activities to teach these subcompetencies)

II. *ADEQUACY OF SOCIAL AND INTERPERSONAL NETWORK* (Halpern, 1985)

(Enabling Objective #2)

A. *Personal-Social Skills Activities*
  1. achieving self awareness
  2. acquiring self confidence
  3. achieving socially responsible behavior
  4. maintaining good interpersonal skills
  5. achieving independence
  6. achieving problem solving skills
  7. communicating adequately with others

(Categories of Activities from Brolin, 1983. See Brolin for a further breakdown of the above into 33 subcompetencies and for suggestions for specific activities to teach these subcompetencies)

III. *EMPLOYMENT* (Halpern, 1985)
           (Enabling Objective #3)
   A. *Occupational Guidance and Preparation Activities*
      1. knowing and exploring occupational possibilities
      2. selecting and planning occupational choices
      3. exhibiting appropriate work habits and behaviors
      4. exhibiting sufficient physical-manual skills
      5. obtaining a specific occupational skill
      6. seeking, securing, and maintaining employment
        (Categories of Activities from Brolin, 1983. See Brolin for a further breakdown of the above into 27 subcompetencies and for suggestions for specific activities to teach these subcompetencies)

Although we have included Brolin's categories of competencies, districts could elect to generate their own categories or use some other system of categorization. We chose Brolin's simply because we find it to be logical and complete, and because Brolin has published his curriculum in widely available form (Brolin, 1983). We believe, however, that his specific activities need to be modified to make them consistent with the Holland theory. We will discuss ways of integrating the Holland theory with curriculum in a later section of this chapter.

## THE THEORETICAL FOUNDATION

We have selected John Holland's theory as the philosophical and theoretical foundation for our career/vocational model. Although we have described this theory in depth in Chapter Three, we will provide a review of the theory in this chapter. We will also present the seven assumptions that provide the foundation on which the theory was developed.

### A Review of the Holland Theory

Holland refers to this theory as *A Theory of Vocational Personalities and Work Environments* (1985a). He proposes that a person's career choice is a reflection of that person's personality and vocational style. He hypothesizes six personality types and six occupational environments including: Realistic (R), Investigative (I), Artistic (A), Social (S), Enterprising (E), and Conventional (C). According to the theory, individuals who work in environments congruent with their personality types are more likely to be satisfied with their jobs, be better employees, and less likely to change jobs than those who work in environments incongruent with their personalities. Following is a brief review of the six Holland types:

The *Realistic* personality is characterized by aggressive, antisocial, and masculine behaviors. Realistic people see themselves as having mechanical ability and lacking ability in human relations. They tend to view the world in simple, tangible, and traditional terms. They enjoy engaging in physical, highly-concrete activities, and they avoid abstract problem situations.

A Realistic environment stimulates people to perform realistic activities such as manipulating objects, using machines and tools, and working with animals. This environment rewards people for the display of conventional values and goods, money, power, and possession.

Like the Realistic individual, the *Investigative* personality avoids close interpersonal contact. However, unlike Realistic types, Investigative people enjoy abstract problem-solving; they can be described as analytical, complex, curious, independent, and intellectual; and they see the world in complex, abstract, independent, and original ways.

An Investigative environment encourages scientific competencies and achievements, and it rewards people for the display of scientific values.

The *Artistic* personality is similar to the Investigative type in terms of dealing with abstractions and being asocial. Artistic people can be described as expressive, original, intuitive, nonconforming, and as having artistic abilities such as acting, writing, and speaking. They view the world in complex, independent, unconventional, and flexible ways.

The Artistic environment stimulates people to engage in artistic activities, fosters artistic competencies and achievements, and rewards people for the display of artistic values. It is characterized by demands and opportunities that entail ambiguous, free, unsystemized activities and competencies to create art forms or products.

Individuals with a *Social* orientation prefer close interpersonal situations, enjoy helping others, and are skilled in interpersonal relations. They see themselves as liking to help others, understanding of others, cooperative, and sociable. They see the world in flexible ways.

The Social environment stimulates people to engage in social activities, fosters social competencies, and rewards people for the display of social values. It is characterized by demands and opportunities that entail the manipulation of others to inform, train, develop, cure, or enlighten.

*Enterprising* personalities have interpersonal skills equal to those of Social types. However, instead of using their skills to help and support other people, these individuals prefer to manipulate and dominate others. Enterprising people see themselves as aggressive, popular, self-confident, sociable, and possessing leadership and speaking ability. Enterprising individuals see the world in terms of power, status, responsibility; and in stereotypic, constricted, dependent, and simple terms.

The Enterprising environment stimulates people to engage in enterprising activities such as selling, or leading others; fosters enterprising competencies and achievements; and rewards people for the display of enterprising values and goals such as money, power, and status. It is characterized by demands and opportunities that entail the manipulation of others to attain organizational or self-interest goals.

Finally, *Conventional* types exhibit concern for rules and regulation, practice self-control, and have a desire for order, both of things and people. They often subordinate their personal needs and have a strong respect for individuals who have power and status. Conventional types see themselves as conforming, orderly, nonartistic, and as having clerical competencies. They see the world in conventional, stereotypic, constricted, simple, dependent ways.

The Conventional environment stimulates people to engage in conventional activities, such as recording and organizing data or records; it fosters conventional competencies and achievements; and it rewards people for display of conventional values such as dependability and conformity. This environment is characterized by demands and opportunities that entail the explicit, ordered, and systematic manipulation of data. Examples include keeping records, filing materials, reproducing materials, organizing written and numerical data according to a prescribed plan, and operating business and data processing machines.

According to Holland (1985b), the theory's typology is based on seven assumptions that were elaborated to create a typology of persons and environments and their interactions. These assumptions include the following:

1. *Most people can be categorized as one of six personality types labeled Realistic, Investigative, Artistic, Social, Enterprising, or Conventional.* These are theoretical or ideal types against which the real person can be measured.

Cultural and personal forces such as parents, social class, culture, and the physical environment shape people in different ways. Because of these experiences, people learn to prefer some activities over others. Later, the preferred activities become strong interests which lead to a specific group of competencies. Finally, these interests and competencies create a particular personal disposition which causes an individual to think, perceive, and act in special ways. This developmental sequence continues to evolve throughout a person's lifetime.

2. *There are six kinds of environments: Realistic, Investigative, Artistic, Social, Enterprising, and Conventional.* Each environment is dominated by given types of personalities and activities. For example, a Realistic environment is dominated by Realistic types of people, and it often requires interaction with mechanical objects.

People tend to surround themselves with others like themselves who share their interests, competencies, and outlook on the world. Thus, where people congregate, they create an environment that reflects the types they are.

3. *People search for environments that will let them exercise their skills and abilities, express their attitudes and values, and take on agreeable problems and roles.* For example, Realistic types seek Realistic environments, Social types seek Social environments, etc. To a lesser extent, environments search for people through friendships and recruiting practices. According to Holland (1985b), the person's search for an environment is carried on in many ways, at different levels of consciousness, and over a long period of time.

4. *A person's behavior is determined by an interaction between his or her personality and the characteristics of the environment.* Certain outcomes of pairing an individual with a specific environment can be forecast by using knowledge of personality types and environmental models. These outcomes may include choice of vocation, job changes, vocational achievement, personal competence, and educational and social behavior.

5. *The degree of congruence between a person and an occupation (environment) can be estimated by a hexogonal model* (this model is illustrated in Chapter Three). On the hexagon, the shorter the distance between the personality type and the occupational type, the closer the relationship. For example, an R-person and an R-job are most congruent. An R-person in an S-job is in the most incongruent situation.

6. *The degree of consistency within a person or an environment is also defined by using the hexagonal model.* Types adjacent on the hexagon are most consistent and have compatible interests, personal dispositions, or job duties. Types located directly across from each other on the hexagon are most inconsistent and have personal characteristics or job functions that are usually unrelated. For example, a person whose two highest SDS scales were Artistic and Conventional would have an inconsistent two-letter code because these codes are opposites on the hexagonal model, and they imply numerous oppositions. An intermediate degree of consistency is defined by alternate types on the hexagon such as Investigative-Social, Conventional-Social, and so on.

Consistency is associated with a more stable work history and is assumed to be conducive to vocational achievement and clarity of goals.

7. *The degree of differentiation of a person or an environment modifies predictions made from a person's SDS profile, from an occupational code, or from their interaction.* Some persons or environments are more clearly defined than others. For example, an individual may closely resemble a single type and show little resemblance to other types. Likewise, an environment may be dominated largely by a single type. In contrast, a person who resembles many types, or an environment that is characterized by about equal numbers of people representing the six different types are labeled undifferentiated or poorly-defined.

Differentiated, or well-defined, people or work environments are most likely to exhibit the characteristics attributed to their code. On the other hand, poorly-defined types or environments are least likely to exhibit the expected characteristics or influence.

## Maladaptive Vs. Adaptive Career Development

Holland (1985a) believes that maladaptive career development results from failure to develop (a) a consistent and differentiated personality pattern, (b) a clear sense of vocational identity, or (c) a career in an occupation congruent with one's personality. Holland lists seven contributors to maladaptive career development including:

1. Lack of personal experiences leading to development of clear-cut interests, competencies, and self-perceptions.
2. Lack of exposure to a variety of occupational environments.
3. Personal experiences that have led to unclear understanding about one's interests, competencies and personal characteristics.
4. Personal experiences that have led to unclear understanding of major work environments.

5. Difficulty translating personal characteristics into occupational opportunities, possibly resulting from ineffective interpersonal skills and/or emotional instability.
6. Lack of ability to carry out career/vocational plans due to limited personal, educational, or financial resources.
7. Inability to find work congruent with personality due to economic or social barriers.
(Adapted from Holland, 1985a)

## TRANSMITTING THE CULTURE OF WORK

Since the above conditions result in maladaptive career development, public school curricular activities should be chosen that will prevent their occurrence. Past efforts of the public school have been ineffective because of failure to recognize the importance of identifying and transmitting the *culture of work*. A contributing factor to this failure has been the conviction that work-related skills and information are best taught using an *infusion* approach or a *job-skill-specific* approach.

We believe that work-related skills and information are too important to be left to infusion alone. Use of an analogy with reading may be instructive at this point. Reading is considered highly important in our culture and the teaching of reading receives a great deal of time and effort in our schools. Reading is infused into most other subjects in schools, but *reading is also considered a separate subject as well!* Work should be accorded this same emphasis.

By *work* we are referring to a concept much broader than that of *career or job*. In short, work is as much a major part of the human condition as love, sex, hunger, etc. In other words, we are referring to an innate human need that cuts across many human activities. For example, we all must *work* at developing leisure time activities. Keeping our homes clean and orderly, developing rewarding interpersonal relationships, etc. We have all experienced the work involved in learning to play a new game; learning a new motor skill such as riding a bicycle; or engaging in a hobby such as stamp collecting, dancing or rock collecting. In fact, Ernest Hemingway was said to be a meticulous planner of social gatherings involving his friends, and invitations to these events were consequently highly prized.

As we previously suggested, we believe that work should be thought of in the same way that we think about basic subjects such as reading, writing, and arithmetic. In fact, perhaps we should think of four, rather than three basic subjects: reading, writing, arithmetic, and *work*. If we could accomplish this change in thinking, we could avoid the periodic educational shifts in emphasis from *basic skills* to *career/vocational* material, since *work would be one of the basic school subjects*.

Just as reading, writing, and arithmetic curricula have been developed from theoretical perspectives, the same must be true of work curricula. Thus, the remainder of this chapter will be devoted to some general suggestions to guide such curriculum development within the theoretical perspective given to us by John Holland.

## INTEGRATING THE CURRICULUM WITH THE HOLLAND THEORY

The Holland theory is organized around the six categories of vocational personalities and work environments. Therefore, a school curriculum based on this theory should be organized around the same six categories.

Holland (1985a) has provided some brief guidelines for translation of the theory into educational strategies:

1. Provide students with relevant school and nonschool experiences. This means giving them the opportunity to experience the six curricula *and* the six kinds of nonschool experiences. This orientation implies that unless schools, parents, or other agencies provide a full range of experiences, they lessen students' abilities to understand themselves and their future possibilities.
2. Provide students with accurate and accessible information about themselves and jobs over a long time span rather than at a few critical decision points.
3. Provide students with translations of personal characteristics and jobs that are readily accessible and easily comprehended. The typical use of tests violates this principle. Test information is usually inaccessible, not clearly translated, incomplete, and unintegrated with other data. (p. 150)

We will discuss a plan for curriculum development at the elementary and the secondary levels.

### The Elementary Curriculum

Holland suggests that the first two strategies above are appropriate for building curriculum in the elementary school. Understanding of self and understanding of the work environment is crucial at this level. We will suggest related activities taken from the curriculum outline presented earlier in this chapter.

We suggest these specific activities because young children can profitably engage in them. However, even though they are introduced in the elementary grades, they should be reinforced in the secondary curriculum as well.

The reader is referred back to the curriculum outline presented earlier in this chapter. Under Enabling Objective #1, Quality of the Residential Environment, the Daily Living Skills Activities we believe are most appropriate for emphasis in the early elementary years are numbers three, five, and six: *caring for personal needs, buying and preparing food,* and *buying and caring for clothing.*

Under Enabling Objective #2, Adequacy of Social and Interpersonal Network, the Personal-Social Skills Activities should include numbers one through four, six, and seven: *achieving self awareness, acquiring self confidence, achieving socially responsible behavior, maintaining good interpersonal skills, achieving problem solving skills,* and *communicating adequately with others.*

Under Enabling Objective #3, Employment, the Occupational Guidance and Preparation Activities should include numbers one and three: *knowing and exploring occupational possibilities,* and *exhibiting appropriate work habits and behaviors.*

We believe that, whenever possible, these activities should be related to Holland's typology. They should be specifically implemented in the Work curriculum and generally infused into the entire curriculum.

Perhaps the greatest strength of the Holland theory is its simplicity. Therefore, the Holland categories should be explained to students at a very early age although no attempt should be made to actually measure individual student interests until later. If a good foundation in work education is laid in the elementary grades, then necessary prerequisites will have been established so that adequate measures of occupational interests and personalities can be obtained by the time students are twelve or thirteen years old.

At the elementary level, relating the activities to the six Holland categories is not always possible. Therefore, the activities we have identified for the elementary curriculum must be augmented with continuing explanations, demonstrations, and field trips related to the six Holland categories. For example, elementary teachers should make sure that field trips are taken to job environments falling all around the Holland hexagon. Guest speakers representing all six personality types should be invited to discuss their occupations with the class, emphasizing what it is they like and dislike most about their work.

We believe that goals and objectives of the elementary work curriculum should include thorough understanding of the six Holland categories. In addition, students should be exposed to a wide variety of jobs representative of each of the six Holland work environments. Finally, students should gain understanding and appreciation of the importance of the concepts of congruence, differentiation, and consistency.

## The Secondary Curriculum

Holland suggests that the secondary school work curriculum incorporates the last of his three strategies. This strategy focusses on providing students with translations of personal characteristics and jobs that are readily accessible and easily comprehended. Thus, the content of the secondary work curriculum will be more specific to the community and will require categorizing community employment sites according to their Holland classification.

Also, as we have previously stated, if the elementary curriculum has provided a thorough foundation in work-related skills and concepts, necessary prerequisites will have been met for adequate measurement of personalities and interests of entering secondary students. These measures then can be used as guides for curriculum development, counseling strategies, and specific skill training.

While the goal of the elementary work curriculum was general understanding of the Holland theory, the goal of the secondary work curriculum is personal application of the theory. For instance, students should be able to relate their own measured interests to greater self-awareness and to potentially satisfying work environments in the community.

In addition, administrators, counselors, teachers, and students themselves could use students' measured Holland codes as guides for placement with individual teachers and into individual courses that are congruent with student interests and personalities. Holland (1985a) provides an example of a two-year post-secondary institution that actually used the Holland classification system to code college courses. There is no reason why secondary schools could not use the same scheme. For instance, secondary schools might publish a catalog of courses with Holland codes assigned to each course. Thus, a course in auto mechanics would be identified as a Realistic environment, a physics course as

Investigative, a literature course as Artistic, a public relations course as Social, a course in free enterprise as Enterprising, and an accounting course as Conventional.

Although it is not feasible to expect that students could avoid *all* courses that are incongruent with their personalities and interests, *some* could be avoided. Also, if students are required to enroll in incongruent courses, knowledge of Holland's theory would give them understanding of why they might experience dissatisfaction or difficulty in such courses. Thus, they would be less likely to feel like failures if they were not successful in such classes. In addition, matching students and teachers who have similar Holland codes could promote better student-teacher relationships.

We believe there should be a separate work curriculum at the secondary level as well as at the elementary level. In addition to the Holland activities presented above, activities from the model curriculum outline should also be incorporated into the work curriculum. These activities were outlined earlier in the chapter, and the secondary activities are much easier to relate to Holland categories than are the elementary activities. For the sake of brevity, we will not discuss each of these activities. The reader should assume that all activities not begun at the elementary level should begin at the secondary level. For example, under Enabling Objective #3, Employment, one Occupational Guidance and Preparation Activity appropriate for junior high/middle school might be number two, *selecting and planning occupational choices.* Students could be provided with information pertaining to the variety of occupational choices congruent with their measured interests and personalities, and they could begin investigating those possibilities. Thus, by the time they entered high school, they should have a good idea of what courses they should take to prepare them for chosen occupations.

## Applications for Mildly Handicapped Students

We believe that if the proposed model curriculum is instituted properly in the public schools, it will be as appropriate for most mildly handicapped students as for nonhandicapped students. For those students who may have difficulty with the *regular* work curriculum, then adaptation and modification of the curriculum will be just as important as for the *reading* or *mathematics* curriculum. In addition, implementation of the Holland theory in the work curriculum will prevent training for and placement of handicapped students into occupational environments reflecting a narrow, stereotypic view of their abilities and interests. Finally, if the proposed model work curriculum is properly implemented, then only the most cursory transitional program will be required for these students.

## SUMMARY

In this chapter, we have presented a model *work* curriculum based on Holland's Theory of Vocational Personalities and Work Environments. The proposed curriculum assumes that an innate need to work is part of the human condition, that instruction in work is as important as instruction in other basic school subjects, and that knowledge of work contributes as much to total life functioning as does learning to read, write or calculate.

We have not presented a complete operational curriculum, only a plan for devising such a curriculum. Much remains to be done including the following: (a) determination of a logical K-12 scope and sequence, (b) delineation of specific activities, and (c) validation of the curriculum through empirical investigation.

While this approach is similar to more traditional ones in terms of recommending early institution of career/vocational education and integration of handicapped students with nonhandicapped peers, we are hopeful that its theoretical orientation will provide a unique and appropriate approach to meeting the *work* needs of all students.

# BIBLIOGRAPHY

Adelman, H. S., & Taylor, L. (1986a). The problems of definition and differentiation and the need for a classification schema. *Journal of Learning Disabilities, 19*(a), 514-520.

Adelman, H. S., & Taylor, L. (1986b) *An introduction to learning disabilities.* Glenview, IL: Scott, Foresman and Company

Alley, G., & Deshler, D. (1979). *Teaching the learning disabled adolescent: Strategies and methods.* Denver, CO: Love Publishing Company.

Azrin, N. H., & Besalel, V. A. (1980). *Job club counselor's manual: A behavioral approach to vocational counseling.* Baltimore: University Park Press.

Barker, S. B. (1978). *An evaluation of the development of the Self-Directed Search for use by visually disabled individuals.* Doctoral dissertation, College of Education, Florida State University.

Bellamy, G. T. (1985). Transition progress: Comments on Hasazi, Gordon, and Roe. *Exceptional Children, 51*(6), 474-477.

Bennett, G. K., Seashore, H. G., and Wesman, A. G. (1969). *Differential Aptitude Tests (DAT).* New York: Psychological Corporation.

Benz, M. R., & Halpern, A. S. (1986). Vocational preparation for high school students with mild disabilities: A statewide study of administrator, teacher, and parent perceptions. *CDEI, 9*(1), 3-15.

Biller, E. F. (1985a). Career development of the learning disabled adolescent: A focus on career maturity. *Career Development for Exceptional Individuals, 8*(1), 17-22.

Biller, E. F. (1985b). *Understanding and guiding the career development of adolescents and young adults with learning disabilities.* Springfield, IL: Charles C Thomas.

Bingham, A. (1978). Exploratory process in career development: Implications for learning disabled students. *Career Development for Exceptional Individuals, 4*(2), 77-80.

Blau, P. M., & Duncan, D. D. (1967). *The American occupational structure.* New York: Wiley.

Blau, P. M., Gustad, J. W., Jessor, R., Parnes, H. S., & Wilcox, R.S. (1956). Occupational choice: A conceptual framework. *Industrial Labor Relations Review, 9,* 531-543.

Bordin, E. S. (1943). A theory of interests as dynamic phenomena. *Educational and Psychological Measurement, 3,* 49-66.

Botterbusch, K. F. (1976). *A guide to job site evaluation.* Menomonie, WI: University of Wisconsin-Stout, Stout Vocational Rehabilitation Institute, Materials Development Center.

Bowe, F. (1978). *Handicapping America: Barriers to disabled people.* New York: Harper and Row.

Braginsky, D., & Braginsky, B. (1971). *Hansels and Gretels.* New York: Hold, Rinehart and Winston, Inc.

Brickey, M., Brauning, L., & Campbell, K. (1982). Vocational histories of sheltered workshop employees placed in projects with industry and competitive jobs. *Mental Retardation, 20,* 52-57.

Brickey, M., & Campbell, K. (1981). Fast food· employment for moderately and mildly mentally retarded adults: The McDonald's project. *Mental Retardation, 19,* 113-116.

Brimer, R., & Rouse, S. (1978) Post-school adjustment: A follow-up of a cooperative program for the educable mentally retarded. *Journal for Special Educators of the Mentally Retarded,* 1978, *14,* 131-137.

Brody-Hasazi, S., Salembier, G., & Finck, K. (1983). Directions for the 80's: Vocational preparation for secondary mildly handicapped students. *Teaching Exceptional Children, 15,* 206-209.

Brolin, D. E. (1972). Value of rehabilitation services and correlates of vocational success with the mentally retarded. *American Journal of Mental Deficiency, 76,* 644-661.

Brolin, D. E. (1978). *Life-centered career education: A competency based approach.* Reston, VA: The Council for Exceptional Children.

Brolin, D. E. (1982). *Vocational preparation of persons with handicaps.* Columbus: Charles E. Merrill.

Brolin, D. E. (1983). *Life centered career education: A competency based approach* (Revised Ed.). Reston, VA: The Council for Exceptional Children.

Brolin, D. E., & D'Alonzo (1983). Critical issues in career education for handicapped students. *Journal of Special Education, 17*(1), 93-98.

Brolin, D. E., Durand, R., Kromer, K., & Muller, P. (1975). Post-school adjustment of educable retarded students. *Education and Training of the Mentally Retarded, 10,* 144-149.

Brolin, D. E., & Elliott, T. R. (1984). Meeting the lifelong career development needs of students with handicaps. *Career Development for Exceptional Individuals, 7*(1), 12-21.

Brolin, D. E., Elliott, T. R., & Corcoran, J. R. (1984). Career education for persons with learning disabilities. *Learning Disabilities, 3*(1), 1-14.

Brolin, D. E., McKay, D. L., & West, L. W. (1978). *Trainer's guide for life centered career education.* Reston, VA: The Council for Exceptional Children.

Brolin, D. T., & West, L. L. (1985). Career development: Services for special needs learners in postsecondary education programs. *The Journal for Vocational Special Needs Education, 7*(2), 29-30, 34.

Bryan, J., & Bryan, T. (1984). The social life of the learning disabled youngster. In J. D. McKinney & L. Feagans (Eds.), *Current topics in learning disabilities, Vol. 1.* Norwood, NJ: Ablex Publishing Co.

Buehler, C. (1983). *Der menschliche lebenslauf als psychologisches problem.* Leipzig: Hirzel.

Campbell, D. P. (1974). *Manual for the Strong-Campbell Interest Inventory T325 (merged form).* Stanford, CA: Stanford University Press.

Campbell, D. P., & Hansen , J. C. (1981). *Manual for the SVIB-SCII.* Stanford, CA: Stanford University Press.

Carter, H. D. (1940). The development of vocational attitudes. *Journal of Counseling Psychology, 4,* 185-191.

Cartledge, G., & Milburn, J. F. (1986). *Teaching social skills to children* (2nd ed.). New York, NY: Pergamon Press.

Cegelka, P. T. (1979). Career education. In D. Cullinan & M. H. Epstein (Eds.), *Special education for adolescents* (pp. 155-184). Columbus, OH: Charles E. Merrill.

Cegelka, P. T. (1981). Career education. In J. M. Kauffman, & D. P. Hallahan (Eds.) *Handbook of special education,* Englewood Cliffs, NJ: Prentice-Hall.

Cegelka, P. T. (1985). Career and vocational education. In W. H. Berdine & A. E. Blackhurst (Eds.), *An introduction to special education,* (pp. 572-612). Boston: Little, Brown and Company.

Chaffin, J., Davison, R., Regan, C., & Spellman, C. (1971). The follow-up studies of former mentally retarded students from the Kansas work study project. *Exceptional Children, 37,* 733-738.

Chalfant, J. C. (1984). *Identifying learning disabled student: Guidelines for decision making.* Burlington, VT: Northeast Regional Resource Center.

Chelser, B. (1982). ACLD vocational committee completes survey of LD adult. *ACLD Newsbriefs,* No. 146, 5, 20-23.

Clark, E. T. (1967). Influence of sex and social class on occupational preference and perception. *Personnel and Guidance Journal, 45,* 440-444.

Clark, G. M. (1979). *Education for the handicapped child in the elementary classroom.* Denver, CO: Love Publishing Company.

Cobb, R. B., & Larkin, D. (1985). Assessment and placement of handicapped pupils into secondary vocational education programs. *Focus on Exceptional Children, 17*(7), 1-14.

Collier, S., & Bruno, R. (1984). Teaching safety skills: A problem solving approach for special needs students. *The Journal for Vocational Special Needs Education, 7*(1), 15-16, 20.

Collins, A. M., & Sedlacek, W. E. (1972). Comparison of satisfied and dissatisfied users of Holland's Self-Directed Search. *Journal of Counseling Psychology, 19,* 393-398.

Conte, L. D. (1983). Vocational development theories and the disabled person: Oversight or deliberate omission? *Rehabilitation Counseling Bulletin, 26*(5), 316-328.

Cox, S. (1977). The learning disabled adult. *Academic Therapy, 13*(1), 79-87.

Crawford, D. (1985). The Heritage Foundation Report handicaps the handicapped. *ACLD Newsbriefs,* No. 158, 18-19.

Crimando, W., & Nichols, B. (1982). A model for vocational exploration and selective placement of the learning disabled. *Vocational Evaluation and Work Adjustment Bulletin, 16*(3), 98-102.

Croft, D. B. (1976). *Predictors of success in college for low prior educational attainment multicultural students.* (Grant No. OEG-0-74-1912) Educational Research Center, Las Cruces: New Mexico State University.

Cummings, R., & Maddux, C. D. (1984). Learning-disabled children: Parental expectations. *Techniques: A Journal for Remedial Education and Counseling, 1,* 81-87.

Cummings, R. W., & Maddux, C. D. (1985a). The Holland theory: Implications for the handicapped. *The Journal for Vocational Special Needs Education, 8*(1), 3-6,10.

Cummings, R. W., & Maddux, C. D. (1985b). *Parenting the learning disabled: A realistic approach.* Springfield, IL: Charles C Thomas.

Cummings, R. W., & Maddux, C. D. (1987). Self-administration and scoring errors of learning disabled and nonlearning disabled students on two forms of the Self-Directed Search. *Journal of Counseling Psychology, 34.*

Cummings, R., & Maddux, C. (In press). Holland personality types among learning disabled and nonlearning disabled high school students. *Exceptional Children.*

D'Alonzo, B. J., Marino, J. F., & Kauss, M. W. (1984). Mesa Public School comprehensive career and vocational education program for disabled students. *Career Development for Exceptional Individuals, 7*(1), 22-29.

Dawis, R. (1973). A theory of work adjustment. In J. G. Cull, and R. E. Hardy (Eds.), *Adjustment to work* (pp. 51-63). Springfield, IL: Charles C Thomas.

Dawis, R. V., Lofquist, L. H., & Weiss, D. (1968). *Minnesota studies in vocational rehabilitation: XXIII, a theory of work adjustment (Rev. ed.).* Minneapolis: Industrial Relations Center, Work Adjustment Project, University of Minnesota.

DeVoge, S. (1975). Personality variables, academic major, and vocational choice: A longitudinal study of Holland's theory. *Psychological Reports, 37,* 1191-1195.

Dineen, J. (1981). Survey of Washington developmental centers and sheltered workshops. The Employment Training Program, University of Washington, Seattle, Washington (unpublished).

Donohoe, I. (1976). Learning center blueprints for real-life skills. *Instructor, 86*(1), 64-66.

Drew, C. J., Logan, D. R., & Hardman, M. L. (1984). *Mental retardation: A life cycle approach.* St. Louis: Times Mirror/Mosby College Publishing.

Edge, D., & Burton, G. (1986). Helping learning disabled middle school students learn about money. *Journal of Learning Disabilities, 19,* 46-50.

Fafard, M., & Haubrich, P. (1981). Vocational and social adjustment of learning disabled young adults: A follow-up student. *Learning Disability Quarterly, 4,* 122-130.

Farber, B. (1968). *Mental retardation: Its social context and social consequences.* Boston, MA: Houghton Mifflin.

Federal Register. (1978, September). Position statement on comprehensive vocational education for all handicapped persons. *43*(186).

Ford, L., Dineen, J., & Hall, J. (1984). Is there life after placement? *Education and Training of the Mentally Retarded, 19*(4), 291-296.

Foss, G., & Bostwick, D. (1981). Problems of mentally retarded adults: A study of rehabilitation service consumers and providers. *Rehabilitation Counseling Bulletin, 25,* 66-73.

Gage, N. L. (1963). Paradigms for research on teaching. In N. L. Gage (Ed.). *Handbook of research on teaching.* Chicago: Rand McNally & Co.

Gardner, D. C., Beatty, G. J., & Gardner, P. L. (1984). *Career and vocational education for mildly learning handicapped and disadvantages youth.* Springfield, IL: Charles C Thomas.

Geib, B., Guzzardi, L., & Genova, P. (1981). Intervention for adults with learning disabilities. *Academic Therapy, 16*(3), 317-325.

Gerber, P. (1981). Learning disabilities and eligibility for vocational rehabilitation services: A chronology of events. *Learning Disability Quarterly, 4,* 122-130.

Gillet, P. (1983). It's elementary: Career education activities for mildly handicapped students. *Teaching Exceptional Children, 14,* 199-205.

Ginzberg, E., Ginsburg, S. W., Axelrad, S., & Herma, J. L. (1951). *Occpational choice: An approach to a general theory.* New York: Columbia University.

Goldhammer, K. A. (1972). A career curriculum. In K. Goldhammer, & R. Taylor (Eds.), *Career education: Perspectives and promises.* Columbus, OH: Charles E. Merrill.

Goldstein, A., Sparfkin, R., Gershaw, N., & Klein, P. (1980). *Skill-streaming the adolescent: A structured approach to teaching prosocial skills.* Champaign, IL: Research Press.

Gottfredson, L. (1977). A multiple labor market model of occupational achievement. Research Report No. 225. Center for Social Organization of Schools, Johns Hopkins University, Baltimore, MD.

Gottfredson, L. S. (1981). Circumscription and compromise: A developmental theory of occupational aspirations. *Journal of Counseling Psychology, 26,* 319-328.

Gottfredson, G., Holland, J., & Ogawa, D. (1982). *Dictionary of Holland occupational codes.* Palo Alto, CA: Consulting Psychologists Press.

Graubard, P. S. (1973). Children with behavioral disabilities. In Dunn, L. M. *Exceptional children in the schools* (2nd ed.). New York: Holt, Rinehart and Winston, Inc.

Gray, R. (1981). Services for the LD adult: A working paper. *Learning Disability Quarterly, 4*(4), 426-434.

Greenan, J. P. (1982). Problems and issues in delivering vocational education instruction and support services to students with learning disabilities. *Journal of Learning Disabilities, 15*(4), 231-235.

Greenan, J. P., Miller, S. R., & White, M. (1985). Research and development problems in the delivery of career development programs for exceptional individuals. *CDEI, 8*(1), 33-41.

Greenan, J. P., & Phelps, L. A. (1982). Delivering vocational education to handicapped learners. *Exceptional Children, 48,* 408-411.

Gross, E. (1964). The worker and society. In H. Borow. (Ed.), *Man in a world at work.* Boston: Houghton Mifflin.

Gross, E. (1967). A sociological approach to the analysis of preparation for work life. *Personnel and Guidance Journal, 45,* 416-423.

Grossman, H. (Ed.). (1973). *Manual on terminology and classification in mental retardation.* Washingtn, DC: American Association on Mental Retardation.

Grossman, H. (Ed.). (1983). *Manual on terminology and classification in mental retardation.* Washington, DC: American Association on Mental Deficiency.

Gysbers, N. C., & Moore, E. J. (1975). *Improving guidance programs.* Englewood Cliffs, NJ: Prentice-Hall.

Halpern, A. S. (1973). General unemployment and vocational opportunities for EMR individuals. *American Journal of Mental Deficiency, 78,* 123-127.

Halpern, A. S. (1985). Transition: A look at the foundations. *Exceptional Children, 51*(6), 479-486.

Halpern, A., & Benz, M. (1984). Toward excellence in secondary special education: A statewide study of Oregon's high school programs for students with mild disabilities. Unpublished manuscript, University of Oregon.

Halverson, P. M. (1974). Career development in the elementary school: A rationale. *Elementary School Journal, 75*(2), 122-128.

Hanson, L. S. (1977). *An examination of the definitions and concepts of career education.* Washington, DC: U. S. Government Printing Office.

Harnden, G., Meyen, E. L., Alley, G. R., & Deshler, D. D. (1980). Performance of learning disabled high school students on the Armed Services Vocational Aptitude Battery (Research Report 24). Lawrence, KS: Institute for Research in Learning Disabilities, The University of Kansas.

Hasazi, S. B., Gordon, L. R., & Roe, C. A. (1985). Factors associated with the employment status of handicapped youth exiting high school from 1979 to 1983. *Exceptional Children, 51,* 455-469.

Havighurst, R. J. (1964). Youth in exploration and man emergent. In H. Borow (Ed.), *Man in a world at work.* Boston: Houghton Mifflin, 1964.

Heber, R. (1961). *A manual on terminology and classification in mental retardation (2nd Ed.). American Journal of Mental Deficiency,* Monography Supplement.

Heller (1981). Secondary education for handicapped students: In search of a solution. *Exceptional Children, 47,* 582-583.

Hewer, V. H. (1965). Vocational interests of college freshmen and their social origins. *Journal of Applied Psychology, 49,* 407-411.

Hewett, F. M., & Taylor, F. D. (1980). *The emotionally disturbed child in the classroom* (2nd ed). Boston: Allyn and Bacon.

Hightower, M. D. (1975). Status is certain death. *Journal of Rehabilitation, 42,* 2.

Hoffman, F. J., Sheldon, K. L., Minskoff, E. H., Sautter, S. W., Steidle, E. F., Baker, D., Bailey, M. B., and Echols, L. D. (1986). Needs of learning disabled adults. *Journal of Learning Disabilities, 20,* 43-52.

Hohenshil, T. H. (1984). School psychologists facilitating career development programs in secondary education. *Career Development for Exceptional Individuals, 7*(2), 51-58.

Hohenshil, T. H., & Warder, P. (1978). The emerging vocational school psychologist: Implications for special needs students. *The School Psychology Digest, 1,* 5-17.

Holcomb, W. R., & Anderson, W. P. (1977). Vocational guidance research: A five-year review. *Journal of Vocational Behavior, 10,* 341-346.

Holland, J. (1977). The Vocational Preference Inventory. Palo Alto, CA: Consulting Psychologists Press.

Holland, J. (1979). *Professional manual for the Self-Directed Search.* Palo Alto, CA: Consulting Psychologists Press.

Holland, J. (1985a). *Making vocational choices: A theory of vocational personalities and work environments* (2nd ed.). Englewood Cliffs, NJ: Prentice-Hall.

Holland, J. L. (1985b). *The Self- Directed Search: Professional manual—1985 edition.* Odessa, FL: Psychological Assessment Resources.

Hollingshead, A. B. (1949). *Elmtown's youth.* New York: Wiley.

Holt, J. (1964). *How children fail.* New York: Pitman

Horner, C. M., Maddux, C. D., & Green, C. (1986). Minority students and special education: Is overrepresentation possible? *NASSP Bulletin, 70*(492), 89-93.

Houck, C. K. (1984). *Learning disabilities: Understanding concepts, characteristics, and issues.* Englewood Cliffs, NJ: Prentice-Hall, Inc.

Hoyt, K. B. (1975, June). *Career education and the business-labor industry community.* Paper presented at the National Apprenticeship and Training Directors Conference, Washington, DC.

Hoyt, K. B. (1977). *A primer for career education.* Washington, DC: U.S. Government Printing Office.

Hoyt, K. B. (1980, June). *Career education for persons with visual handicaps.* Paper presented at the Helen Keller Centennial Conference, Boston.

Hyman, B. (1956). The relationship of social status and vocational interests. *Journal of Counseling Psychology, 3,* 12-16.

Ianacone, R. N., & Leconte, P. J. (1986). Curriculum-based vocational assessment: A viable response to a school-based service delivery issue. *Career Development for Exceptional Individuals, 9,* 113-120.

Irvine, P., Goodman, L., & Mann, L. (1978). Occupational education. In L. Mann, L. Goodman, & J. L. Wiederholt (Eds.), *Teaching the learning-disabled adolescent.* Boston: Houghton Mifflin.

Johnson, S. W., & Morasky, R. L. (1980). *Learning disabilities,* (2nd Ed.). Boston: Allyn and Bacon.

Kanner, L. (1964). *A history of the care and study of the mentally retarded.* Springfield, IL: Charles C Thomas.

Kapes, J. T., & Parrish, L. H. (1983). Career guidance and assessment tools for handicapped persons. *New Directions in Testing and Measurement,* n20, 47-61.

Keddie, N. (Ed.) (1973). *The myth of cultural deprivation.* Harmondsworth, Middlesex, England: Pinguin Education.

Kendall, W. (1981). Affective and career education for the learning disabled adolescent. *Learning Disability Quarterly, 4,* 69-75.

Kerr, C. (1979). Giving youth a better chance: Options for education, work. *Carnegie Council of Policy Studies in Higher Education.* San Francisco: Jossey-Bass.

Kidd, J. W., Cross, T. J., & Higginbotham, J. L. (1967). The world of work for the educable mentally retarded. *Exceptional Children, 33,* 648-649.

Kiernan, W. E., & Petzy, V. (1982). A systems approach to career and vocational education programs for special needs students grades 7-12. In K. P. Lyncy, W. E. Kiernan, & J. A. Stark (Eds.). *Prevocational and vocational education for special needs youth: A blueprint for the 1980s.* Baltimore, MD: Paul H. Brookes.

Kimball, R. L., Sedlacek, W. E., & Brooks, G. C. (1973). Black and white vocational interests in Holland's Self-Directed Search (SDS). *Journal of Negro Education, 42,* 1-4.

Kirk, S. A. (1962). *Educating exceptional children* (1st ed.). Boston: Houghton Mifflin.

Kirk, S. A., & Chalfant, J. C. (1984). *Academic and developmental learning disabilities.* Denver: Love Publishing Co.

Kirk, S. A., & Gallagher, J. J. (1983). *Educating exceptional children* (4th ed.). Boston: Houghton Mifflin.

Kirk, S. A., & Gallagher, J. J. (1986). *Educating exceptional children* (5th ed.). Boston: Houghton Mifflin.

Knight, O. B. (1972). Occupational aspirations of the educable mentally retarded. *Training School Bulletin, 69,* 54-58.

Kokaska, C. J. (1968). The occupational status of the educable mentally retarded: A review of follow-up studies. *Journal of Special Education, 2,* 369-377

Kokaska, C. J. (1983). Career education: A brief overview. *Teaching Exceptional Children, 15,* 194-195.

Kokaska, C. J., & Brolin, D. E. (1985). *Career education for handicapped individuals.* (2nd Ed.). Columbus, OH: Charles E. Merrill.

Kokaska, C. J., & Kolstoe, O. P. (1977). Special educators' role in career education. *Journal of Career Education, 3,* 4-18.

Kokaska, C. J., Lazar, A. I., & Schmidt, A. (1970). Vocational preparation at the elementary level. *Teaching Exceptional Children, 2,* 63-66.

Kolstoe, O. P., & Frey, R. M. (1965). *A high school work-study program for mentally subnormal students.* Carbondale: Southern Illinois University press.

Krivatsy, S. E., & Magoon, T. M. (1976). Differetial effects of three vocational counseling treatments. *Journal of Counseling Psychology, 43,* 112-118.

Kronick, D. (1978). *Social development of learning disabled persons.* San Francisco: Jossey-Bass.

Kronick, D. (1981). *Social development of learning disabled persons.* San Francisco, CA: Jossey-Bass.

Kuder, F. (1966). *Kuder Occupational Interest Survey.* Chicago: Science Research Associates.

Kuder, F., & Diamond, E. E. (1979). *General manual for the Kudar DD Occupational Interest Survey.* Chicago: Science Research Associates.

Kuhn, E. A. (1966). A comparative analysis of the nature of EMR adolescents' expressed level of understanding of selected occupations. Unpublished Doctoral Dissertation, Michigan State University.

Lerner (1985). *Learning disabilities: Theories, diagnosis, and teaching strategies.* Boston: Houghton Mifflin.

Levinson, E. M. (1984a). A vocationally oriented secondary school program for the emotionally disturbed. *Vocational Guidance Quarterly, 33,* 76-81.

Levinson, E. M. (1984b). Vocational/career assessment in school psychological evaluations: Rationale, definition, and purpose. *Psychology in the Schools, 21,* 112-117.

Levitan, S. A., & Taggart, R. (1976). *Jobs for the disabled.* Washington, DC: George Washington University Center for Manpower Policy Studies.

Lewis, A. H., & Sedlacek, W. E. (1972). Socioeconomic level differences on Holland's Self-Directed Search. *Proceedings, 80th Annual Convention of the American Psychological Association,* 587-588.

Lignugaris/Kraft, B., Rule, S., Salzberg, C., & Stowitschek, J. (1986). Social interpersonal skills of handicapped and nonhandicapped adults at work. *Journal of Employment Counseling, 23*(1), 20-29.

Lofquist, L. H., & Dawis, R. V. (1969). *Adjustment to work.* New York: Appleton-Century-Crofts.

Maddux, C. D., & Cummings, R. E. (1986). Alternate-form reliability of the Self-Directed Search — Form E. *The Career Development Quarterly, 35,* 136-140.

Marino, J. F. (1981). *Vocational education: Available but allusive for handicapped students.* Phoenix: Arizona Department of Education.

Marland, S. P. (1971). Career education now. Speech presented before the annual convention of the National Association of Secondary School Principals, Houston, TX.

McCary, P. M. (1982). *Vocational evaluation and assessment in school settings.* Menomonie, WI: Stout Vocational Rehabilitation Institute.

McDaniel, L. (1982). Changing vocational teachers' attitudes toward the handicapped. *Exceptional Children, 48,* 377-378.

McGowan, A. S. (1977). Vocational maturity and anxiety among vocationally undecided and indecisive students: The effectiveness of Holland's Self-Directed Search. *Journal of Vocational Behavior, 10,* 196-204.

Meehan, D. A., & Hodell, S. (1986). Measuring the impact of vocational assessment activities upon program decisions. *Career Development for Exceptional Individuals, 9,* 106-112.

Mercer, C., Hughes, C., & Mercer, A. (1985). Learning disabilities definitions used by state education departments. *Learning Disability Quarterly, 8*(1), 45-55.

Mercer, J. (1973). *Labeling the mentally retarded.* Berkeley: University of California Press.

Miller, D. C., & Form, W. H. (1951). *Industrial sociology.* New York: Harper & Row.

Minner, S. (1982). Expectations of vocational teachers for handicapped students. *Exceptional Children, 48,* 451-453.

Mori, A. A. (1982). Career attitudes and job knowledge among junior high school regular, special, and academically talented students. *Career Development for Exceptional Individuals, 5*(1), 62-69.

Mount, M., & Muchinsky, P. (1978). Person-environment congruence and employee job satisfaction: A test of Holland's theory. *Journal of Vocational Behavior, 13,* 84-100.

Nadolsky, J. M. (1981). Vocational evaluation in the public schools: Implications for future practice. *The Journal of Vocational Special Needs Education, 3*(3), 5-9.

National Assessment of Education Progress. (1978a). It's what you don't know that hurts. *NAEP newsletter, 11*(5), 1(a).

National Assessment of Education Progress. (1978b). Wrap-up: Social studies/citizenship. *NAEP Newsletter, 11*(5), 1-2(b).

Neubert, D. A. (1986). Use of vocational evaluation: Recommendations in selected public school settings. *Career Development for Exceptional Individuals, 9,* 98-105.

Newcomer, P. L. (1980). *Understanding and teaching emotionally disturbed children.* Boston: Allyn and Bacon.

Nowicki, S., & Strickland, B. (1973). Nowicki-Strickland Locus of Control Scale. *Journal of Consulting and Clinical Psychology, 40,* 148-154.

Office of Civil Rights Report (1979). Washington, DC: U. S. Department of Health, Education and Welfare, Office of Education.

Office of Civil Rights Report (1980). Washington, DC: U. S. Department of Health Education, and Welfare, Office of Education.

Olshansky, S. (1969). An examination of some assumptions in the vocational rehabilitation of the mentally retarded *Mental Retardation, 7*(1), 51-53.

Osipow, S. H. (1975). The relevance of theories of career development top special groups; Problems, needed data, and implications. In J. S. Picou, & R. E. Campbell (Eds.), *Career behavior of special groups* (pp. 9-22). Columbus, OH: Charles E. Merrill.

Osipow, S. (1983). *Theories of career development* (3rd ed.). Englewood Cliffs, NJ: Prentice-Hall.

Peterson, M. (1982, December). *Vocational assessment of the visually impaired.* Paper presented at the annual meeting of the American Vocational Association. Anaheim, CA.

Peterson, M. (1986). Work and performance samples for vocational assessment of special students: A critical review. *Career Development for Exceptional Individuals, 9,* 69-76.

Phelps, L. A. (1985). Special needs students: Redefining the challenge. *VocEd, 60*(3), 24-26.

Phelps, L. A., & McCarty, T. (1984). Students assessment practices. *Career Development for Exceptional Individuals, 7*(1), 23-28.

Phillips, S. D., Strohmer, D. C., Berthaume, B. L. J., & O'Leary, J. C. (1983). Career development of special populations: A framework for research. *Journal of Vocational Behavior, 22,* 12-29.

Pierce-Jones, J. (1959). Vocational interest correlates of socioeconomic status in adolescence. *Educational and Psychological Measurement, 19,* 65-71.

Plue, W. (1984). Employment patterns of the mildly retarded. *The Journal for Vocational Special Needs Education, 7*(1), 23-28.

Poplin, P. D. (1981). The development and execution of the vocational IEP: Who does what, when, to whom. In T. H. Hohenshil & W. T. Anderson (Eds.), *School psychological services in secondary vocational education.* Blacksburg, VA: Virginia Tech.

Porter, J. R. (1954). Predicting vocational plans of high school senior boys. *Personnel and Guidance Journal, 33,* 215-218.

Porter, M. E., & Stodden, R. A. (1986). A curriculum-based vocational assessment procedure: Assessing the school-to-work transition needs of secondary schools, *Career Development for Exceptional Individuals, 9,* 121-128.

Postman, N., & Weingartner, C. (1969). *Teaching as a Subversive Activity.* New York: Dell.

Prediger, D. J. (1982). Dimensions underlying Holland's hexagon: Missing link between interests and occupations? *Journal of Vocational Behavior, 21,* 259-287.

*President's committee on mental retardation: Trends in state services.* (1976). Washington, DC: U. S. Government Printing Office.

Razeghi, J. A. (1979). *Final report of supplement to consumer involvement in career and vocational education.* Washington, DC: American Coalition of Citizens with Disabilities.

Redmond, R. E. (1973). Increasing vocational information-seeking behaviors of high school students. (Doctoral dissertation, University of Maryland, College Park, 1972). *Dissertation Abstracts International, 34,* 2311A-2312A. (University Microfilms No. 73-17, 046).

Reese, H. W., & Overton, W. F. (1970). Models of development and theories of development. In L. R. Gulet and P. B. Baltes (Eds.). *Life-Span Developmental Psychology.* New York: Academic Press.

Rhodes, W. C., & Paul, James, L. (1978). *Emotionally disturbed and deviant children: New views and approaches.* Englewood Cliffs, NJ: Prentice-Hall.

Rimland, B. (1969). Psychogenesis versus biogenesis: The issues and the evidence. In Plog, S. C., and Edgerton, R. B. (eds.). *Changing perspectives in mental illness.* New York: Holt, Rinehart and Winston.

Ringness, T. A. (1961). Self-concepts of children of low, average, and high intelligence. *American Journal of Mental Deficiency, 65,* 453-461.

Roe, A. (1956). Early determinants of vocational choice. *Journal of Counseling psychology, 4,* 212-217.

Rogers, C. R. (1942). *Counseling and psychotherapy.* Boston: Houghton Mifflin.

Rogers, C. R. (1951). *Client-centered therapy.* Boston: Houghton Mifflin.

Rogers, C. (1969). *Freedom to learn.* Columbus, OH: Merrill.

Rosenberg, M. (1957). *Occupational and values.* Glenco, IL: The Free Press.

Rusch, R. R., & Mithaug, D. E. (1980). *Vocational training for mentally retarded adults.* Champaign, IL: Research Press.

Schalock, R. L., Wolzen, B., Ross, I., Elliott, B., Werbel, G., & Peterson, K. (1986). Post-Secondary community placement of handicapped students: A five-year follow-up. *Learning Disability Quarterly, 9*(4), 295-303.

Schumaker, J., Pederson, C. S., Hazel, J., & Meyen, E. L. (1983). Social skills curricula for mildly handicapped adolescents: A review. *Focus on Exceptional Children, 16*(4), 1-16.

Sears, P. S. (1940). Levels of aspiration in academically successful and unsuccessful children. *Journal of Abnormal and Social Psychology, 35,* 498-536.

Sewell, W. H., & Shah, V. P. (1968). Social class, parental encouragement, and educational aspirations. *American Journal of Sociology, 73,* 559-572.

Sheldon, J., Sherman, J., Schumaker, J., & Hazel, J. (1984). Developing a social skills curriculum for mildly handicapped adolescents and young adults: Some problems and approaches. In S. Braaten, R. Rutherford, & C. Kardash (Eds.), *Programming for adolescents with behavioral disorders* (pp. 105-116). Reston, VA: Council for Exceptional Children.

Siconne, E. R. (1983). A strategic new vision for education. *Education Network News, 2,* 2-3.

Sitlington, P. L. (1979). Vocational assessment and training of the handicapped. *Focus on Exceptional Children, 12*(4), 1-11.

Sitlington, P. (1981). Vocational and special education in career programming for the mildly handicapped adolescent. *Exceptional Children, 47,* 592-598.

Sitlington, P. L., Brolin, D. E., Clark, G. M., & Vacanti, J. M. (1985). Career/vocational assessment in the public school setting: The position of the Division on Career Development. *Career Development for Exceptional Children, 8,* 3-6.

Sitlington, P. L., & Wimmer, D. (1978). Vocational assessment techniques for the handicapped adolescent. *Career Development for Exceptional Individuals. 1*(1), 74-79.

Stephens, R. K., & Confar, C. F. (1984). Teaching technical skills to behavior disordered adolescents. *Teaching Exceptional Children, 16,* 146-149.

Stodden, R. A., & Boone, R. (1986). The role of vocational educators in planning vocational assessment activities for handicapped students: An indepth review of a six step model. *The Journal of Vocational Special Needs Education, 8*(3), 23-27.

Stodden, R. A., & Ianacone, R. N. (1981). Career/vocational assessment of the special needs individual: A conceptual model, *Exceptional Children, 47,* 600-608.

Stodden, R. A., Ianacone, R. N., & Lazar, A. L. (1979). Occupational interests and mentally retarded people: Review and recommendations. *Mental Retardation, 17,* 294-299.

Strain, P. S., & Odom, S. L. (1986). Peer social initiations: Effective intervention for social skills development of exceptional children. *Exceptional Children, 52*(6), 543-551.

Strickland, C. G., & Arrell, V. M. (1967). Employment of the mentally retarded. *Exceptional Children, 34*, 21-24.

Super, D. E. (1957). *The psychology of careers*. New York: Harper & Row.

Super, D. E. (1976). *Career education and the meanings of work*. Washington, DC: U. S. Government Printing Office.

Super, D. E. (1982). Comments on Herr, Good, McClosky, and Weitz: "Career behavior." *Journal of Vocational Behavior, 21*, 254-256.

Super, D. E. (1983). Assessment in career guidance: Toward truly developmental counseling. *The Personnel and Guidance Journal, 61*(9), 555-561.

Super, D. E., & Bachrach, P. B. (1957). *Scientific careers and vocational development theory*. New York: Bureau of Publications, Teachers College, Columbia University.

Super, D. E., Crites, J., Hummel, R., Moser, H., Overstreet, P., & Warnath, C. (1957). *Vocational development: A framework for research*. New York: Bureau of Research, Teachers College, Columbia University.

Super, D. E., Thompson, A. S., Lindeman, R. H., Jordaan, J. P., & Meyer, R. A. (1981). *Career development inventory forms III and IV: Manual for research and field trial*. New York: Columbia University.

Swanson, H. L., & Watson, B. L. (1982). *Educational and psychological assessment of exceptional children: Theories, strategies, and applications*. St. Louis: C. V. Mosby.

Tenth Institute on Rehabilitation Services. (1972). *Vocational evaluation and work adjustment services in vocational rehabilitation*. Washington, DC: Rehabilitation Services Administration, Office of Human Development.

The National Commission on Secondary Vocational Education (undated). *The unfinished agenda: The role of vocational education in the high school*. (Series No. 289). Columbus, OH: Ohio State University, The National Center for Research in Vocational Education.

Thompson, L., & Wimmer, D. (1976). Organizational parametes in planning for a work/study program. In *Parameters of planning: The work-study coordinator*. Lawrence: University of Kansas, Habilitation Personnel Training Project.

Timmerman, W. J., & Doctor, A. C. (1974). Special applications of work evaluation techniques for prediction of employability of the trainable mentally retarded. Stryker, OH: Quadco Rehabilitation Center.

Tobias, J. (1970). Vocational adjustment of young retarded adults. *Mental Retardation, 8*(3), 13-16.

Tucker, J. A. (1985). Curriculum-based assessment: An introduction. *Exceptional Children, 52*, 199-204.

Turner, T. N. (1982). The newspaper — a "New" resource for career education.

U. S. Office of education (1975). *Proceedings of the conference on reseach needs of the handicapped*. Washington, D. C.: Department of Health, Education, and Welfare.

Vautour, J. A. C., Stocks, C., & Kolek, M. M. (1983). Preparing mildly handicapped students for employment. *Teaching Exceptional Children, 16*, 54-58.

Vinup, A. (1986, January/February). The Carl D. Perkins Vocational Education Act now in effect. *ACLD Newsbriefs, 163*, 18.

Virginia Commonwealth University. (1966). *Proceedings of a training institute in work evaluation.* Richmond, VA.

Washburn, W. Y. (1975). Where to go in voc-ed for secondary LD students. *Academic Therapy, 11,* 31-35.

Wehman, P., Kregel, J., & Barcus, J. M. (1985). From school to work: A vocational transition model for handicapped students. *Exceptional Children, 52*(1), 25-37.

Weisgerber, R. A., Dahl, P. R., & Appleby, J. A. (1981). *Training the handicapped for productive employment.* Rockville, MD: Aspen Sytems Corporation.

Weizenbaum, J. (1976). *Computer power and human reason.* San Francisco: W. H. Freeman.

West, L. (1985, August). Implications for inservice training for vocational teacher educators in facilitating the transition from school to work. *Interchange,* 2-5

White. W. J. (1985). Perspectives on the education and training of learning disabled adults. *Learning Disability Quarterly, 8,* 231-236.

White, W., Deshler, D., Schumaker, J., Warner, M., Alley, G., & Clark, F. (1983). The effects of learning disabilities on postschool adjustment. *Journal of Rehabilitation, 49*(1), 46-50.

Wiggins, J. (1976). The relation of job satisfaction to vocational perference among teachers of the educable mentally retarded. *Journal of Vocational Behavior, 8,* 13-18.

Will, M. (1984a). Let us pause and reflect—but not too long. *Exceptional Children, 51,* 11-16.

Will, M. (1984b). *OSERS programming for the transition of youth with disabilities: Bridges from school to working life.* Washington DC: Office of Special Education and Rehabilitative Services.

Will, M. (1984c). *Supported employment for adults with severe disabilities: An OSERS program initiative.* Washington, DC: Office of Special Education and Rehabilitative Services.

Will, M. (1984d, June). Bridges from school to working life. *Interchange,* 2-6.

Wilms, W. W. (1984). Vocational education and job success: The employer's view. *Phi Delta Kappan, 65*(5), 347-350.

Wilson, R. M., & Barnes, M. M. (1974). *Survival learning materials.* York, PA: Strine.

Zigmond, N., & Brownlee, J. (1980, August). Social skills training for adolescents with learning disabilities.

# INDEX